THE
NEXT
CANADIAN
ECONOMY

THE
NEXT
CANADIAN
ECONOMY

Dian Cohen
Kristin Shannon

Eden Press
Montréal · London

THE NEXT CANADIAN ECONOMY
by Dian Cohen and Kristin Shannon

ISBN: 0-920792-44-8

Credits:
Cover Illustration & Design: J.W. Stewart
All cartoons are reprinted with permission as follows:
Aislin, MacPherson, Larter, and Peterson: reprinted with permission of the
Toronto Star Syndicate.
Edd Uluschak: Miller Services Ltd.
Gable: reprinted with permission of The (Regina) *Leader-Post*.
Pritchard: reprinted with permission of Denny Pritchard.
Dewar: reprinted with permission of Susan E. Dewar.
Davis: reprinted with permission of Susan Davis.

Printed in Canada at Imprimerie Gagné Ltée.
Dépôt légal — quatrième trimestre 1984
Bibliothèque nationale du Québec

Eden Press
4626 St. Catherine St. West
Montreal, Quebec, Canada H3Z 1S3

Canadian Cataloguing in Publication Data

Cohen, Dian
The next Canadian economy

ISBN: 0-920792-44-8

1. Canada--Economic conditions. 2. Economic
forecasting--Canada. I. Shannon, Kristin
II. Title.

HC113.C57 1984   330.971   C84-090186-0

TABLE OF CONTENTS

Acknowledgments

The fullness and joy that comes with hard work on a challenging project is due so much to the support, warmth and good humor of friends and colleagues. Many deserve special thanks:

Diana Wickham collaborated in the development of Chapter 3; valuable assistance was also provided by Pauline Couture.

The labor relations research for Chapter 5 was provided in large part by Brian Parsons and Howard (Buzz) Gibbs.

Diana Wickham collaborated on Chapter 10 and was in charge of research, with contributions from Brian Parsons and Johanna Schalkwyk.

The Honorable William Hamilton provided the impetus and irrepressible curiosity about the tough questions conceived in the "Star Wars" chapter.

Kent Farrell collaborated in the development of Chapter 12, with significant contributions from Paul Osborne, Brian Parsons and Diana Wickham.

"The Soft Revolution," Chapter 14, was co-authored by Brian Parsons and Kristin Shannon.

In Chapter 15, thanks are due to Frank Tyaack who suggested that a larger audience might be interested in "Tit For Tat."

We would also like to thank the public, corporate and government sponsors of the *Canadian Trend Report* research network for urging us to go public with some of the proprietary research findings included in this book because they felt it was timely to put these questions to a wider audience. Particular thanks are due to Jean Cormier, Vic Drury, and one wise mandarin without whose early support this book would not have been written.

We deeply appreciate those who gave generously of their time and best thinking in the detailed interviews that often took two hours from a busy day. In addition to those quoted by name, there are many others who provided "deep background" and opened their private files. The Niagara

Institute gave us a very special environment for quietly exploring the crucial issues with thoughtful companions.

We would also like to thank Eden Press for the good grace they showed in taking us through this process; the multi-talented Susan Davis for her original art work, and Terry Mosher, who so kindly permitted us to rummage through his wealth of excellent cartoons.

Special thanks to the Silicon seven who laid bare their hacking skills; Gerry Davis who is always at the leading edge; David Thomas for the map to the IMMEDIA network; Camilo Wilson for giving us the Volkswriter Deluxe vehicle; Jim Baird and Buzz Gibbs whose technical wits kept us on the road; and most of all to Bill Watson, who not only navigated, but drove.

On a personal note, Dian Cohen would like to add thanks, appreciation and respect to Lisa Cohen, Pauline Couture, Jon Kalina, and the staff of *Canadian Trend Report*. My family helped considerably, having to fend for themselves during the long weeks of preparing the manuscript. My gratitude to Jack Weldon, who first introduced me to the mysteries of economics; to Max Cohen and Marty Goodman, who had confidence long before I did; to Marvin Wexler and Khalil Geagea, and to the many people over the years who have read, listened, responded and otherwise made it all worthwhile.

Kristin Shannon adds her deep appreciation to the crew from *CTR*, including Alexis, Marnie, Gaye, Sean, Toni, Jan, Ned Riley for his renowned flexibility and superb journalistic skills, and Renate Kiechle for her diligence in overseeing the data bank. Thanks go also to Peter, for his sensitivity and humor, T. George Harris, for giving the right advice, and Julian, for having given us a second start. Warm coaching and support came from family and friends, especially Sanora Babb, Will Blazer, Larry and Zoe Boxer, Jean Cormier, Bill Ennes, Rosalie Fedoruk, the Fichmans, the Hartwells, Mary Kohler, the Kriegels, Keiko Leonard for her Buddhist wisdom, Susan Marx, Norene MacLeod, Charlotte Nusberg, Louis Patler, Frank Stanton, and Shelley Ehrenworth, who is the best and most sensitive of Canadian "networkers" and a valued friend. Former associate John Naisbitt taught the unforgettable lesson that in his lexicon, "eleemosynary" means "freely taken." Additional thanks are due to Michael Phillips, who not only provided valuable insight, but whose timing is impeccable, and to George McRobie, for the very best temperance songs, north and south. Special thanks to my co-author for her friendship and the warm writing haven of her Québec raspberry farm.

Preface

"We believe that in grappling with the human condition, speculation can be as useful a tool as observation and analysis, and we focus on the future as much as . . . the past and present.

"We have three basic speculations: 'What if . . . ?' 'If only . . . ?' and 'What if this goes on . . . ?' In the third and simplest of these, we extrapolate the present into the near or far future to determine what course the human race is presently steering. In the second, we try to invent a fictional world superior to this one, and puzzle out ways to get there from here. In the first and hardest, we introduce one or more 'wild cards' into the equation—the way life frequently does—and study the results for whatever insights they offer on our present situation."[1]

In this book, we explore what will happen to Canada in the transition to the *next* Canadian economy, "If this goes on . . ." In the last chapter, we speculate as to what might happen "If only . . . ," and throughout, we take a look at some of the "wild cards" being tossed our way with the new technologies bumping up against institutions left over from the last economy, particularly the habits of mind we all fell into during the industrial age.

Economics, history, and politics are brought to bear on these basic speculations about our future, along with a set of intimate portraits of the people who are supposed to be minding the store. We left out the sad portraits of those who are still waiting for the return of the good old days. In our profiles of leaders, and emerging leaders, we concentrated on those people who have the courage to ask, out loud, the questions we all need to examine as we build towards the next Canadian economy.

Spider Robinson, Canada's best known contemporary writer of science fiction, describes his craft as "the only branch of literature which insists on asking the *next* question." Well, maybe not the only branch. But he correctly argues that a "reader who has lived in many different fictional worlds is more sophisticated, less provincial, than one who has not, and a reader who can change fictional worlds without trauma, for fun, is forever insulated against future shock."[1]

You might not be "forever" insulated against future shock, but certainly you'll be better prepared to map out *your* place in the next Canadian economy. And hopefully, *much* better prepared to ask those who are supposed to be running this show whether or not *they* are asking the right questions about the shape of the next Canadian economy, and how, and by whom, that transition will be managed.

Kristin Shannon & Dian Cohen

Montreal, October, 1984

For Frank Stanton and Marty Goodman

THE
TRANSITION

Chapter 1

IS ANYONE MINDING THE STORE?

As we move towards the *next* Canadian economy, there is a wrenching contrast between the optimism we feel about the long-range future, and the fear we feel, not just of the unknown ahead, but a legitimate, uneasy leftover fear from the troubled times of the last few years when our expectations were shattered in so many ways at once.

We feel great enthusiasm for the world our grandchildren will discover; but we are not nearly as comfortable about the world our children will inherit, or what our own retirement will bring. We may have been frustrated about our place in the *last* Canadian economy, but at least we knew what it looked like, what we were supposed to aspire to, how to fight fair, and who was supposed to be in charge.

Talking with people around the country, it is clear that they feel there are dramatic changes in our economy. Canadians are confused and disillusioned about their own personal prospects, and very uncertain about what the future holds. We are going through a profound transition from the old industrial-age order to the next economy. No wonder that over and over again we hear the question: *"Is anyone minding the store?"* And so we set out to find out.

After interviewing dozens of businessmen, labor leaders, mandarins, politicians, and other members of the so-called establishment, it is easy to be struck by how many of them are asleep or in shock, quietly mumbling yesterday's platitudes or waiting anxiously for growth in the U.S. economy to roll across the border and bail out Canada.

By contrast, face-to-face meetings with bitterly disgruntled members of the public, and research findings from *Canadian Trend Report* point to a sharp divergence between what many of our lagging leaders believe needs to be done and what the Canadian public believes needs to be done in order to face the challenges of the next economy.[2] Worse yet is the discrepancy between what people suspect our choices might be and what many of our leaders believe we might "be ready" to hear about the next economy.

People who work, study, and wait in line in the hopes of finding a job *know* that something is happening that may be irreversible; they know that the world we grew up to expect has not turned out to be exactly the way we were taught it would be. They don't want to be simply reassured. They want to get a clear picture of what is coming, what is of value in the next economy.

After all, we certainly thought we knew the source of our own prosperity in the *last* Canadian economy. Our images of Canada's wealth and abundance have endured for decades: fields of waving wheat, bracketed by familiar arguments with the railroads about how that grain gets to market and who pays the freight. Flatcars moving forests of trees towards the mills, pulled by a thriving demand for new homes. Sure there were some cyclical ups and downs, but for thirty years the direction was clear: an ever-expanding market.

And, of course, our energy, our ticket to being a power player in the international arena. The energy equation: hydro-electricity, abundant oil and gas equals power, equals security, equals the dream and secret smugness that we could be independent; a not too well-hidden belief that if push came to shove, we could go it alone.

Grafted on top of that pride and sense of security is the belief that we are a modern nation; we are a developed, "industrialized" country. This belief is so strong that when we examine our common language of economic expectations, it is the "industrial" metaphor, not the "agricultural" one which predominates.

"Industrial" connotes mechanized assembly lines, blast furnaces belching fire, freight-trains full of raw materials, waters fouled with industrial residue, and sometimes, violence on the picket line. The images are of fixed, heavy, vertical structures, fixed wages and collective-bargaining rituals, a huge input of raw resources, heavy and constant transport costs to massive, centralized production facilities, a rigid hierarchy of management, and enormous wastage factors such as pollution. It is, in short, a "hardware" view of the economy.

A consistent and fairly narrow range of values is assumed to be required to support the well-oiled machinery of production. The assumptions of a cohesive workforce, a reasonably large domestic market of consumers, and a political consensus on the supporting role for government presuppose a near universal code of values and behavior. Our industrial society implies a dominant, comprehensive value system tied to the goals of material growth and the accumulation of wealth; measures of success are mostly quantitative. We invent whole professions to count the things that we produce.

These images of a fiercely competitive industrial world carry harsh imperatives for policy choices, even when they are masked by an era of rapid growth. The assumption that we are constantly growing permits us to be a liberal culture: a post-war expanding economy, a dynamic youth culture fed by the baby boom. An ever-increasing standard of living propels business and political leaders past one year's unfinished agenda and into the next year's budget.

Our tacit social contract with one another is "if we didn't get around to giving you what you want this year, we'll manage to do it next time."

But now there are clear signals to our leaders that our patience is wearing thin. Growth appears to have stalled, the U.S. recovery didn't quite roll across the border on schedule, and Canadians have noticed that things aren't quite what they expected. Voters, for example, aren't sure that their programs will *ever* be funded if they really do have to wait until the deficit comes down.

The Next Canadian Economy   If past patience with political leaders, security in national pride, and personal confidence were tied to a vision of a rich and growing country, well-managed by public and private sector executives, then the impatience we now feel is linked to a decline in trust; a blurring of that clear vision of what our next political economy is supposed to do for us.[3]

There is a growing discomfort with the problem of how we get from here to there. How do we travel from the daily realities of deficits, unemployment, and the declining value of the Canadian dollar, to the wonderful world of the future with an ordered culture that features bio-tech and plenty of wealth to go around?

It is the management of the transition to the next economy that has us feeling most uncomfortable. There is less assurance that we are going to make it from here to there with any grace. There is uncertainty about *who* among us will be guaranteed secure jobs and ample pensions.

3

The people once trusted to "mind the store" don't seem to be listening. Even if they are listening, they can't always respond. Many of them show few signs of understanding the severity of the crisis that we face coming out of the worst depression since the thirties. They seem stuck with a picture of the world they formed in the go-go years of the sixties. If they can't let go of that picture for themselves, how can they help us?

Profile: A man holding slack reins of power: the chief executive officer of a huge resource-based conglomerate. In the resource-hungry world in which he grew up, every move he made brought in millions of dollars. Then came inflation, OPEC, short-term borrowing for long-term debt, and Third World countries so desperate for hard currency that they sell their resources, the same commodities he has to sell *below* the cost of production. He comes to the office each morning and gets the latest computer printout of commodity prices; his hands tremble with anger. Commodity prices have been dropping for two years, and there's not a damn thing he can do about it. Damn the recession. Damn the government. Damn the Third World countries. He has no control over the world price for his product.

Twice a day his assistant brings him up to date. Twice a day he holds the little slip of paper and stares at it—ten straight quarters of losses. Very little that he can control within the borders of Canada will change that reality. Sometimes as he stares out the 57th-floor window the paper slips to the floor.

It is understandable that he is disheartened, maybe even somewhat bitter . . . he sees so much of the world he knew, and used to be able to control, slipping out of his grasp. Not all corporate managers have fully recovered from the abrupt changes in their world. Others who are doing better have been aware for a far longer time that they live in an interdependent world economy. Says David Culver, president and CEO of Alcan: "If you want to find the good ones, you're likely to find them in the international businesses rather than in the purely Canadian businesses. There's something about having to make your way in the world that toughens you up a little."

Profile: A provincial finance minister three weeks before budget night, shouting at three other cabinet members: "You don't want me to raise taxes, you don't want me to cut spending, you don't want me to tell the public the truth about what we are facing, you want me to promise on budget night that they *can* have it all, and you don't want to have to retract that wildly unrealistic forecast about the strength of the recovery four months from now! Now tell me, what do you want to give up? I am a lawyer, not a magician!" An aide quietly closes the outer door.

4

If the powerful leaders from the last economy are feeling helpless, who is minding the store?

We frequently hear that businesses and governments are deeply committed to long-term strategic planning, that millions are being spent on government economic forecasting, and that our big corporations are commissioning studies and reading the entrails of the newest econometric models. It sounds very rational, very professional, and very comforting. After all, twenty million dollars is being spent on *just one* commission to enquire into the future of the Canadian economy. Why don't we feel reassured?

It is not just because they aren't giving us the right answers; they aren't even asking the right questions! The first report of the Macdonald Commission, for example, landed with a thud because even the questions had been sanitized, homogenized and made bland beyond belief. No sense of urgency was reflected in those dry pages, and there was very little indication that the commission staff had, in fact, listened carefully to any of the briefs presented to them.

Asking the Tough Questions Out Loud   What is keeping us from bluntly asking the right questions, confronting the future (no matter what shape it's in) and getting on with the job of putting together a short list of realistic options? One of the big barriers to getting on with the job of deciding on our options in this transition to the next economy is that we seem to be hesitant to ask those tough, starting-point questions *aloud*. Many of our leaders don't think that it is wise to ask difficult questions openly, especially in public. We don't hear much of the realistic and challenging forecasting; it is diluted or conveniently lost in the bureaucratic maze.

Bankers and politicians and finance ministers too often see it as their responsibility to be mechanically "optimistic" about the future. If they show a tendency to break out of the mold, their well-paid public affairs advisors tell them it is bad practice to be the first kid on the block to make public anything that could be labeled as a "gloomy" forecast. Gloomy forecasts are not in fashion. Some futurists have made a career of being flamboyantly optimistic, why not follow the pattern? The classic example was, of course, the American futurist, Herman Kahn.

"Kahn was always publicized as the greatest optimist among futurists. At the opposite end was Lester Brown of the Worldwatch Institute; or Dennis Meadows of the original Club of Rome *Limits to Growth* studies, who were regarded as gloom and doomers," observes John Kettle, editor of *Futureletter* and consultant to the Hudson Institute.

"Kahn said, 'Certainly the world can sustain a population three or four times its present level with a per capita income around the world of an

5

upper middle-class American.' But when you look closely at his numbers, what he actually forecast for North America was a growth rate in the next twenty, thirty or forty years of about 3 percent. Sometimes he was slightly more optimistic, sometimes less, forecasting 2-1/2 percent. But, I've noticed that in his published forecasts over the last ten years that the growth rates steadily decline. . . . Not that the economy would decline, but the economy would grow at a slower percentage rate.

"When I translated the rates into absolute levels, I found over and over again that he was forecasting, in fact, straight-line growth. In Canada's case, we're growing by about $15 billion a year. Kahn's figures would suggest that the Canadian economy will continue to grow at $15 billion a year (in constant 1984 dollars). But that really means a *smaller* growth rate because $15 billion will be a *smaller* proportion of the total.

"Interestingly, if you go to other forecasters—Data Resources, Informetrica—they are making similar forecasts without saying the same glowing things. Therefore I run the risk of being portrayed as the 'gloomiest' of all, forecasting a growth rate of 2 percent, even though I consider myself an optimist."

The most important thing that comes out of Kettle's analysis is the fact that so-called "gloomy" and so-called "optimistic" forecasters are only 1/2 a percentage point apart. Kahn got lots of great mileage in the press for taking issue with the gloomy guys, but his own forecasts were only slightly different. What is genuinely remarkable, is the extent to which forecasters agree that growth is likely to range from 2-1/2 percent to 3 percent maximum. Yet, here in Canada, we assumed constant growth of at least 5 percent a year, an assumption that was not questioned for two decades.

Effective business leaders like David Culver don't fret about how their forecasts sound. Culver talks instead about the need for a pragmatic frame of mind: "I started my business career in Switzerland and I decided many years ago that the best businessman's state of mind I know is the Swiss. It never seems to change, it's always the same: if you ask him how business is going he says, 'Well, last month was all right, but next month I'm very worried about it.' I've never had a different answer out of a Swiss businessman: last month was quite nice, but next month looks difficult. And that's the best state of mind to approach the business world."

There is one other reason why politicians and bankers try to avoid "gloomy" or even pragmatic forecasts; why they always want to be quoted as "optimistic." *They are trying to build our confidence.* They are trying to negotiate a kind of self-fulfilling prophecy; "we think that things will be getting better and if you think so too, maybe they will." This "mood-management" takes the form of repeated assurances, with an occasional side-swipe at anyone who dares to question:

> "Recovery *is* taking place. There are plenty of encouraging statistics to prove it—job creation, housing starts, inventory levels, retail spending and so on," says a banker.

> "Pessimism is the greatest danger to the Canadian economy," says a finance minister.

The translation is simple. What they are really telling us is: "We want things to get better, therefore *you* go out and borrow; *you* go out and lead the spending, and we'll have a consumer-led recovery!"

Macpherson

7

In short, they hope that if we go out and borrow, if we go out and spend our savings, that that might lead to a new growth cycle. The assumption is that if the Canadian public adopts an optimistic, albeit unrealistic attitude about the future, and then takes risks, maybe that will drive a sustained recovery. Or at least it will tide us over until we have a better idea. So what is wrong with this picture? Mostly, if we are afraid to talk about the toughest problems that confront us, afraid that we might be called "pessimistic" or even downright unpatriotic by calling it as we see it—then we'll never get around to facing our choices. We won't even know how to *weigh* the trade-offs.

These pressures to be optimistic are amplified in an election year in which very few candidates stood out from the pack. For example, in the last election, the only prime ministerial contender who had the courage to seriously confront these uncomfortable longer-term issues was Don Johnston. He was rewarded for his courage with the respect of many young people across Canada, and by other candidates cautiously following him a little ways out onto the ice. But certainly he was not rewarded, yet, with the job.

Prime ministerial candidates are not very brave about making detailed economic forecasts, especially if they are tying the financing of their election promises to economic improvements. The summer of '84 election campaign was a classic example of the caution with which the candidates approached the future of the economy. "There's nothing wrong with Canada," declared John Turner, promising at least $5.1 billion worth of new spending, and also promising to halve the $30 billion deficit within seven years.

"Better delivery of services and eliminating waste" will get Canada growing again, said Brian Mulroney, owning up to only $4.3 billion in new programs "with little or no increase in discretionary spending." There was virtually no mention of projected rates of growth, or of the likelihood of job creation. But even before the election, Finance Minister Michael Wilson was advisedly cautious, carefully tying additional expenditures to a pattern of future, as yet unknown, growth.

Even our supposedly more independent economic forecasters are being muzzled, sometimes by their own institutions. The Conference Board in Canada had, almost since the beginning of 1984, been lowering its expectations for growth in the economy. Each time they did it, they got blasted, not only by the politicians, but by the media for being "gloomy." The day after the official GNP figures were released in the last week of the election campaign, Conference Board economists were directed to make "no further public comments" on their own forecasts.

The private sector is equally uncomfortable with slow growth forecasts. Perhaps this chapter should be dedicated to the chairman of the board who rejected research findings because of a correct, but pragmatic forecast on the likely Canadian economic performance for the next eighteen months. His vice-president for public affairs, a very charming and highly political fellow, said apologetically, "Well, those things that were said about the bank's economic forecasts being wrong were very unsettling, and, after all, our chairman is on the bank's board, . . . and we really wanted to hear something, you know, more upbeat."

As we questioned various leaders around the country, we found the most revealing question was: "Do you believe that the changes we are experiencing are *cyclical*, and that we'll soon be back to business as usual, or do you think the changes are *structural* and long-term?"

Another telling question was about unemployment. Again we asked, "How long do you think we are going to have double-digit unemployment?" If anyone answered, "Only until the next election," we moved on gently to other matters, as these people were highly resistant to even confronting the question. They clearly did *not* want to face the thought of managing their businesses (or finding revenues for their governments) in a period of prolonged financial drought or slowed growth.

When urged to respond, however, they almost always came up with one of three solutions. *The first solution offered was reflation, the second, war, and the third—well, the most polite translation was "why don't we go back to the good old days and f— like rabbits, . . ."* in other words, find a way to get another surge in population and start the growth cycle all over again.

The common denominator of all the conventional thinkers is that they are hunting for some way to trigger a new round of rapid growth; growth will take care of everything. After all, through most of their adult professional lives, they felt the welcome anticipation of next year's growth, which would carry them over the shallows of this year's judgments. No need to change the basic way we think, or manage, or set policy; this is just a short-term problem. That line of thinking implies that "we can just coast."

Although each person used a slightly different vocabulary, there was a striking amount of agreement among those whose values and patterns of success had remained relatively unexamined during the upheaval of the last decade as they waited for business to "return to normal."

Reflation   "What was so bad about inflation, anyway? People seemed to be so much happier then, . . ." is one way that those interviewed backed into suggesting a mild reflation as a way out of the current economic malaise. Reflation means stimulating the economy with tax cuts and easy credit, so that the demand for goods and services rises, and people go back to work. But in the process, we also get renewed inflation.

9

In Canada, this perspective is heard mostly from the old-time liberals, and from the NDP. But a surprisingly large number of conservatives, after a few drinks at lunch or dinner, also expressed a deep longing for the good old days. They, too, had made a lot of money on real estate during the seventies, and did pretty well in the stock market. They, too, found something comforting about upward lines on the chart, even when they knew it was partly illusory, swollen with "gains" due only to inflation.

Ironically, these were often the same conservatives who would name the deficit as a key national problem. They would then go on to say that in a slightly more inflationary environment, people would at least have the "feeling" of progress, and that, in turn, might fuel confidence, which might, in turn, increase the velocity of spending. And voilà—a recovery that might be sustained! Back to the good old days.

War   This isn't the solution that most of our leaders like to feature in their public pronouncements, nor in their bedtime stories, yet it lurks just beneath the surface in their minds. "After all, we really would never have gotten out of the last depression without a war."

"The stimulus of a wartime economy really helped us. It may not be fashionable to talk about it these days, but I lived through that era and I know that we really didn't get the economy cranked up again until the U.S. economy boomed under the pressure of the war. It was a boon to us here."

These views are stated very quietly in Canada, and often voiced indirectly in comments such as, "I understand what Ronald Reagan is trying to do; I know what is implied in that American defense budget, and it may make sense for them to pursue that course of action. And of course, we will benefit here from related defense manufacturing contracts."

There is almost a wink and a nod when the conversation moves around to this perspective, as if this is something that the *real* grownups get to talk about. Grownups *know* that the way the world got out of the depression was to go to war; grownups *know* that, unfortunately, it might take another war to get things going again.

Mate Like Rabbits   "If only we had another baby boom coming along, most of this would settle itself out. . . . Another growth push would take care of most of our economic problems. We need a return to traditional roles . . . perhaps the women's movement has played itself out—I am sure that it has screwed up our unemployment numbers, anyway."

Not surprisingly, this set of views came most often from conservative males from both major parties. But a large number of those who would describe themselves as socialists (in the European tradition of a labor party) hold these views.

10

Pritchard

For example, the Parti Québecois policies in Québec, self-described as "socialist" and "progressive," reflect this clash of values on the question of women in the work force. On the one hand, there is lip service paid to feminist concerns, such as requiring a special form to be signed if a newly married woman wants to use her husband's name. On the other, the PQ government continues to develop financial incentives for women to stay home, and reproduce.

The labor movement, too, shows a lot of conflict about the mate-like-rabbits solution. While passing resolutions in support of women's rights, the Canadian Labor Congress is, in its policy statements, looking for a return to the good old days of more rapid growth, and implicitly, an upsurge in the population.

Perhaps the unemployment numbers have been "screwed up" by the large number of women in the work force. But with a majority of new mortgages requiring *two* paycheques to get approved, it may be a while before we return to mating like rabbits and generating another big population surge.

11

While once the economy *permitted* us to experiment with one wage-earner families, economic forces are now *driving* women out of the home and into the work force. While working outside the home might once have been a "frill" or a hobby for most of the middle-class women in the country, this is no longer the case.

Times have changed. Cheap money, for example, meant affordable mortgages. The high cost of money has done lots to reduce the residual romanticism of the family where the husband is the sole breadwinner; fewer than half of Canadian families now fit the traditional pattern. The shift into the service economy quite frequently means that the male head of household loses a factory job, and that the female "dependent" is more adaptable, picking up a new service-sector job, although for lower wages.

While these economic driving forces predominate, there is also evidence of cultural change throughout the industrialized world. The choice to have fewer children varies directly with the educational level of the population: more schooling equals fewer kids.

If the only answers they come up with are reflation, war, or mate-like-rabbits, then *these* leaders aren't as forward-looking as they would like us to believe. And if we are further being enjoined by leaders not to dwell on "gloomy" forecasts because, after all, "pessimism is the greatest enemy of the Canadian economy," then we are indeed, in a classic double-bind.

Technofix In addition to the three "solutions," we found an inchoate belief that a sudden breakthrough in technology might smooth the transition to the next economy. Computers to make us faster and smarter; new telecommunications toys to link us with the wider world; lasers for microsurgery. But the greatest fascination is with bio-technology.

Those interviewed hope that bio-engineering will improve the world's food supply, maybe even fast enough to reduce the terrifying risk of nuclear war. Genetic engineering will strengthen our resistance to disease, maybe even to the pain associated with the decline in old age; maybe this will happen quickly enough to help us deal with the bulge in the deficit caused by medicare costs. We don't like to think about the potential holes in our social safety net if it doesn't happen fast enough.

There is a sense of excitement about the possibilities of the next economy, the post-industrial era, but the images that *Canadian Trend Report* has collected and analyzed are surprisingly abstract, almost surreal. The future is often portrayed in soft focus, hard to point to, smell or taste. It is hard to "see" a fibre-optic infrastructure, or "taste" an information economy (perhaps it tastes like plastic poker chips). It is much easier to smell acrid smoke, or to touch products rolling off an assembly line. We know the feel of grease, the loud grinding noise of a factory, the shiver of massive machinery in the next room. But how do you touch, or caress, the slippery and shiny and sometimes invisible components of the "information age?"

To compensate, we call our robots "R2D2," and make them heroes; we give our massive mainframe computers voices and personalities, as well as names like "HAL" (a play on the famous letters IBM). We call our personal computers after living things like "apples," and hope that our hardware and software designers will make these forbidding machines into "user-friendly" companions.

That's what they call us, users. We have user groups to try to outwit the unfriendly "documentation" handbooks that come with the machines, and to try to outwit the social cost of part of the transition. User groups reduce the isolation and frustration of confronting these intractable little machines, alone, late into the night.

Meanwhile, despite the friendly bleeps and whistles and supposedly soothing artificial voices telling you that "you forgot to put on your seat belt," we worry about the master-servant relationship with these new toys. Using the new computer-aided design/computer-aided manufacturing systems (CAD/CAM) may increase the productivity of a draftsman many times over. But just over the horizon is CIM—computer-integrated manufacture, which enables an engineer to sit at the terminal and transform his specifications directly into a product. No more draftsman required.

Fears of long-term unemployment abound. The job displacement, this time, is not treated as "cyclical" and "temporary," but as "structural" and "long-term." It's not just hands and bodies that are candidates for replacement this time, but brains and eyes. And soon, ears and voices.

Not only do we worry about robots taking over assembly line jobs, but there are the new expert systems to take over white collar professional jobs. These "expert systems" are computer software that contains the logic process of clever people from well-paying professions. You can buy an accounting package for a few hundred dollars that may save a small business thousands of dollars on auditing fees. Or you can buy a self-teaching language or math program that leaves you free to learn at home, on your own time, without embarrassment, and without having to pay tuition.

Sounds pretty exciting. But these same new packages of friendly expert-system software are also a little threatening to those middleclass professional guilds of accountants and teachers. They aren't quite as amused by the long-term prospects for their fields, which depend, in part, on their control of proprietary information for their survival. We needed what they knew, and had to hire them in order to have access to their specialized knowledge. Now, we don't need them quite as much.

International Interdependence   We no longer look at our Canadian problems in isolation. Canadians, especially the younger ones, are aware that their choices are contingent on events happening elsewhere on the planet. We worry about global overpopulation straining resources. The membership of the planet is scheduled to grow by nearly two billion souls in the next twenty years, up from a current population of 4.5 billion to over 6.2 billion in the year 2000. And since the rate of growth is much higher in the south, the northern industrialized countries are likely to have only 20 percent of the population at the end of this century. That means a big political shift from North to South, and a different role for Canada.

Another global issue that is far from solved is the energy problem at home, not to mention outside the country. Canadians are now acutely aware of energy interdependence; we feel the impact of global deforestation, of the lack of cooking fuel in Africa. The development of a wider range of energy choices affects our options for the next Canadian economy. We are well aware, too, that our commodity prices are subject to shifts in the volatile international market place. Cartels, local wars, and the actions of other governments can increasingly make us rich, or shock our incomes down several notches. Nothing we do in isolation at home can prevent this.

What other governments do with their budgets will affect us. If they are solvent, or if they are over their heads with bad debt, it matters to us domestically. Alcan's David Culver reminds us: "A lot of our strain is due to the pain-sharing aspects of the less-developed countries' debt problem. The LDC debt problem will be paid for by everybody in the Western world; you, me and everybody else. Our devaluation is part of our payment of the LDC debt situation."

Or, if a major economy such as the U.S. tries to buy its way out of the recession with a huge structural deficit, that will raise our domestic interest rates, and make it harder for small business to get loans. The possibility of a "made in Canada" interest rate looks pretty dim, unless we also want "made in Canada" exchange controls.

Will there be thermonuclear war? Will there be peace? These are not questions Canada can decide alone. We have to shout to be heard at the peace table. Yet the cruise missile is being tested in our skies. And our citizens are questioning NATO obligations.

All these factors make us aware of our strong interdependence with others on the planet. It also calls into question, on both moral and practical grounds, the once prideful certainty that we always had the option of closing

14

the doors and going it alone. We feel more vulnerable, and uneasy about the world our children are entering, and sharing. Other nations' wars in far-off Iran quickly become our risk, too.

Some other cultures appear to be more sure of their ability to manage their transition to the next economy. We lack the confidence displayed by Japanese workers, for example, as they watch new aluminum plants being mothballed. They appear to trust the commitment of their decision-makers to rapidly develop replacement jobs. We don't.

The Soft Revolution   It is a soft, almost silent revolution, altering the tissue of society in profound but difficult-to-capture ways. It was much easier to see the dramatic social disturbances of the late sixties and early seventies, especially in Québec. Changes could be recorded, they could be photographed. The soft revolution of the late seventies that is changing so many of our Canadian institutions, and which is the focus of part of this book, is much harder to grasp.

We waver, torn between the uncertainty and the excitement; angry with our leaders for abandoning their part of the bargain, to lead us out of the current economic mess and to give us a vision of the next economy. We are even angrier with ourselves for having depended on them.

Canadians will stubbornly resist a transition to the next economy if we cannot be assured that its spoils and risks will be divided fairly. We get very impatient with those who try to reassure us, with their mechanical smiles and their Star-Wars imagery of a wonderful future, that "if only we will hang on, close our eyes, and trust them," it will all work out in the end. No wonder research findings show that the Canadian public doubts whether anyone is minding the store or even asking the right questions! And so the chasm widens between the attitudes and choices of leaders and the so-called led.

New Vision   Not content to leave it at that, we went looking for those in business, in politics, in the labor movement, and in charge of our pension fund monies to find those who had thought beyond the three solutions we found so limiting. We also sought emerging leaders, and those individuals who had the courage to speak for the record. We focused on people who believed that it is OK to have doubts in public, and that it is *very* important to ask the right questions. What we found was reassuring.

We found people very generous with their time and their thinking. We found people who were ready to open up, who were only too glad to pursue the tough questions, probing for more significant solutions. Many were hunting for a forum to express their doubts that "coasting" was the best solution for an economy undergoing a wrenching, and involuntary,

15

transition. We found deep commitment and passionate concern. We found a willingness to wrestle with integrity and the complex agenda that accompanies a serious look at long-term structural problems.

It is all right not to know the answers in detail, not to know exactly where it is going to come out, but *not* all right to deny that it is going to be a tough transition. It is crucial that we question our personal and institutional values to see if they are helping us understand the difficult choices implied by the transition to the next Canadian economy.

And finally, the best of the crop seemed willing to experiment, test the water, try to find a way to enable themselves, their families, and the institutions that they run to adapt to the transition to the next Canadian economy. Unlike their colleagues, they were not content to "muddle through."

David Culver: "I suppose the single greatest surprise for me in the seventies was the tranquillity with which Canadians accepted a slowly slipping, steadily falling standard of living in relative terms. I'd always thought that we were more competitive minded than that and that we'd get more upset than we did. So I began asking questions: Why is that so?"

To answer David Culver's question about our complacent set of mind, it is useful to reflect on the "good old days." There is a reason why they have such a hold on our values and put such dull blinders on our vision; the good old days made fewer demands.

Chapter 2

THE GOOD OLD DAYS

Perhaps we didn't know what worked back in the good old days of the sixties and seventies. But we thought we did, and that was good enough.

The end of World War II marked the beginning of great times for much of the world. Canada was one of the first in line. At the start of the war, Canada was still an agricultural country; we came out of the war as an industrial nation, champing at the bit to grow bigger and richer.

There was nickel production in Sudbury, gold in Ontario and Québec, and plenty of copper and platinum. There was asbestos in the Eastern Townships, titanium at Allard Lake, aluminum from Arvida, silver and cobalt in the Cobalt-Gowganda area, and iron ore from the St. Lawrence region. The war had stimulated the metals and minerals industry, but peace seemed even better for business. Continued high prices led to a huge expansion. Everyone knew, for example, that there were massive reserves of high-grade iron ore close to the surface on the Québec-Labrador border. But only after the war did it become economically feasible to exploit them.

War-financed aircraft improvements meant better airplanes and helicopters were available for prospectors. Modern geophysical techniques reappraised old mineral deposits and discovered new ones. New power developments helped to open up these new resources, as did the roads and railways that had to be built to get them out.

As the demands for war goods declined, new technology provided new markets. The car industry absorbed tons of nickel; so did the aircraft, railroad equipment, radio, diesel engine and machine tools industries.

Asbestos was in high demand for roofing, building materials, insulation, and brake linings.

The pulp and paper industry boomed. The war had checked exports from Scandinavia; pulpwood resources in the United States were depleted just as the demand for paper for advertising and cheap reading material was rising in the wake of the U.S. GI Bill that guaranteed education for returning soldiers. The world turned to Canadian suppliers. The industry soon became Canada's largest, with a total value greater than that of grain, and equal to that of the mineral industry.

The pulp and paper industry became the best customer for hydro-electric power, and our biggest source of exports. Energy development right across the country proceeded rapidly: hydro-electricity in British Columbia, Ontario and Québec; petroleum and natural gas in Alberta and Saskatchewan.

The resource boom was coupled with an industrial boom. By 1950, industrial production, including steel, cars, planes, textiles, electrical equipment, railway rolling stock, and housing, had more than doubled from its pre-war level. The pent-up demand of consumers who had waited six years for new cars and other goods provided thousands of jobs for returning soldiers.

More cars meant more roads. More money and the extension of roads meant the development of suburbs around each major urban centre. The trans-Atlantic air service begun by the government during the war was turned over to Air Canada (née Trans-Canada Air Lines), which then expanded its services to the United States. Canadian Pacific Air Lines was organized in 1942. By 1949, CP Air was flying to Australia, New Zealand and the Far East.

To stave off the anticipated post-war depression, Ottawa introduced family allowance payments in 1948. They needn't have bothered. There was no depression, and returning military men and their wives needed no additional incentive to increase the birthrate. The population grew more rapidly in Canada during the post-war period than at any other time in this century.

All this prosperity looked so attractive that Newfoundland decided to join the federation in 1949.

The decade of the fifties, even while we were still living it, was known as the Fabulous Fifties, with growth averaging 5.3 percent a year. Governments had just begun to grapple with their appropriate role in the workings of the economy. By the start of the sixties, they had decided that one of their major responsibilities was to maintain an economy that worked smoothly.

18

When needed, the state would turn entrepreneurial; all political parties created Crown corporations to serve as chosen instruments.

Governments gradually came to see their job as two-fold. First, they should not, for any length of time, allow the economy to operate below its potential, and thereby inflict unemployment on the work force. Second, they should not permit excessive inflation, which would erode the value of both incomes and savings.

But the science of "stabilization" was in its infancy. The recession of the late fifties, for example, was gravely aggravated by policy-makers largely ignorant of how the economy worked. They were fortunate, however, as Canadians were equally ignorant. Most of us still believed that recessions, like the Great Depression, were "acts of God."

Eventually, the Fabulous Fifties gave way to the Soaring Sixties. Most of today's leaders grew up in those golden years. As they matured, they assumed values appropriate to a rapid growth era, and acquired certain attitudes about how the world works.

Economists as Heroes During the sixties, professional economists really came into their own. All round the world, they began to believe that their knowledge about the way the economy works would allow them to define policies for achieving a healthy balance in the country's economic performance. We believed them as well.

Both economists and politicians felt that the 1962-65 recovery confirmed their ability to manage the economy scientifically. Coordinated and "enlightened" economic policy—low taxes and low interest rates—contributed to an economic expansion that saw unemployment drop from 7.6 percent in 1961 to 4 percent in late 1964. Meanwhile, the consumer price index rose less than 2 percent.

It seemed obvious to all that by making the appropriate scientific adjustments to economic policy, the excesses of boom-and-bust business cycles and the accompanying unpleasantness of unemployment and inflation could be avoided.

It was during this period that economists began to take themselves very seriously indeed as "scientists." We began to take them seriously as savants, and as trusted advisors to those politicians who believed that we could "manage" the economy.

Economics became the Golden Profession. Suddenly, economists had all the "right answers." Economic forecasts were bang on. Economic policy recommendations worked. The sixties saw economic growth average 6 percent a year, just as economists said it would. Economists were hailed as the

19

new priesthood that could keep the economy on a stable and prosperous growth path.

Graduate, undergraduate and extension students flocked to economics, and to its younger brother, business administration. Both fields gained status and became professionalized. Governments and industry hired hundreds of economists and supported MBA degree programs. The Economic Council of Canada was established in 1964 to be the federal government's economic advisory arm, and to disseminate the new-found wisdom as widely as possible.

By the end of the decade, the profession would be accorded even greater legitimacy. The Nobel Committee in Stockholm announced a new category of recognition: an economist would be honored each year with a Nobel Prize.

As Canadians prepared for their 1967 Centennial Year, the outlook for the economy seemed bright and infinitely promising. Except for a few clouds on the horizon, all signs pointed to accelerating, uninterrupted economic growth. It had never seemed so worthwhile to be a Canadian. With such glowing prospects, the excesses of smugness and self-congratulation that occasionally characterized the observance of our 100th birthday are understandable. After all, didn't we deserve just a little wave of the flag for having the good sense to live in such a stable and prosperous country at a time when much of the world was awash in economic and political turmoil?

The sixties brought to fruition the hopes and expectations that accompanied nearly twenty-five years of economic expansion. It seemed clear, on the eve of our 100th birthday, that our already considerable prosperity was almost guaranteed to grow. We could look forward to increasing incomes; we could expect to be better housed, better clothed, better fed. We could anticipate vastly improved health care services for our families. We would even have money to waste on some of the luxuries and frivolities which add spice to the getting-and-spending routine of living.

Who would blame us for enthusiastically singing "O Canada," when our economy was as buoyant and lively as the sky rockets that would soon explode nightly over the Expo site? How could we have known then that our prosperity was in fact every bit as fragile and transitory as these same fireworks, and would shortly begin a quiet, dark descent?

We weren't alone in our confidence about the course of social events. One economic philosopher wondered aloud at the enthusiasm (and perhaps hubris) rampant in North America at that time:

The present generation of adults passed its formative years in a climate of extraordinary self-confidence regarding the direction of social change. For the oldest among us, this security was founded on the lingering belief in "progress" inherited from the late Victorian era— a belief suffused for some with expectations of religious and moral perfectability, for others with more cautious but no less sustaining beliefs in the solid prospects for bourgeois society.

This was a time when one spoke of social problems as so many exercises in applied rationality: when economists seriously discussed the "fine tuning" of the economy; when repair of the misery of a billion human beings was expected to be attained in a Decade of Development with the aid of a few billion dollars of foreign assistance, some technical advice, and a corps of youthful volunteers; when "growth" seemed to offer a setting in which many formerly recalcitrant problems were expected to lose their capacity for social mischief.[4]

Most of today's leaders, whether in business, labor, government, or the universities, learned their values in these comparatively unusual times when our economic destiny seemed so clear. No one wanted to be reminded that compared to the long sweep of history, this was an almost unparallelled period of growth.

Politicians were more than eager to go along with the businessmen and the economists because they were led to believe that they would never have to make tough, unpopular choices. If they didn't get around to some issue this year, they could simply add it to next year's budget. *The best advice of the day was that we could afford to do anything we wanted to do.*

When research in the early sixties showed that improved education meant increased economic growth, spending on post-secondary education doubled, trebled and quadrupled. Money to fund such projects was no problem, the governments' coffers were full. In 1966, when universal medicare and hospitalization insurance were introduced, we could afford it.

Evidence started to appear by the end of 1968, however, that the gap between our great potential and our actual achievements was in fact widening, not lessening. But it wasn't easy to abandon the familiar assumptions that had been with us throughout the entire post-war era. After all, we were doing well by many measures. The value of our measurable output of goods and services grew 57 percent from 1961 to 1968; unemployment averaged only 4.1 percent. Inflation had averaged less than 1.7 percent in the first half of the decade. In view of these spectacular gains, it should not have been surprising that when from 1966 to 1968, the consumer price index more than doubled, there was no huge cry of protest.

21

It was too early then to see clearly that the world we thought we were inheriting was fast disappearing. The momentum of a new Liberal government, elected on the promise of a Just Society, would continue for several years longer. No wonder the new prime minister wasn't interested in the economy; he didn't have to be. The economy could obviously take care of itself. The only real issue was what to do with the surplus.

We quickly found places to put it: in 1968, the Canada and Québec Pension Plans came into being. A new Guaranteed Income Supplement was tacked onto the Old Age Security program, promising at least a minimal income for the most needy of our citizens.

The year 1969 was in many respects a watershed for Canada. Canada left the decade of the sixties and entered the decade of the seventies with a startled awareness that we would have to fight inflation. The textbook way to fight inflation is to raise taxes (thereby taking money out of the pockets of both producers and consumers) and to raise interest rates (to inhibit borrowing). The Canadian government did both. And it went one step further, establishing a Prices and Incomes Commission to "jawbone" down the rate of inflation.

Unlike the made-in-Ottawa recession of the late fifties, which was accepted by Canadians as unavoidable, the blunders that were visited on them by their government in the late sixties did *not* go unnoticed. The higher taxes worked to create more unemployment. The higher interest rates (way above the American rates) attracted massive amounts of foreign money anxious to get the best deal. Those American dollars, German marks, French francs, and so on, had to be changed into Canadian dollars before they could be invested here. This great demand for the Canadian dollar boosted its price in the international money markets.

Unhappily for policy makers, they forgot that they had pegged the Canadian dollar to the American dollar after the two-year recession at the end of the fifties. Speculators, sensing that the Canadian government couldn't hold the Canadian dollar at its pegged rate of 92.5 American cents, stepped in to buy even more Canadian dollars than legitimate investors wanted. This was the straw that broke the camel's back: on May 31, 1970, the Canadian dollar was cut loose to float.

The result of this first "war on inflation" was spectacular. In less than a year, the Canadian dollar floated up from 92.5 cents to 95 cents, to par. With a much more valuable Canadian dollar, imports became noticeably cheaper. The evidence in the Consumer Price Index was there for all to see—the domestic inflation rate dropped abruptly. The pleased government declared that inflation had been "wrestled to the ground."

22

It did not take Canadians long, however, to recognize that the victory over inflation would be short-lived, while the damage to the economy would endure for years. The high interest rates, originally imposed to curb inflation, contributed to rising unemployment. The higher value of the Canadian dollar made all Canadian exports more expensive; foreigners cut back on their orders, creating even more unemployment in Canada.

The Canadian government, worried by the rising level of unemployment, and pressed by angry and outspoken Canadians, instructed the Bank of Canada to crank up the printing presses. With easier money, they hoped to reduce interest rates, stimulate growth, and create jobs. They did not lower unemployment, as just at that time the first of the massive baby boom generation entered the labor force. They *did* ensure that the respite from inflation would be short-lived, buoyed, in part, by the international shock waves caused by the inflationary side-effects of the Vietnam war.

Canadians were becoming less willing to accept economic policy pronouncements as gospel, but it was difficult to put together exactly what was going wrong. So many things were going wrong, and all at once. Even while the "fine-tuning" of the priesthood was coming apart at the seams, Canada embarked on the most radical tax reform in fifty years. Family allowance payments were increased three-fold. The unemployment insurance system was reformed to make it one of the most generous in the world. Personal income taxes were indexed to shield taxpayers from the effects of inflation.

These programs were becoming increasingly burdensome to the economy, but we were happy to ignore the implications because the economy was still growing. Government spending to pay for these perks, however, was growing faster than the economy as a whole.

The first really big shock came in August, 1971, when U.S. President Richard Nixon put wage and price controls on the American economy, and trade and currency sanctions on the rest of the world. It was the first time Americans were no longer willing to freely exchange their currency for gold at $35 an ounce.

For Canadians, the "special relationship" with the U.S. broke down: for the first time, Canada was not exempted from the 10 percent surcharge that the Americans put on imports from the rest of the world. The Americans had always treated Canada as a benign neighbor, and had always exempted Canada from its isolationist and protectionist policies. This time, Canada was not given special consideration, and this marked the start of a decade of decline in mutual consideration. It also marked, within the government, an upward swing in economic nationalism. Not long after, FIRA was created.

23

Aislin

The next surprise came in the form of an idea in the following year, when the Club of Rome's *The Limits To Growth* became a best seller. For years, indeed generations, we had grown up with the belief that economic growth was limited only by our ingenuity, certainly not by our natural resources. *The Limits to Growth* argument turned out to be premature, but in 1972, the idea that resources could run out and the whole system could collapse caught on like wildfire.

Indeed, there were visible shortages in many areas. There had been crop failures in dozens of countries, driving up grain prices. The anchovy harvest off the coast of Peru—the largest source of protein meal for livestock feed—failed, adding to the cost of other meats. Commodity markets around the world boomed, driving up inflation that had begun as a whisper only a few short years before.

24

Canada's tax reform contributed to our own inflation. The tax reform introduced capital gains to Canada, with the single exemption of owner-occupied homes. That exemption sparked a real estate boom that saw house prices double in five years.

Then came yet another unexpected shock—OPEC. Arabs, according to the popular view of the day, were primitives in robes whose only other resource was sand, and who were ecstatic to receive ten cents a barrel for a commodity they were too poor and too underdeveloped to use themselves. No one knew how to handle the effect of quadrupling oil prices. When inflation shot up in '73 and '74, analysts blamed it on the oil price rise. But economists and advisors failed to see that if people were spending more on oil and oil by-products, they would have less to spend on other things. The recession that began in 1974 was not understood until long after it was underway in the United States.

Canadian policy-makers made their decisions based on the assumption that we could insulate ourselves from both the inflation and the recession that was rocking the rest of the world. That mind set was a product of the times. We didn't need to worry about interdependence; we didn't need to consider overpopulation. We thought the nuclear bomb was behind us, and besides, we had a 200-year supply of energy, according to the best information of the day.

Government spending and intervention in the economy escalated. The money supply exploded. Governments' share of the gross national product grew from 30 percent in the mid-sixties to 41 percent in the mid-seventies, and even that wasn't enough. Governments began to borrow heavily to pay for their current expenses.

Political belief and domestic policy combined to set the stage for continued, but slower, economic growth. Huge profits were generated by the spectacularly high prices of our resources. In this atmosphere, companies and governments were willing to award wage settlements larger than they could afford if they were to stay internationally competitive. During the two years when the U.S. was leading the rest of the world out of recession, Canada's inflation rate shot up, and the Canadian dollar plummetted.

Nothing was working out the way it should. Wage and price controls were imposed, but the dollar continued to drop. Offshore, investors looked at the country and didn't like what they saw. Foreign investment funds began to drop off. Canadian investment lagged.

While Canada didn't share the mid-seventies recession with the rest of the world, it did share the economic phenomenon that followed. The economic expansion up to 1979 was the weakest in history. Unemployment and unused production capacity increased, but inflation did not decline for any length of time. "Stagflation" was added to our lexicon to describe a condition not found in any textbook.

This was a new economic condition that did not respond to the long-accepted remedies; dealing with inflation made unemployment worse, and vice versa. "Quite suddenly," says *The Economist* in an end-of-the-decade review, "twenty-five years of belief in ever upward growth fell to pieces."

The world order itself changed. Robed Arabs now bought power stations and communications systems from us. Third World countries started industrializing just as Japan had, and knocked the stuffing out of western competitors with their low wage costs and fancy new plants.

The 'boom' years

Uluschak

If "a series of shocks" is the phrase that characterizes the seventies, "lower expectations" is the expression that best characterizes the first few years of the eighties. While once we were sure that energy was our ticket to being a power player internationally, suddenly every move the government made seemed to worsen our position. In particular, the 1980 National Energy Program was poorly timed, coming years too late to get in on the boom, and just in time to get the blame for making the cycle of lowering prices even worse, especially for Western Canada. As the price of energy went down and the cost of capital shot up, the much-vaunted word "megaproject" disappeared overnight, with even the huge Cold Lake project becoming a *"mini-mega"* project.

The MacEachen budgets in 1981 and 1982 further compounded the widespread feelings of frustration and uncertainty. These demoralizing changes came at a time when Third World countries and domestic capital needs were threatening to bankrupt not just the western banks, but the whole developed world. At home, we suddenly realized our supposedly prudent banks were held hostage both by foreign governments and by domestic energy companies such as Dome.

Not even the decline in the inflation rate was enough to change the mood. Our political hopefuls, captains of industry, labor militants, and leaders everywhere, had grown up in a golden era of expansion. When their success came to them, management was quite a lot of fun. Then, without warning, the rules changed. What they now face is a world they never thought they'd have to run.

Chapter 3

INFORMATION: THE CURRENCY OF THE NEW AGE

In the good old days, we knew what to expect. We shared a common vision of our society and our place in it. Canadian society was expanding and growing, and our place in it was supposed to improve steadily. But as the gulf between our high expectations and our more modest experience widens, this vision is blurring. We aren't yet sure what will replace the old social glue of common, constantly rising expectations that once held our community together. Vision-poor, we are information-hungry.

Information is the currency of the new age, yet its traditional purveyors and guardians are still caught up in the metaphors of the past. While we stand on the edge of a "wired world" in which the role of the media as information broker is reaching a new threshold, many of its practitioners agree that the media are unschooled in, if not insensitive to, those transformations.

Peter Desbarats, Dean of Journalism at the University of Western Ontario and a journalist of 30 years' standing: "My own feeling is that journalists, generally, are not all that aware of the kind of change that you're talking about, even as it affects them! You're talking about the information economy."

Peter Trueman, anchorman and managing editor of *Global Television News* in Toronto states: "I used to kid myself that if I did my job properly

29

as a television anchorman I would be stimulating people to rush off to buy books and magazines and newspapers to find out more about the subject. I don't kid myself about that anymore. More and more Canadians are relying only on television for their news, and we're still locked into a one-minute-thirty-second format."

Desbarats suggests: "Journalists now have an obligation to look up from their notebooks, typewriters, video display terminals, microphones and TV cameras to consider more seriously the effects of their work. In a complex world where mass media of all kinds are essential and informative—in a world that already is referred to as the information society, journalists can no longer refuse to look critically at what they do to the news and what the news does to everyone else."

Most of the media people we interviewed agreed on two essential roles for the media in our society: "to give the public enough facts so that they can make intelligent decisions" (Peter Trueman), and "to function as an agent of change . . . not just to reinforce people in the status quo, but to challenge them in all kinds of ways" (Peter Desbarats). In other words, to ask the right questions.

Peter Trueman: "Certainly it's the media's job to suggest a variety of alternatives so that the public can make decisions, and I don't think they've really done that." Few of those we interviewed feel that the Canadian media are fulfilling either of those roles with any degree of success. Their search to identify the possible causes of this failure converged on a number of aspects of the media's particular "culture" that undermine the ability to provide a realistic map of these uneasy times or to contribute meaningfully to a dialogue on our collective future.

Within the culture of the media, few were trained to deal effectively with the issues of the last economy. They learned to report on the economy in the way they reported on wars and sports: who is losing, who is gaining. Or, they used a style learned in political journalism, where the press appropriately sees itself as the loyal opposition. Here, the ground rules are clear—smoke out the hidden bad news and challenge the government. Still without a theory of how to approach reporting on the *last* economy, reporters face the transition to the *next* with only the borrowed tools of a journalistic tradition oriented to war, sports, and politics. This yields a conflict orientation, a tendency towards bad-news reporting.

A comment made by Peter Desbarats reflects the key dilemma: "While our political culture has traditionally accorded the media an important role as loyal opposition, with 'freedom of the press' our guarantor that government won't turn into Big Brother, the rules—and responsibilities—governing economic reporting have not been as clear. The question that has to be asked now is whether that journalistic instinct for bad news is appropriate in the reporting of economic events. There is no doubt about it being one of the most influential factors in the selection of economic and financial news. It is there because it is a traditional part of the journalist's mental equipment.

"But economic affairs today are so complex and the role of information so influential in our society that the old-fashioned instincts of the police desk, operating unchecked in this area, may be not only ridiculously primitive but destructive. Watergate-style investigative journalism is almost useless in most types of economic and business reporting. The recession, for example, cannot be blamed on a single villain. When a major industry lays off thousands of workers, there is no corruption to expose. *No 'Deep Throat' is going to explain the mysteries of inflation.*"

The critical question here is not whether or not economic "bad news" should be reported, but whether the expertise necessary to weigh events, to provide balance and context is present in an economic environment where many of the ground rules have changed dramatically.

For example, there are fewer clear-cut heroes and villains in Canada's economic news. Even in management-labor disputes these days the real fight might be offshore, in another country which has just decided to compete vigorously in a business that used to be very profitable in Canada. Although the tensions may mount, the real adversary might be across the sea, not across the bargaining table. These stories are not easy to report, and the drama is harder to pin down, more diffuse, slower to evolve. It requires a different kind of digging than a political patronage scandal.

The public hungers for knowledge of the economy, as reflected in the spectacular marketing successes of expanded business sections in many North American newspapers. Yet, consumers of economic news and media alike agree that the picture they receive in the press is often a distorted one, lacking in substance, but most importantly, missing a framework that places the facts in context. For example, in one three month period, when the Canadian dollar was dropping, the *Globe and Mail*'s "headline writers were never at a loss for evocative terms—the heads were peppered with words such as jitters, tumbles, fever, record low, looms, disappearing dollar, fails to prop, nervous, plunges, slides, falls," claims R.A. Richardson, in a letter to the *Globe*. The dollar's decline produced 14 front-page stories, while the subsequent rise inspired no front page stories at all.

The second dilemma for the media, identified by many of those we interviewed, stems from poor training in journalism. Peter Trueman thinks most media people don't understand much about economics, adding, "I include myself in that condemnation." He feels that the newspapers give

31

consumers the bare bones of statistical material, "if you know where to look for it, but there isn't much interpretation. . . . One tends to assume, wrongly, in this business that the people who are interested in these things know something about economics and that there's no need to explain things. That tends to leave the general public out in the cold."

Tim Padmore, financial editor of the *Vancouver Sun*, points out that, lacking any understanding of macro-economics, most journalists have a habit of keeping background explanations short. Instead, they endlessly repeat stock phrases. Desbarats says, "Everything that I had picked up about economics and business, I just picked up on the run as a working journalist. I learned how to read a government budget by writing stories about government budgets. I read a lot of popular articles about economists and became sufficiently glib, sometimes, that it sounded like I knew something, but I was always aware that I was treading on very thin ice."

Lacking a good grasp of what made the last economy tick, few journalists are in any position to probe our passage to the next one. Without a solid understanding of economic dynamics and principles, few journalists are able to assess fundamental changes in those relationships and are poorly equipped to challenge others' interpretations of economic events.

These same limits also apply to those political events that fall outside of the formal political process. There are new facets of political life that are largely missed by Canada's newswatchers, who depend heavily on wire service copy which is slanted to traditional Ottawa-centered political reporting. They miss a lot of the smaller, softer, evolving events. For example, issue-based politics is hard to cover.

The issue-based "networking" style of political activity characteristic of the politics of transition (see Chapter 12) is process-, not image-oriented. The journalism of power politics is at sea in this "informal" political netherworld. Standard parliamentary press gallery training provides few tools to aid in tracking the agenda of this informal polity. It is hard to choreograph a scrum around an issue-based group as there are few high-profile leaders and leaders often rotate. Alignments fit no easy classification and certainly no clear ideological label. Political conventions are few; platforms often only momentary.

This brings us to another issue identified by those we interviewed: the tendency of the business press to reflect and promote the status quo. Says media consultant and freelance journalist Barrie Zwicker: "The trouble is that the people in charge of the bubble will never tell you it's going to burst . . . and generally, the media are 'bubble-oriented.' They will not put out the warning signals. They are profoundly conservative in the sense that new ideas, let alone alternative visions, are marginalized and trivialized." Edgar Friedenberg, in his book *Deference To Authority: The Case of Canada*, echoes Zwicker's point: "The Canadian media usually treats opposition to the established position on any issue as a breach of taste, to be ignored or ridiculed but not seriously refuted."

While this bias applies to all forms of reporting, let's look more closely at the ways in which this affects economic news. Canadian Press business reporter Gordon McIntosh suggested the following example of how business and economic stories are "sanitized." The 1984 annual meeting of Dominion Stores Ltd. was, according to McIntosh, the scene of "a goddamn riot." At issue were the actions of management. According to McIntosh, many of the minority shareholders present were senior citizens who thought that they had bought safe food-chain shares to provide a reliable dividend for their retirement, but who now saw themselves holding stock in a mining hybrid due to a series of corporate mergers engineered by CEO Black and his brother Conrad. At the annual meeting, the dissatisfaction surfaced; management received a lot of verbal abuse, with the CEO being called a "pirate."

The following day's version of the meeting in the "Report on Business" in the *Globe and Mail* was a curiously flat account of profit figures, with the standard quotes from the CEO. Only the Canadian Press story filed by McIntosh made any mention of the confrontation at the annual meeting. While McIntosh feels strongly that small shareholders and their concerns deserve to be covered, he sees himself as being in the minority. He speculates that part of the problem is that business journalists are hard to find. They're often recruited directly out of university, and, he says, "this makes for an elitist point of view, because these reporters tend to identify more with business; they don't see things that appeal to the common person."

Financial Editor Tim Padmore: "We really encourage our reporters to do business stories that don't just talk about the dollars, but bring the people along. But there are reporters right across the spectrum who shy away from reporting embarrassing incidents. They don't want to take the risks associated with that style of reporting—if you're not absolutely accurate you can be sued. It takes a higher order of skill to do it fairly and safely.

"And for some reporters, it just makes them uncomfortable. There are personal payoffs—there's a higher status in getting clapped on the back and congratulated for a good story by a ranking corporate executive than, say, by a jock that a sports reporter would write about."

Trapped in the Language of the Last Economy   The financial pages tend to get bogged down by the images and formulas of the last economy because they focus on the established, well-known business leaders and recognized sources. This is a conservative process, made even more so by over-reliance on yesterday's models. Lacking the tools to challenge the traditional economic assumptions and sources effectively, this institutional bias on the part of the media acts as a form of self-censorship.

Diane Francis, writer and columnist for the *Toronto Star*: *"The Financial Post, Financial Times, Report on Business* are not newspapers; they're trade-papers. They talk in a form of jargon which is boring; it's grey, there are no pictures, no controversy. Most of the reporters run around and do rewrites of Dow Jones wire copy and put their bylines on it. They print press releases verbatim, intact; they don't do any big pictures or trend pieces."

Even Desbarats says "It's the duty of a journalist to look for the bad news in a political system, but if you apply the same rule and he starts looking for the bad news economically, it may be more destructive. It may not be an appropriate instinct in the area of economic reporting."

The cumulative impact of these layers of media self-censorship is awesome. The product that results—an overview of political and economic life—has a win/lose "spectator-sport" approach. It is oriented to the status quo, and is carefully constructed to tread a fine line among business's fears of worsening the economic climate, economists' fears of being wrong, and journalists' fears of flying blind.

In this environment, financial page reports over the past two years documenting Canada's struggle to shake off the recession have largely reinforced the conventional wisdom, that this is just a business cycle downturn, with some businesses winning, and some losing in the struggle to adapt. Oriented to the status quo, the press has acted largely as a conduit for government and business mood managers, who hope their optimism about a return to "business as usual" will prove a self-fulfilling prophecy. They cover institutional economists uncritically, despite the fact that these economists have sought safety in a cautious middle ground, and in clinging to old models. *The fundamental question of whether this is a cyclical or a structural change, was rarely addressed.*

Jack Scott, CEO of General Foods, says, "It's difficult to read the business press today and get a good sense of what's taking place. There's a sense of self-fulfilling prophecy that comes from most of them, as you try to look through the next five years and really plan your business. . . . The way it's written and the slant that they take, week in week out, gives us a warm feeling as we read it. Or it gives us a warm feeling about their prognosis. But I'm not sure it gives us the hard-edged information that's necessary to plan and to run your business."

"Too brass-oriented and not enough grassroots-oriented" is the way Barrie Zwicker sees it, reflecting a view that keeping track of how average Canadians are coping with the upheavals underway in our economy would have provided better insight than the analysis of the financial press.

By contrast, general news reporters, trained to look for the human side in any story and less hamstrung by the economic indicators that serve their financial-page colleagues, are proving to be the more able chroniclers, not only of social, but of economic change. They are also less afraid to venture into the "soft" news, or future story area. While the language these journalists speak is likewise often bound by industrial-age metaphors, their more colorful stories on the behavior of individual Canadians tell their own tale.

Canadian Trend Report's research findings over the past few years have consistently shown a strong divergence between the preoccupations of the general news pages and those of the financial press. *Canadian Trend Report* research uses content analysis, a system that records and analyzes the *pattern* of news events across Canada to identify key shifts in the public's behavior. These emerging patterns provide early signs of social change and a good indicator of future economic behavior.

In the last few years, for example, the *financial* pages have been absorbed with charting the hopeful quantitative signs of a "consumer-led" recovery. Movements in spending and saving rates, housing starts, indicators of growth in the economy were closely followed. The stories kept hunting for an upward turn in the business cycle (and profits), anticipating that investment would follow a consumer-spending lead.

But other indicators of new consumer attitudes, the self-help groups of jobless, penny auctioneers and the barter networks recorded on the *general* news pages have told a very different story. These events profiled a middle class hard-hit by the recession, reaching for personal security in informal networks of exchange and community resourcefulness. Moreover, their concerns reflected an extraordinarily long-term perspective. They spent more on long-term security, less on impulse purchases. While the *financial* pages optimistically heralded near-at-hand recovery once corporate balance sheets were "cleaned up," individuals were *acting* in ways that suggested a long-term shift in their attitudes and assumptions about their collective and personal prospects.

Behind the behavior of these middle-class Canadians—once secure participants in the economic mainstream—hover uneasy questions about personal survival: *Will our household be able to withstand a prolonged economic strain? Should I borrow, or save? Will inflation be back again? Are there any invest-*

DIFFERING PERSPECTIVES ON RECOVERY

Financial-Pages Focus

- Consumer Spending and Savings Rates
- Corporate Profits
- Inflation
- Interest Rates
- Productivity and Labor Relations

General-Pages Focus

- Unemployment—Current and Anticipated
- Disposable Income
- Welfare Rolls
- Interest Rates
- Government Management of the Recovery

---

ments I can make to protect myself? Should I try to live more simply, or will the neighbors notice if the car is getting old? What are the benefits and risks of partici-pating more fully in the informal economy? Is the middle class likely to disappear? These are not questions that can be answered in isolation. Yet, an important, traditional medium of dialogue on alternatives is still waiting for consumer confidence to lead a recovery. The financial press still reflects only a bland, largely unquestioning view of conventional options and opportunities.

As individuals and as voters, Canadians are asking: *As a Canadian citizen, what are my rights to the basics: food, clothing, shelter, medical care, pensions? How can government programs be funded? Who will pay the costs of transition? What should my values be in this transition? Do I go backward to find a code, or forward? Is my Canadian identity a high priority? Is loyalty to a region, a neighbor-hood, or my family a better bet? How large will the deficit be? Will my grandchildren still be paying for our mistakes? Is Canada* really a *"developed" nation?*

Standard business reporting rules don't provide a means of address-ing questions of this scope. Floundering, most journalists fall back on the phrases and measures of the last economy. They talk and write about cycl-ical upturns and downturns, short-term adjustments. Although the word "structural" has finally crept hesitantly into the vocabulary of the financial press, the issue was understood by many unemployed Canadians well in advance of its debut on the financial pages. The following graph shows the virtually unprecedented crossover of concerns between short- and long-term unemployment issues.

Will I have this job ten years from now? Should I get retrained? If so, for what? Who knows, anyway? How do I stay adaptable, employable? What can I control?

UNEMPLOYMENT

SHORT-TERM versus LONG-TERM

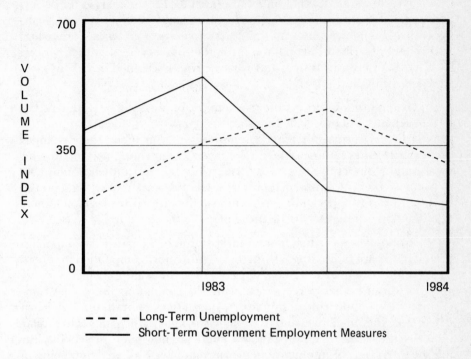

- - - - Long-Term Unemployment
──────── Short-Term Government Employment Measures

How can I become more self-sufficient? Independent? Flexible? Adaptable? Am I better off with a full-time job and a reportable income, or a collection of part-time activities, for cash? What is work, what is free time, and what is real *compensation?*

New Information Brokers for the Next Economy Today's journalists are faced with the task of addressing their own future and mapping their own transition to an information economy, while at the same time informing us about our options. Their monopoly on the transmission of information is dissolving rapidly; their role as broker is being challenged and demystified as the public gains access to new information technologies.

With direct access to these new technologies, consumers can now "bypass the middle man" when they go into the market for information and ideas, as well as for goods and services. Just as consumers are beginning to do their comparison-shopping on their home computer screen rather than in the classifieds and discount flyers, they are personalizing their information sources by letting their computer "do the walking." These expanding choices make it tougher for traditional media to get the attention of their formerly contented audiences.

37

This growing competition is being felt first in the passive media, the traditional publishing realms. "The advantages of an electronic substitute will be large enough to threaten a substantial part of the market for books, newspapers and magazines in the home, office and school," points out Adam Osborne in his book *Running Wild: The Next Industrial Revolution*. Forecasters in this field describe a day, not too far in the future, when a subscriber can specify what he wants to see, and what he wants screened out of his electronic morning newspaper.

The reorganization of the marketplace of ideas will be traumatic for all participants, but especially for established publishers who are committed to a particular format for mass communication. For them, these changes are a source of great uneasiness; they face a fragmenting market, and an increasingly competitive one, with former "buyers" and audiences now able to compose their own information scans. Getting stock market data on the car phone or through a Quotron machine in the office provides more timely reading than waiting for the financial pages in the morning.

Not only is there heightened competition in the passive media (magazines, newspapers, classifieds), but there is also more competition in the so-called interactive media. Radio talkback shows, for example, which serve as vehicles for an exchange of viewpoints in the community, now meet competition from non-broadcast sources. As the audiences for these shows learn to use electronic mailboxes and to form networks of participants with similar interests, they create their own shows. There are now huge guidebooks listing the thousands of interactive networks that have exploded into being in the last two years.

The advent of cheap portable computers has generated a huge new audience for this kind of activity. Hook one up to your telephone, and for $10 an hour, you too can be a network participant.

In the electronic networks, the firm distinction between sellers and buyers of information is collapsing. *The currency of exchange is information*; your ticket to an "on line" conversation is having something interesting to contribute. Everyone using a carrier network such as the Source, for example, can become his own investigative reporter, and his own publisher. If his readers like what he does, his "pay" is often in the form of feedback, personalized messages from others on the network.

Compared to the more rigid formats of published materials, even computer-assisted data bank scanning is much more user friendly than traditional approaches. Well-designed information access systems can respond closely to the user's hierarchy of needs. The range of alternatives is vast; the abilitiy to search, select and interpret boundless, and the filter through which the data must pass is self-defined. The user is *no longer dependent* on the optic of the reporter, editor, or publisher. The creativity and control provided by these new technologies is very seductive.

But the capacity to become isolated is also unprecedented. Narrowcasting and tightly focused computer networks offer participants an opportunity to screen out unwanted viewpoints and perspectives. Certain religious groups, for example, can "tune in" only to their own beliefs on a twenty-four hour a day basis. This means they also "tune out" contradictory value systems. These closed-loop communications systems are reinforcing for the participants in very powerful, often negative ways—they *never* hear dissenting views.

There is very little quarrel with the use of specialized narrowcasting or networking technologies when they are applied to the search for information and the enhancement of knowledge capital. Where there are serious questions being raised, they focus on contrasting the useful socializing effects of the *broad*casting services, versus the potentially isolating impact of overly specialized *narrow*casting media. Just as readers of the financial pages alone miss key events in the surrounding culture, those who tune in to only one view of reality through the new technologies miss an opportunity to participate in the creation of a wider culture.

The principal excitement in the new media technologies is their potential for interactive and participative invention of both the questions the culture should be asking and of the answers. While the conventional media's role as information broker may be diminishing, the role as an essential communicator of common values and goals—our "social glue"—assumes much greater significance.

"Print and broadcast media are unidirectional, so the public can only choose between tuning in or tuning out. With computer-based media it is like having an unlimited magazine rack in your own home, with one big difference—at a magazine rack in the store a sign discourages browsing on the rack, 'Don't read. Don't break the seal.' We are now moving into a medium which says 'Do read. Do break the seal.' "

In his career, Bob McConnell has been a journalist, an editor and a publisher. He has had broad experience in the world of the traditional mass media. He points out: "They are powerful because of the strength of their *signal*—they are built to reach our entire population but they are weak because each of them can only send out a single message. The new media will make it possible for us to choose amongst a wide variety of messages, but we now become editors." This is a big change, not only in the distribution of power but in the fundamentals of what we value about information control.

"When I started as a reporter for a small newspaper, all the value—recognition, advancement, pay—came from *exclusive* possession of the knowledge that could turn into a news story. As a publisher my focus was widened to include not only the knowledge that my editorial staff created, but the scope was widened through the power and size of the distribution system. Now in my new role as president of Infomart, the emphasis is on the *quality* of the electronic interactive medium itself."

These new media not only broaden the range of information but encourage the network participant to tailor the selection, direction and presentation to individual needs. "For example, the slaughter of trees to print detailed stock market quotes is probably the most wasteful use of our nation's timber resources that has ever known to man. Only a tiny fraction of readers have the slightest interest in what the stock market is doing. Electronically, we can now offer not only the stock quotation, but simultaneously provide an historic comparison in sophisticated graph form on the same screen."

As we move into the next economy, the media's crucial challenge is to mind our common store—of values, attitudes, images. Yet our sense of the common purpose is still found largely in yesterday's headlines—the good old days.

We need a new map of our collective path to tomorrow. We could use some tougher probing by the media to help us find our way. If they don't help us explore the alternatives and help to synthesize the fragments of a transition culture, we may all be in trouble when the bubble bursts.

THE
PATHFINDERS

Chapter 4

THE ECONOMISTS

C anadian economists, and their counterparts around the globe, are walking on quicksand. Trying to navigate, or just to keep their balance, is a sufficiently difficult task without compounding it by asking them to forecast the future behavior of the next economy.

Those we talked with were generally unwilling to predict more than a few quarters ahead. When we looked at their published track records, we found that their modesty on behalf of the profession was well-advised; they had been none too accurate about the last thirteen months. After all, most of them had assumed that the much vaunted U.S. recovery would bail out Canada. All we had to do was sit back and wait, and the recovery would roll across the border; but that did not happen on schedule.

So why don't they want to go on record with a firm forecast? Why are they hesitating? Partly, the hesitation is tied to their training: what economists are supposed to learn, and supposed to do. They learn about "models" of how an economy works, and then they are supposed to use those models to better understand and anticipate the directions of movements in the business cycle. Some of them decide to spend their lives improving the models, others focus on applying them.

The trouble is, most of the models they are working from are based on the assumptions of the *last* economy, the industrial economy, and they are very out of date. Not only is a theory of measurement for the information age non-existent, but standards of value for the information-age economy have yet to be established.

We have had clear evidence that Canadian values have been changing in a variety of ways for some time; these changes have just become far more visible, and the pace has accelerated over the last decade. These values will continue to change even more rapidly over the next decade as the transition to the next economy speeds up. Without a clear consensus on value, we also find ourselves on slippery ground when we try to talk about *wealth*.

For example, economists used to assume the value of energy was stable, even neutral, in modeling equations. That made energy costs effectively *invisible*. Policy makers never had to examine alternatives to fossil fuels until the painful price shocks of the early seventies made the cost "visible." Similarly, technology gets treated as a relatively stable variable in most industrial-age models, although we know now that subtle changes in technology have a profound effect, not only on wealth, but on job creation.

Where does that leave economists, who are supposed to be able to help us count, measure and create wealth? Well, they are caught between the formerly firm ground of their rapidly outmoded measures and the uncomfortable need to build a better bridge of understanding to the next economy.

The priesthood, having been confident of an ability to "fine tune the system" only fifteen years ago, is now defending its modeling capacity and being extremely cautious about predictions. After all, weren't the banks using their own economists when they permitted all those energy businesses to over-leverage themselves [borrow more money than they can reasonably expect to pay back]? Yet everyone was supposed to know that the energy business is a capital-intensive, highly cyclical business!

In answer to the question of why so many bank forecasts were optimistic long after it was clear to other Canadians that the world was not quite so rosy, Dr. Hari Thakur, former vice-president of Banque Nationale, replied: "There was some wishful thinking. But don't forget, we're part of the group. We're affected if our major clients are in trouble."

Don Jackson, executive vice-president of Trimac, the biggest bulk carrier in Canada, points out: "What everybody believed in 1980, ourselves included, against all rational odds, was that the business was no longer cyclical. That it would be onward and upward. That once you remove the cycle from a capital-intensive industry, you can increase the financial leverage. And the banks got sucked into that the same way the operators did. So all of a sudden, you had a business that was 90 percent leverage. The banks were happy to lend you 90 cents on the dollar, because it was going ever onward and upward. Then the bust came, and the bust was a shock to all of us.

"The Dome bail out was, in many ways, more a bail out of the banks than of Dome. I think of the 1980-1981 kind of manic activity as a classic boom/bust cycle. It's like Florida swampland, or Dutch tulip bulbs. And in all of those classic examples, everybody gets carried away. Nobody seemed

42

Dewar.

to see it. And the banks are part of that. They got involved as individuals and institutions in the manic phase of a boom."

Almost all the Canadian banks got caught in the cycle, despite their elaborate in-house economic models. When pressed to explain why certain econometric methods failed to accurately forecast the onset, the depth, or the length of the last recession, economists are often forced to reply: "Why, our econometric model was good; it is just that so many of the things that happened were due to *exogenous* factors."

An "exogenous factor" is a fancy label for something that happens outside the model; something that economists don't anticipate. More frequently, exogenous events are things that the economist can't count or measure and therefore, by definition, they do not fit into a mathematical model of the globe.

The trouble is, the whole changeover to the next economy is riddled with exogenous variables; attitudes, changing modes of production, changing pay scales, new standards of value and wealth. Pity the poor economist; it's not much fun being an expert in how to count when a society hasn't quite made up its mind *what* to count or what to value.

We've already been through one dramatic move in this century, from an agricultural to an industrial economy, in both our employment profile and in our thinking. Now we are going through another, and it has taken a very long time for economists and government policy-makers to catch up in their thinking. John Kettle, editor of *Futureletter,* describes the last transition quite eloquently:

"If we look back a hundred years or so, Canada was an agricultural economy. More than half our work force and our output was in agriculture and renewable resources. We were a society of people wringing a living from the soil.

"But, from there on, we were quite clearly industrializing, slowly increasing our output from industry, manufacturing, construction, and non-renewable resources. Meanwhile, service-sector employment went up. *I have tentatively identified 1953 as the peak year for the industrial sector in Canada.* In that year, forty percent of Canadian output came from the industrial sector. At that point, we were about forty percent industrial, twenty percent agricultural, and forty percent services.

"After 1953, the downward trend started. Since then, we have been steadily de-industrializing. Less and less of our total output is from industry. Less and less of our employment is in agriculture. Since 1953, we've been on the road to a post-industrial economy. Whether or not we've arrived there is another question. But at least we can see those two stages, the agricultural and the industrial, very clearly. Now some third stage is in the works."

Not only are we slow to identify the changes, but what has caught us off guard in the last few years is that this long-term change has accelerated, just as we are facing a severe downturn in the shorter business cycle.

"We are being challenged by both cyclical and structural events. And it is very difficult to detect which is causing what at this particular moment. Sometimes the cyclical and structural reinforce each other and then it's nearly impossible to tell which is which. Other times, they are operating against each other, and once again, it becomes very difficult to detect them," explains top Wall Street economist Brian Fabbri.

Dr. David Dorenfeld, manager, economic analysis for Imperial Oil concurs: "We face both a cyclical and structural change in Canada. The cyclical unemployment, for example, is reflected in the high number of unemployed in the prime working age group. But the youth unemployment problem, well, that is structural. We need to define different policy responses for the two types of unemployment."

How do we grapple with this difficulty? "You have instincts. It's at this time that you have to divorce yourself from the econometric models, which are essentially built upon past data and ideal worlds. They are sheltered little greenhouses. You've got to get out of the greenhouse. You've got to get out of the laboratory if you're going to do more than create a controlled experiment for an investor, or corporate financier. And you have to apply judgment, for whatever that judgment is worth. Use judgment and intuition and whatever information you might have about certain trends and how they might be differentiated from other cycles," suggests Brian Fabbri, who believes "that's the interesting thing that makes economics so endearing to those that profess it . . . when you recognize that you're at a new stage in the cyclical development of the nation and the world."

Perhaps Fabbri is one of the most successful and highly paid economists in the world these days (U.S. $1.9 million, including bonuses) because he does step out of the greenhouse. Salomon Brothers, where he works, traded over $2 trillion of securities last year. Fabbri wastes very little time defending old econometric models.

Regrettably, many of our economists, as well as our politicians and business leaders, are still mired in the values and expectations they acquired in another epoch, and they are still using the economic models developed for the last economy. Meanwhile they are hunting for formulas and magic potions to help us get by without confronting the underlying structural issues.

Old Models and Measures   In the corporate and government worlds, the two most prominent buzzwords used in formulas to rescue Canada are "hi-tech," and "productivity." The hi-tech infatuation we explore in the chapter entitled "Star Wars." As for the second expression, "productivity," we don't even know how to measure it or even talk about it sensibly in terms of the information age, much less *stimulate* it effectively.

For example, all our vocabulary about productivity increases is tied to the manufacture of tangibles, material goods which are churned out by factories, with or without robots. These things are designed to be used up; but on their way to oblivion, they can be measured, weighed, and counted as part of our national productivity. Our GNP, the gross national product, is the convenient way to keep track of how well we are doing.

Gross national product is the measure which has ruled the life of industrial nations for almost forty years. It was invented late in the Great

Depression and early war years in order to give policy makers some idea of the total *output* of the commercial sector. How much is consumed? How much used by government? How much is available for war purposes?

By the end of the fifties, GNP was in use as an index, not only of the output of the commercial sector, but of the effectiveness of government, a measure of national vitality, and the test of the economic system. Growth measured by the GNP, became an automatically "good thing." Somehow during that period, growth = good = increasing GNP became the basis of our faith in progress.

But by the end of the sixties, although the GNP was still expanding, it was becoming clearer that such expansion did not necessarily always improve our well-being. There are several difficulties with a reliance on GNP measures and a "growth-is-always-good, more-is-always-better" philosophy. These difficulties also give some indication why a pause in growth may not be such a bad thing if it gives us room to understand more clearly the values that are appropriate to the next economy.

The first problem is that reliance on an aggregate measure such as the GNP does not give us much help in setting priorities. It says nothing about how the output is distributed within Canada, and has nothing to say about quality, an increasingly important issue in international competitiveness. Nor do crude increases in GNP tell us anything about whether or not we would wish to live in Canada, since the non-material, intangible values of cultural, spiritual, or community life are not counted in this measure.

With respect to the question of priorities, GNP counts as equal "wealth" generated by purchases that make a substantial *new* contribution to our lives, and money spent on *remedial* problems, such as cleaning up acid rain—having to invest in smokestack scrubbers, for example. By contrast, investments in preventive health care are almost invisible: "Health is a very important personal asset, and we barely know how to measure it positively; our institutions get very little credit for the steps they take towards prevention," says economist Russell Robinson, assistant deputy minister for Policy, Consumer and Corporate Affairs.

On the distribution issue, for example, one of the things that even economists have noted when talking about the reasons we're unlikely ever to have another Great Depression is that we now have a better, more even distribution of incomes than we did back then. Canadian-born John Kenneth Galbraith points out that "in 1929 . . . it seems certain that the 5 percent of the population with the highest incomes received approximately one third of all personal income. . . . This highly unequal income distribution meant that the economy was dependent on a high level of investment or a high level of luxury consumer spending or both. The rich cannot buy great quantities of bread. . . . This high-bracket spending and investment was especially susceptible . . . to the crushing news from the stock market."

Nowadays, we can be cheered by the knowledge that our incomes are more evenly distributed, but the GNP figures would not warn us if those trends were to reverse—and many forecasters suggest that the income curves may be far less evenly distributed in the next economy. They suggest that we might have far fewer people in the middle-income brackets, but with many more on the "rich" end (households with two working professionals), coupled with many more on the "poor" end (households with two people who have service jobs in, for example, the tourist industry).

If we do wind up with a cluster of super-smart, well-to-do computer engineers on one side of the scale, and "technopeasants" whose skills are in the finger dexterity end of the employment spectrum at the other side, with a sharp decline in the number of people who would describe themselves as "middle class," the consequences sound very disruptive to the comfortable Canadian way of life. But the chairman of the Economic Council of Canada, David Slater, tells us bluntly that "the loss-of-jobs issue is mostly bunk, and the potential decline of the middle income group is exaggerated."

So much for the distributive issue. As to the question of quality not being appreciated by GNP measures, the consumer has been telling us for several years that quality is becoming a more important issue than price in some instances. For example, consumers will pay a slightly higher purchase price for an energy-efficient refrigerator with an advantage over the long-term maintenance and electricity charges of cheaper models. And Canadian suppliers have noticed marked changes in purchasing policies:

"We've always been known as a quality supplier, but the difference in the last few years is that we get paid for durability . . . instead of having to meet the lowest cost supplier. Now some of the people we sell to are going big on quality—Ford, IBM, Xerox, for example. And we're finding that even in the white goods—fridges and washers—they're beginning to require quality. They are beginning to realize that repairs are costly, returns are costly, and consumers want quality," points out Dr. James Fleck, head of Fleck Industries.

Our initial depression and wartime need to measure material output eclipsed many other not-so-easily measured values in our society. Now, as we start to move rapidly into the next Canadian economy, we are paying the price of having to catch up. We have to clarify what we value, and what really constitutes wealth.

Industrial-age models were never designed to measure anything other than the commercial output of society. It's not the fault of the models that our demands have become more sophisticated—that we are more concerned with *both* quality *and* quantity. Economists *can* be faulted, though, for failing to devise other measures when they noticed that their models were being used, not just to make the economy run smoothly, but to measure growth and welfare, too. These economic models were just too narrow to perform those tasks.

"I was trained as an economist, so you start out optimistic, with the belief that at least we can organize our perceptions of our economic life. I even built some models, but I guess I wasn't esoteric enough to want to stay with that, I was always interested in what the economists call the 'applied' side. Being very concerned about public policy, I taught tax policy at university, and then got an invitation to go to Ottawa. Of course, I accepted, thinking maybe I can help. Well, I lost that virginity very quickly. It only took two months inside the government to realize that I could never teach class the same way again. Policy making is such a complicated and rich process—it has so many perspectives feeding into it. Economic, research-based analysis is only one part, and can easily be overruled by another set of concerns. However, once you broaden your thinking, you are no longer simply a research economist, you become something else," muses Russell Robinson.

While we are moving out of the industrial age, we still have economists and politicians talking about "getting this country moving again," seemingly entranced with growth as the the only way out. Not only are leftover economic models from another age inappropriate, but the vocabulary for grappling with how we should measure things in the next economy hasn't been developed yet. That makes it difficult to address productivity in the next economy.

Productivity   Although most observers agree that people are the sources of wealth in the next economy, we are just beginning to look at how to measure information age "outputs." Our traditional input/output measures such as GNP are heavily focussed on the manufacture of goods, and *are not much help* when it comes to measuring the more subtle forms of productivity in the information age. Although we are very good at counting things, we lack a measurement vocabulary for assessing the movement, for example, of electronic blips across a liquid crystal screen, the rearrangement of electron patterns in a bubble memory, or the significance of a skilled expert spending all afternoon selectively wiping files from a computer's memory bank.

And so in some Canadian companies we find ourselves faced with the humiliating practice of trying to count the number of keystrokes a computer operator makes in an hour. That's far from a sophisticated, qualitative approach. Is that what we mean by taking steps to improve productivity in Canada? *Is that how we are going to measure Canadian productivity in the next economy?*

Meanwhile, in Silicon Valley, some of the best and most productive innovators of information age hardware and software systems do not follow any of the industrial-age work rules, and they certainly don't punch a clock! They have been known to disappear for weeks, gone off trekking in the high Sierras, returning for a 36-hour marathon session which might be worth seven man-years in effectiveness. *How do you measure that?*

In the current environment, we don't even, for example, move real money around any more—what we move are blips of information, and what our investment markets bet on is largely speculation on future subtle changes in the flow pattern of these information blips on the screen.

We don't even limit ourselves to buying and selling simple stocks anymore—we've created not only new commodity futures options, but "synthetic" stocks which are made up of bits and pieces of "real" equities, designed by computer systems largely to meet someone's portfolio needs, which are in turn largely dictated by their tax brackets.

Says Brian Fabbri, vice president and senior economist at Salomon Brothers, New York, "We're no longer in the business of just taking a given financial asset and buying, selling or holding it. We reduce it to the sum of its parts. We sell off parts and retain others. The latest development in our financial markets is called interest rate swaps. It's not quite so simple as having one security and swapping it for another, but rather, to swap *parts* of a security with another one. An interest rate swap gives both borrower and lender the ability to minimize or maximize cost (or yield) by altering parts of their portfolio which don't make sense *at the moment*, but may make sense in terms of the investment needs of other parties.

"The process involves synthetically creating securities. It's the dawn of a new era in financial markets. This is the creation of synthetic securities that hedge against various risks whether they be currency, or interest rate risks, and allow investors to participate in various markets that they otherwise couldn't have entered."

Question: As we step through the looking glass, you're now talking not only about a very abstract mathematical model, but synthetic securities.

Fabbri: Created by the same ingenious people that got involved in looking at yield curves.

Question: From the perspective of an average person reading this, . . . is it their pension funds that are going into "synthetic" stocks?

Fabbri: Keep in mind that there is a distinction between a synthetic security and something that doesn't exist. This exists, it's just not in its original form.

Question: Try and make that a little bit more concrete. This is like something out of Borges's *Book of Imaginary Beings*.

Fabbri: The purpose of these synthetic securities is essentially to shed some part of its risk. And that's why you create a security with limited characteristics.

Question: But are you literally taking pieces of actual securities?

Fabbri: Yes, pieces of actual securitites. For example in a zero coupon bond. You take a bond, you take the coupons that would be attached to that bond, which one investor doesn't want or need, and you create a security out of those coupons and sell it to another investor, who may have different risk preferences and return preferences, but he wants the coupons. And you sell it to him in a packaged form, and it's a security.

Question: It's as if you bought a house and sold the bathroom to one guy and the kitchen to someone else?

Fabbri: Except in this case, you don't have to live with the guy in the bathroom and the guy in the kitchen. They can be quite independent. Totally independent once the coupons are stripped.

The concept of synthetic securities is only in its infancy; these securities are also traded in a secondary market, just in case you no longer like the one you bought. It's really just a blip of information. It doesn't connect up, except almost theoretically, with some "real" value somewhere. Asked whether this is so, Fabbri says:

"It's a thought. I don't know even whether I want to comment on where the 'real' value lies. I think there is real value, because the swaps do satisfy particular financial needs. And some institutions benefit enormously by reducing costs, or else achieving some yield with a limited risk. So in that sense there is real value. But whether you can determine it by looking at the balance sheet itself is another matter. Nor could you then unravel the risk involved in the security. *And unraveling what it is that you bought and sold is going to be a very nasty task.*"

In this environment, all of our formerly secure notions about the respective value of land, labor, capital, and equities, along with the notion of "risk," begin to come unglued. When a large chunk of the GNP is made up of information particles tied to speculation surrounding the likelihood of future movements in the markets, people are understandably uneasy about the meaning and stability of wealth.

What is wealth in the information age, anyway? What will be the source of real value in the next economy, and culture, which we are attempting to measure?

What are the productivity measures that will lead us in the direction of those objectives?

What if that baby boom generation decides it has bought enough stuff? Enough televisions, enough sitting in front of a screen watching politics (barely distinguishable from hockey) and—this one really upsets Revenue Canada—what if they have had enough of the current tax system? All these possibilities are already alive, and they will hamper the traditional economist from trying to find things to count and use in industrial-age models.

There are several social and market trends that are going to make an economist's job even harder. These include reducing the use of money. This "demonitization" of the economy—as the middle-class joins the ranks of other members of the culture (farmers, for example) in exchanging things and services more directly—bypasses the culture of money that economists love to count. When people move out of the money system, this also outwits the present state of the art of counting economic transactions.

This barter business was supposed to be a thing of the past, a relic of the rural economies, certainly not part of the modern age. But barter is now on a rapid upswing. Fuelled by trends towards personal privacy and a deep instinct for avoiding transaction taxes, barter systems are now enhanced by new technologies that enable swaps far beyond the geographic barriers of the neighborhood garage sale. The trend towards demonitization of an increasingly large chunk of the culture is not only growing rapidly, but is increasing in social acceptability.

Even *Fortune* magazine, always a little slow on trends, has been keeping track of how large corporations are moving into "countertrade," a fancy name for international barter. These corporations are forced into using barter to cope with the instability in international currency exchange rates or the fact that the countries they want to sell to don't have enough foreign exchange. (Would you like to swap some wheat for a train load of hand-stitched cloth shoes?) Barter is moving uptown and becoming respectably institutionalized in the international trading companies.

Another tough trend for the economists is "disintermediation," the abandonment of the middle-man in the retail transaction. Instead of walking over to buy from a retail store on the corner, consumers are using mail order, discount super stores, or going down to the wholesale markets, even if it means driving an extra two hours. This reduces the number of steps in the economic chain, and may reduce the number of times money changes hands.

Yet both trends, "demonitization" and "disintermediation," make a lot of sense for the Canadian consumer, giving him ways to stretch his dollar. So both are likely to continue and to become more widespread; Chapter 11 looks at these and other things Canadian households are doing to cope with the transition to the next economy.

Hi-Tech and "Jobless Growth"   Technology, like energy, was treated for a long time as a relatively stable element in industrial age economic models. Now that we are going through another revolution in the means and form of production, technology is no longer neutral. The rate at which we are generating job-displacing technologies is accelerating. And the range of human skills which are being displaced is widening. Noted economist Carl Beigie reminds us:

"Technological advance in the industrial era primarily enabled capital equipment to be used to augment the physical skill of people—speed, strength, and dexterity. Technological advance in the information era uses capital to augment the mental skills of people—memory, manipulation of numbers, and decision making. The total dimensions of this era are hard for anyone but science fiction writers to grasp."

Economist Beigie makes clear that we are entering uncharted territory as machines now have the capacity to replace not only those who work with their hands, but also those who supervise, and "decide" things at the plant. This huge leap in the capacity of technology to supplant human labor suggests that we may have to do some massive re-thinking of our labor force needs, as we make the transition to the next Canadian economy.

For the first time, we are being forced to confront the spectre of *jobless growth*, the possibility of an increase in the GNP that is not matched by an increase in jobs. We are seeing signs of a recovery, of improved

52

corporate balance sheets, but we are not certain that this will mean relief from the high cost of maintaining our social safety net—of unemployment insurance and, for the less lucky ones whose benefits have run out, welfare. The presumption in both of these systems that makes them so expensive, and which largely worked for the last economy when they were designed, is that we are only dealing with a "temporary" unemployment problem. Another presumption built into the system is that those who have to make prolonged use of the safety net are at the "margins," the edges of our culture; certainly not the middle class.

If there is any truth to the prospect of jobless growth, then all these assumptions, and the design of our "safety net" system, have to be questioned. It is difficult for a traditional economist to do this. After all, they have been schooled in the belief that growth in itself is magic, and that growth will create jobs. For example, Carl Beigie, in an article entitled "No Need for High Unemployment in Canada," proclaims this view with assurance:

"I want to register my skepticism about forecasts of bleak job market conditions in Canada far into the future. I believe that the government was forced to adopt the strategy of unemployment to brake the momentum of inflation in this country. Inflation is down sharply now, and if we all work hard to keep it down by tying our income expectations more in line with our contributions to the nation's productive capacity, we can continue on the recovery path we began in 1983. Recovery brings growth; growth creates jobs."

Of all the beliefs left over from the last economy that our economic priesthood has inspired, the prospect of jobless growth might be the most shattering. It is also the most pressing question in the minds of the electorate.

Chapter 5

JOBLESS GROWTH

I n the last economy, growth was seen to be the answer to virtually all our economic, if not all our political, problems. Now, the spectre of jobless growth casts a shadow over labor leaders' vision of the next economy. That is not a surprise. They, too, have heard the business leaders on the question of structural unemployment:

Jack Scott, president, General Foods: "We'll probably see unemployment up over 11 percent through the nineties. So I think there have been fundamental changes in the structure of the economy."

Hari Thakur, former vice-president, Banque Nationale du Canada: "The problem of structural unemployment is more critical than cyclical . . . hundreds of thousands of workers—in manufacturing will be displaced. Their jobs will never come back."

Jim Bennett, executive director, Canadian Federation for Independent Business: "We're going through something that's fundamental, structural. It's pervading the whole western economy. You're not going to be able to get back to where we were in the fifties or the sixties where big business and big government were just hiring all the university graduates and whenever there was a problem, we'd throw a program at it."

David Culver, president, Alcan: "For a number of reasons I think that this is a fundamental change and not just another of the cycles that we've had over the last twenty years. There's no getting around the fact that this particular generation of young people is getting a different deal and they—those that survive it—are going to be stronger for it, because human beings respond to challenge with strength."

Adam Osborne, president, Osborne Computer: "It is inevitable that hundreds or thousands of new companies will be spawned around the semi-conductor industry, manufacturing everything from games to robots. How many new jobs will be created? It is hard to say, but compared to the number of jobs eliminated, it will not be very high."

U.S. Chrysler chief Lee Iacocca is another prominent business leader who worries about long-term downsizing and structural unemployment from, among other things, robotics. Does he agree with the longer-term view that we must lower our collective wage expectations? "It worries the hell out of me . . . are we going to be a second class nation? I don't buy the line that everyone is going to have to adjust . . . and I sure as hell don't think it should be our objective."

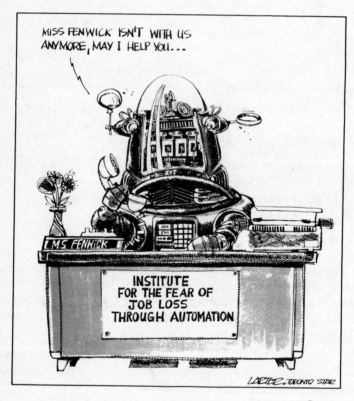

Larter

Perhaps the best informed person in the labor movement on the subject of technological change and the future of employment is Fred Pomeroy, president of the Communications Workers of Canada. He puts it this way: "The change is structural; the hardest thing to come to grips with is jobless growth. We are not going to see increased employment in the next ten years; the new technologies are emphatically not going to bail us out. The 'winners' are downsizing just as fast as the losers. With technology that is on the shelf right now, for example, Bell Canada could, if it chose to, cut its labor force in half.

"Even if the people who believe that technology will create jobs are right, we are still in for what I call a time warp between the destruction and creation of jobs. Workers likely to be displaced aren't the ones likely to get the new jobs. They are disadvantaged when it comes to skills, training, and financially. We have a major unemployment crisis on our hands. . . . We need long term job security as a measure of protection against the impact of technological change."

This sensitive, uncomfortable, and almost unmanageable problem of the future number and distribution of jobs, compounds the labor movement's struggle to define its place in the next economy.

There are three dimensions to the "seige mentality" felt by the leaders of collective bargaining institutions. First, from the outside, labor feels itself under pressure to cope with changing expectations on wages in the surrounding economy. Jack Gerow, of the B.C. Hospital Union, characterizes that province's labor code amendments as examples of a government "hell bent" on de-unionization. Gerow suggests that without "mobilization to take up the challenge . . . there will be no trade union movement left."

Research findings show a steady climb in reports of union accusations of union-busting and "hardball" tactics in all Canadian jurisdictions. Organized labor's responses to what often seems a coordinated public sector/ private sector attack on traditional collective bargaining prerogatives have taken many paths, one of which is more frequent recourse to court challenges under the Charter of Rights. (This path has yielded mixed results, with the Charter reaffirming the "organizing" right, but being less firm on the "means" of attaining labor's objectives, i.e., through picketing, strikes and collective bargaining.)

From the inside, the institution of collective bargaining is being undermined by the lack of a well-defined consensus on anything but survival. The diversifying interests of its members, the difficulty of distinguishing which issues should be negotiated in regular bargaining sessions, and the problems of pulling together a majority view on anything, is making it harder to engineer agreements.

The third area of pressure is truly structural: large labor unions grew up in response to large employers on the other side of the nation's bargaining tables. As big business and government struggle to adapt to the next economy and find themselves operating in smaller scale units, their unions try to find ways to keep their footing. And the areas of new job growth, small business, telecommunications and the service sectors, have been traditionally the hardest to organize. So trade union leaders keep pressing for the principles, if not the rigid forms, of industrial democracy.

New Pressures, New Politics   The traditional political allegiances—attempts to forge an effective political alliance patterned after the European labor parties using the fulcrum of the NDP, are severely strained. Long before the results were in from the last election, there were signs that both the NDP and leaders from the labor movement were looking for a face-saving way to let the bonds loosen.

One of the most consistent findings from the interviews of labor leaders across Canada, especially the younger ones, was that they shared a view that the marriage between the Canadian Labor Congress (CLC) and the New Democratic Party (NDP) was about over. They also agreed that neither party wanted to be the first one to suggest, aloud, that it was time for a divorce. Understandably, very few of them wanted to go on record.

Quietly checking with the NDP, we were surprised to find many of those in the party hierarchy felt the same way, but didn't know how to go about breaking new ground beyond the European model of a labor party. Others wondered whether the old structures would fit the new realities. All sides privately acknowledged that the model was breaking down, and that they could not deliver a reliable vote.

"After all, the largest unions, and some of the best leadership, like the United Auto Workers' Bob White, are tied to the industrial-age models, making cars, making steel, etc. And we don't really have a clear picture of what comes after that," was the sense we got from talking to people at the last CLC convention.

When asked about the possiblity of future growth within the labor movement, the response was: "Well, perhaps in the white collar service sector jobs—maybe the banks are our best prospects. But I am not very optimistic. We've hit a plateau."

Understandable—since the industrial sector as a proportion of the Canadian economy has been in decline since the mid-fifties. Most of the membership growth since then came from the addition of public sector employee unions, mostly legislated.

58

Futureletter Editor John Kettle notes: "The growth of public sector workers is not as striking as the growth of public sector spending, however. While the share of GNP spent in the public sector seems to be accelerating, the public sector's share of employment is decelerating. It is still climbing, but the growth rate is slowing."

Says Jeff Rose, national president of the Canadian Union of Public Employees (CUPE): "Like most institutions in Canada, CUPE is struggling to cope with the impact of a swift succession of social and economic transformations. I think that's also true of our schools and universities, our political parties, our churches, and our business and professional organizations. We're all being forced to adjust to the new realities of the eighties—the end of the boom times, the microchip revolution, the right-wing shift in politics, and all the other changes that buffet us from every side."

Labor leaders in Canada today are clearly feeling the strains and attendant insecurities of slow growth. In addition to this drain, they are currently under seige from the outside, as several government jurisdictions across Canada are in the process of "tampering," from their perspective, with hard-won provisions of the labor code.

Collective Bargaining   Collective-bargaining procedures and practices have long formed the core of the issues labor leaders have been fighting for. And now the collective-bargaining institution itself, seems to be under attack. One of the most tightly defined Canadian institutions, the collective bargaining process has a host of rules and procedures negotiated to define its place and power in our society.

The last generation of labor leaders could count on some firm beliefs about the place of work in the social order: the way a worker prepared for a career, the length of time one worked in a day, a week, a lifetime, until you got pregnant. They also knew appropriate levels of pay, the well-defined rituals of daily management-worker relationships, and the limited role of the corporation outside the basic pay and benefits package.

Although labor disputes could be bitter, they were largely quantitative disagreements and could eventually be resolved through an elaborate collective bargaining system. The structure of the system implied conflict, an adversarial situation, with contracts and penalties for violating the rules of negotiating behavior hammered out over several decades.

Organized labor's role was seen as appropriately adversarial, but within a strict framework of rules. It was "OK" to fight the good fight that was eventually supposed to ensure a good contract for both sides. After all, the adversary system is implicit in a vision of a market place that is competitive and evolving. It is another extension of social darwinism which is in turn tied to a particular view of the nature of man that fit the ground rules of the industrial democracy.

Now, however, the rules are being widely questioned and the premise of the traditional collective bargaining framework is being challenged. *The appropriateness of the adversarial approach* for handling long-term, complex issues with implications for Canada's international competitiveness is being questioned.

Do we know who to fight with, and when? Do we know how to proceed fairly when our labor-management disputes hamper the overall performance of the economy? Do we know exactly what we are supposed to be fighting about? Have the issues changed in subtle and pervasive ways? New constituencies of workers and voters have new perspectives on work; people spend a smaller proportion of their lifetime at work than their parents did.

The economy is no longer widely expected to provide enough fixed jobs to guarantee full employment. And "full" employment is no longer defined as even 97 percent employed, but has become a sliding, changing definition, measured no longer against some quantitative standard, but against current political tolerances. Twelve years ago "full employment" was 3 percent unemployed, now it's 11 percent.

Cultural changes are also placing tremendous stress on the collective bargaining process. The average worker is no longer predictably a male, "head-of-family" wage earner. The wisdom of keeping young people and old people out of the mainstream workforce is doubted. "The office" or "the factory" is no longer seen as the necessary locale for "the job"; as we move into the next economy, "work" can happen anywhere.

Once carefully drawn distinctions between rank-and-file employees and owners are breaking down, especially in the more vital smaller business sector. As a result, labor leaders are experiencing grave difficulties not only in fending off attacks from the outside, but in articulating the needs of their increasingly diverse constituents. As "jobs" become "work," jobs become unbundled, wholly new factors are introduced into collective bargaining. Canadian workers are now looking for a second or third household paycheque, more non-taxable benefits, flexible compensation, flexible job structures and job sharing, take-home work tasks, and the end of sex discrimination.

Many Canadian workers are privately discouraged with traditional collective bargaining as the way to achieve these goals. Published polls show repeatedly that there is virtually no difference between the attitudes of union members and the views of non-union members about these issues.

Union spokesmen repeatedly fail to deliver a union vote in national elections, the new fast-growth industries are not being easily organized, and the overall percentage of unionized workers continues to fall. Some labor leaders have taken the soundings of their constituency group and opened up the political process. Despite the risks, they are saying that their membership doesn't want to be told how to vote.

For example, Gary Doer, president of the Manitoba Government Employees Union, finds: "Our constituency is telling us they do not want their unions to be partisan in a way that makes them subservient, as public sector employees, to any political party. They want their unions to be political on issues, to be strong advocates, but not to limit the way they might have to deal with a particular issue in the future. I see the next economy, and the transition, with political concerns being treated on an issue-by-issue basis; not through partisan political affiliations.

"I think we're going to evolve a unique Canadian political philosophy in the union movement, and I don't see it being the same as it is for the American business unionism, because I don't see the country being the same. Nor the British model. The majority of the union leaders in this country, however, are still subscribing to the European labour party kind of approach, which is inconsistent with what our constituency is really saying.

"We are evolving a different, *Canadian* model. During elections, our union does something that is very, very popular with our constituency. We ask questions about the economic, political and social issues to all the three political leaders and we distribute their answers to our membership. Very popular. They can decide how to vote. They don't want their union leaders telling them how to vote.

"Many positions the trade union movement takes are contradictory. For example, we're 'free-market' in collective bargaining but 'socialistic' in terms of incomes policies. The labor movement is very much pigeonholed in terms of the left-right spectrum, although we don't like to admit that. And that may not help us in the transition to the next economy when 'left' and 'right' will take on new meaning."

Adds Jeff Rose, "My election to the presidency of CUPE last fall reflects on growing membership awareness that the changing times call for new leadership and ideas." There is a less ideological approach in these younger labor leaders; they are conscious of being fiscally responsible, yet they are very sensitive to social concerns.

We need more candor about the economy, says Doer: "In our first 'advisory committee' meeting with the Chamber and the unions and the government, everything we discussed was based on a very positive scenario.

My question to the minister responsible for the planning and the business community (as well as ourselves) is what is our contingency plan if interest rates go up next year and we continue to have a massive rationalization at the same time? There's absolutely no acknowledgement that it might happen at the senior economic levels of government, business, or even labor.

"I suggested that we develop two scenarios, one based on the optimistic perspectives, the other one based on the fact that the American deficit is high and the Canadian deficit is higher. Remember, our Canadian deficit is not as discretionary in terms of social services as the American one is; the Americans always have the option of slowing down military spending. We're in trouble because of our interdependence with the United States, and in our own country, because of our high expectations for the social service net.

"Yet we saw all the leading potential prime ministers of either party talking about not diminishing the safety net, or the deficit, by implication. And that deficit scares me, because I think there's going to be a day of reckoning."

Clearly, the younger leaders of the labor movement are painfully aware of some of the double-binds implied by the ties between the CLC and one political party; they are also deeply concerned with the task of trying to create genuine Canadian labor institutions that are appropriate for the times.

New Leadership Challenges   Another Westerner raises an additional set of challenges, and that is the diversifying nature of the work force. Arthur Kube, president of the B.C. Federation of Labor, states, "In 1965, labor's social policy objectives were directed towards a family unit that had a man as head of the household, who had gone to work right after school, and had a progression of salary increases in a job he could count on keeping till retirement. He pretty well counted on building a home, putting aside life insurance and savings for the future. That's not exactly what the workforce looks like today. Social policy objectives now acknowledge that women are heads of households, that 40 percent of all women will be single parents, that women are paid less than men, that housing is not affordable, that childcare is essential, that two paycheque families are increasing. . . ."

Historically, the underlying premise supporting the collective bargaining process was that workers had similar, almost predictable needs and that affiliation would create security. In the decades ahead, personal security seems more rooted in the individual's capacity to be flexible, to adapt, to control options and to exercise choice according to changing needs at various stages in life. This makes it harder to institutionalize a majority position on all issues. "Building the Solidarity Coalition really taught us some useful skills in appreciating the diverse and subtle needs of different groups," says Art Kube. "All of us—from the community groups to the various labor leaders—learned to hear and respect a wider range of concerns."

Not much on the union leader's internal agenda is likely to remain stable. Traditional bargaining issues will be treated in new ways; it may be wages *versus* benefits, instead of wages *and* benefits, as more benefits are made taxable by revenue-hungry governments. There are new issues forwarded by committed minority interests, such as affirmative action, equal pay for work of equal value, and educational leave. Age differences will expand the range of issues to be dealt with simultaneously. For example, union leadership will be stretched to cope with daycare demands and improved retirement income at the same time.

Some policy questions lack a clear focus of responsibility: they fall somewhere between business and government; for example, environmental health issues. Resolving certain issues will require a cooperative approach, antithetical to the customary adversarial style.

These increasingly diverse personal needs will be at odds with the traditional collective, common-denominator approach to bargaining. During the next decade, union leaders will face a more difficult task in representing their bargaining units. While it may be possible to get a strike vote *against* something, it will become harder to define the points of agreement for returning to work.

The strike is turning out to be too limited a weapon in the defensive arsenal of collective bargaining. Some of the more recent innovative labor and community coalitions, such as B.C.'s Solidarity group, for example, have targetted the necessity of developing a much wider and more flexible set of responses to situations they feel they wish to protest.

"While the right to strike is fundamental, there are far too few gradations in our range of activities; we need to develop a less limited vocabulary of responses. We need to adapt to the changing realities of today's internationally competitive business environment. And that means the response to every dispute cannot simply be to strike.

"We need to develop this broader list of alternatives ourselves. We should not wait for some third party to call it to our attention that labor disputes which seem destined to end in work stoppages are not always in the national, or the provincial interest. On the other hand, we cannot simply walk away when a fundamental issue is at stake," says Art Kube, president of the B.C. Federation of Labor.

"People keep talking in one dimension," says Gary Doer. " 'You've got to be militant or you're going to be weak.' I think you have to demonstrate over a period of time that you're prepared to take on whoever, when it's a matter that is vitally against the best interests of your constituency. If you're perceived to have both a punch in an agreement, and a handshake, you're in a lot better position.

"I think we must admit that the methods that worked in the thirties and forties and fifties, in particular the strikes, are no longer relevant to the great number of people that (a) want representation because of the fear of the long-term economic situation and (b) want the protection of a collective agreement in terms of certain fair ways of dealing at the workplace. They certainly don't always want to go on strike for it, and I understand that. After all, it's a uni-dimensional tool."

To be successful, a labor leader in the next economy will have to have a number of characteristics to fit the demands of these transitional times, and the changing nature and structure of the work force.

First among these characteristics is the ability to manage pluralism. The work force is diversifying so quickly that it is becoming increasingly difficult to find that "typical" unionized worker.

Success also hinges on how well they are able to discriminate *between* issues which are legitimate subjects for collective bargaining and those which would be better dealt with through joint study. For example, the need to be competitive internationally to preserve jobs puts a new light on the productivity debate; gains will require committed *joint* responsibility for dealing with the "enemy across the sea."

R. Heneault, vice-president of Stelco, Inc., feels strongly that "Of all the good and logical reasons that can be advanced in support of a more cooperative management-labor relationship, none is more relevant than the fundamental reality that it is upon the establishment of such a relationship that the survival of Canadian manufacturing and the future economic health of our society will depend." Finding cooperative ground means finding innovative and imaginative ways to resolve conflict, beyond recourse to strikes.

David Culver, president of Alcan says, "You could have a matrimonial dispute but that doesn't mean to say you've got the wrong wife. So it starts from basic respect. You've got to have that basic respect. I don't care how you get it, but you've got to have it. You have to realize that there is no such thing as good Canadians and bad Canadians and rich ones and poor ones. We're all in this boat together and we're either going to ride comfortably together or we're going to ride in a very bumpy way together. Those are easy things to say, but they're important. They affect all kinds of things. They affect your body language. Labor relations are human relations, and often under conditions of stress, body language is important."

"The rules of the game have been drastically changed," says CUPE's Jeff Rose. "And they've changed so quickly that our union structures and methods have not yet had time to adapt. We're still playing by many of the old rules, still trying to bargain with few bargaining rights; still training our people to fight some of yesterday's battles; still trying to address at the local level problems that originate with higher levels of government." That ability to distinguish between national and local issues will need to be more sharply honed in the next several years.

Similarly, it will be important in the transitional period and beyond, to negotiate for the longer term. Canadians no longer believe that there are good and lasting solutions in the short term.

REQUIREMENTS FOR SUCCESSFUL UNION LEADERSHIP

- Manage a diversifying constituency
- Discriminate between collective-bargaining issues and those for joint study
- Develop alternatives to supplement the strike
- Distinguish between national and local issues
- Develop broader policy perspectives
- Negotiate for the longer term
- Choose opponents carefully

Most importantly, being a labor leader in the next economy means embracing a far wider consituency than the union membership. It implies a capacity to identify with a broad range of workplace concerns, which affect both organized and non-organized employees. A new breed of labor leaders, who may not even be the elected heads of trade unions, may evolve to fill the gap in communicating with, for example, small business representatives.

The list is not a bad guide for leadership in general, in the next economy. In particular, the ability to manage pluralism, and to choose opponents carefully, will be needed in every field.

Given the above list of pressures, it is easy to understand why Canadian labor leaders feel themselves to be under seige; their position has gotten harder, their days longer, and their rewards fewer. The reaction of some is to become more entrenched in the logic of the last economy, clinging to models brought over from Europe, and determined to fight to the death to retain yesterday's agenda.

Most of the official CLC platform, and the spokesmen for the organization, have, unfortunately, adopted a public voice and a private one. In public we hear the old rhetoric; in private, at off-the-record meetings, we hear musings that they wished there were a better way to go.

In this look at labor in the next Canadian economy, we talked with some of the leadership that is evoking the themes of change, and talked with some of the labor leaders who are struggling to define, and confront, a new generation of issues.

Art Kube describes labor's broadening perspective that resulted from the Solidarity Coalition experience: "More and more people have become sensitized to each other's needs. Where we started with basically diverse concerns . . . we developed a common ground. We agreed on the right to social services . . . labor's right to organize and negotiate. And then we started to ask deeper questions, for example about incomes policy as it might relate to the question of work sharing, shorter hours, paid educational leaves . . . all this has come up. And we're talking about the question of the desire of people for self-sufficiency. We're also talking about the possibility of cooperative ownership and community control, especially for operations which may not be very profitable, but which could be economically sustainable."

One of the principal things labor leaders agree upon is that the changes we are experiencing are not simply problems with the business cycle, but are long term, structural, and signify vast and potentially irreversible changes in the job market.

Art Kube: "The problems we're facing are largely structural. They're problems we've been facing for quite some time, except that we were able to make certain transfers in terms of employment from the private sector to the public sector. Now it seems like we have reached our maximum capacity for absorbing people in the public sector. What do we do now? That's the next question. We're trying to maximize our benefits from the industrial sector but that can only be done marginally at best. As a matter of fact, I think with the increased application of hi-tech, that sector will continue to shrink."

Fred Pomeroy: "The telephone company is making record profits through the introduction of computers and robots that have done away with thousands of jobs. . . . Employers are getting their money back in record time from investment in new technology—three years in the case of automated telephone systems and about six months for robots installed in the equipment manufacturing sector. Obviously there is some wealth to be shared, and our society would be better off if the available work was spread around. . . ."

Gary Doer: "I don't believe that this 'it's a temporary problem, we're really in a recovery' rhetoric is accurate. I find it more than a little disconcerting that we went to the last Canadian Labour Congress meeting and we had the same slogan up on wall: 'United Toward a *Working* Recovery.' I suppose that's a good slogan for people trying to be elected, but it's not necessarily an accurate one.

"Given the structural changes that are going to take place, if there is no attempt to cooperate with the major components—not the major components as institutions, but the major components as legitimate representatives—we'll have a lot greater cynicism in the workplace. Productivity will go down, militancy in unions will rise in an unguided way or in a negative way for the economy."

David Culver points out that international survival is a very strong motivator and reminds us that the much-vaunted Japanese labor/management cooperation is a post-war phenomenon. "Immediately after the war the U.S. moved in and the first thing they did was to remove the top layer of management from all the major companies, which was the first shock that the Japanese got. One of them told me what happened on that day. His first reaction was to go down onto the floor of the plant to tell the workers that their bosses had been removed by the U.S. military and that it fell to him to be responsible for the business and that he was going to have to fulfill that responsibility.

"He went down there expecting to get support. Instead, they tied him to a chair and burned him with cigarettes. He said to them 'Why are you doing this?' and they said 'Because you are the boss now.' Now this is *not* the picture of Japan that most of the world has today. He said to them 'Look, I'm in the same boat as you are. I know there's no food in your house but I can tell you there's no food in mine either. I'm thirty pounds lighter than I was at the start of the war. Now we've got a choice: Are we going to eat? Or are we going to fight each other?' And this is the kind of atmosphere in which the so-called Japan Inc. has grown and which has fostered the ability of Japanese labor and management to cooperate. It was survival. So I think the lesson we can learn from that is that our own state of mind could also change very quickly." David Culver stresses that management has to change its views, too.

One of the things the emerging leaders shared was a collaborative style, a willingness to explore wide-ranging options. Dick Martin, formerly head of the Manitoba Federation of Labor, now vice-president of the CLC, for example, said he looked forward to a climate when "we could take some of our strike funds, business could put up some capital, and together we could create new enterprises for displaced workers. That would be a real sign of progress. But to do that, there must be trust. And both sides have to work towards that. In order to establish that trust, we can't be fighting for labor survival issues at the same time we are talking about long-term joint goals."

The message we heard again and again from the labor leaders we interviewed was "let's create an atmosphere of trust, and then work on the long term issues together." Misapplication of the adversarial system by either side, they cautioned, will hold us all back. The potential for structural unemployment in the next economy is one of those issues that is *not* readily resolvable by one bargaining unit sitting across the table from one employer. We have to find a better framework in which to consider our mutual options.

Chapter 6

DOWNSIZING: BIG BUSINESS IN THE EIGHTIES

O ne of the truly remarkable experiences we had during the course of these interviews was discovering such widespread agreement on the question of job creation in the eighties. Over and over again corporate presidents and their chairmen told us the same thing: "We have no plans to create new jobs in the foreseeable future."

If "growing," "expanding," "hiring" and "building new facilities" were the common images that were used in talking about big business in the last economy, then "contracting," "getting the balance sheet in better shape" and "facing up to redundancies in the work force" are the current phrases. The captains of industry have clearly started to adapt to the new vocabulary, at least on the surface, and are preparing for the transition to the next economy by "tightening up" their operations.

The CEO of a multinational oil company tells us: "We are no longer stockpiling engineers in expectation of starting another round of mega-projects. Instead, we are downsizing, especially in middle management."

"Downsizing" is the elegant euphemism used as a shorthand for solutions to a host of problems Canadian business, for the most part, didn't foresee. Getting to a more manageable size operation, becoming more cautious about expansion, finding a way to decentralize, a way to get more autonomy to the shop floor, to reduce middle management controls, get rid of the bureaucracy, become more agile . . . all of these expressions suggest

69

that the word "smaller" has entered the language, right after "leaner," and just before "downsizing."

"We can get along in this company with probably exactly the same production, probably half the people," said Paul Paré, CEO of Imasco. Even a strong performer such as Imasco is taking a careful look at its payroll.

"Today's pressure on profits forces concentration on cost containment, and therefore restricts job creation prospects. Growth per se is no longer the god to which we all bow," points out Tony Edwards, president of Hartz Holdings, Inc., which competes effectively in a tough international market.

"We'll be growing only by acquisitions; there are no plans to expand," said Robert McConnell of Southam Press, one of Canada's most successful publishing and information businesses. Even in this promising sector of the economy, there are no plans to hire.

In the last economy, big business enjoyed a powerful, pivotal role, especially the resource-based companies. This was the critical institution that supplied the goods and services we all wanted. There were profits for the shareholders and retained earnings with which to expand operations, creating new wealth and new jobs in the process. Big business supplied us with reliable paycheques; there was security in joining a large, stable enterprise.

Although Canadians argued from time to time about the effects of the multinational giants on the economy, big business was encouraged to grow bigger. In this environment, politicians did not pass more forceful anti-combines legislation because growth for growth's sake—for itself, for us and for the economy—was an article of faith. The bigger the better; the object was to keep the cycle going. The ever-expanding future of large-scale Canadian business was assured. Hardly anyone believes that anymore. Least of all big business.

Now security is sought in developing a lean posture, and in becoming more flexible and adapatable. Business leaders no longer take the future for granted. Trained to look for ways to expand in an era of rapid growth, businessmen are now looking for ways to stay in business. Caught by surprise, and certainly not interested in being the first one to express "gloom" or a "lack of confidence," big business backed the wrong future. Blinded by success in the more affluent times of rapid growth, many failed to see the signals of a dramatically changing world.

"It struck me during the wave of commodity price shocks in the mid-seventies. Suddenly, everyone was talking about cash flow . . . big business never before had to worry about cash flow . . . it was just something you heard about in MBA courses, you know in 'Source and Application of Funds, page 606, read it if you get a chance,' and then all of a sudden it became an integral part of running the business.

"The financial guys started coming in and showing you that your costs were going to out-pace revenues . . . that was the first painful experience we had with downsizing. We had to take people who were institutions in the business and make them redundant. That's the world that I remember—where you could buy a case of beer for five dollars every week—and you never thought about price increases.

"Those were the days when productivity would be greater than costs. . . . When it started to work the other way, we really had to learn a whole new way of managing. In order to maintain our margin we had to increase cost to the consumer. But as we did that, they found substitutes. This produced a decline in volume and suddenly we found ourselves on the horns of a real dilemma, growing costs, decreasing volume . . . that was unheard of. We didn't know how to run that kind of a business," says the CEO of a food products giant.

Says *Futureletter* Editor John Kettle, "All big business does today is fire people and lose money."

"Much of my day is focused on the financial restructuring of a business that was originally predicated on a view that the oil and gas industry would be ever onward and upward," says Don Jackson, president of Trimac, the biggest bulk carrier in Canada.

There is no question about it, the routine of big business has changed, and many business leaders are deeply, if quietly disturbed. Even more shattering for some is the prospect of the transition to the next economy, and the likelihood that we will never return to the business-as-usual world of the last economy. But for others, it is an exciting challenge: "I'm seeing a significant change in the way the whole of the manufacturing and resource industries are being managed—a major structural change as we move into the information age," says Walter Light, CEO of Northern Telecom.

We interviewed dozens of businessmen to get a handle on the place of big business in the next economy. No one knows for sure, of course, but one of the clearest statements experienced executives are making is that "bigger is better" is *not* necessarily always a good guide to the future.

Trevor Eyton, CEO of Brascan, a conglomerate with total assets exceeding $3 billion, feels that "we've had a learning experience in the last couple of years. People are concerned; they're worried and they're wondering, and that's a good thing. It makes you go back and ask, 'What's wrong?' I've been looking at a variety of corporate business plans, both in and out of our group, and it's really quite remarkable how they all sound the same. They're all going back to basics. They're all pushing decision-making down, making people more accountable, making them more active participants in the business process."

Particularly telling is the way Bay Street views the potential of the larger firms. These firms are partially sheltered because much of their equity financing comes from pension fund investments which cannot go offshore. These funds wind up being placed in the large Canadian resource-based firms almost by default. When you examine the choices made by investors with more freedom, there is a different story.

"The marketplace is becoming more sophisticated than it used to be. That's one of the reasons why your so-called household names are having so much difficulty doing financing. Sophisticated investors are able to see that their prospects are in fact not very exciting; they are in some cases marginal, and in some cases very bleak," points out the CEO of Burns Fry, Jack Lawrence, who has the reputation of being the sharpest bond trader in Canada.

He is particularly critical of those business leaders who sat on their hands waiting for the U.S. recovery to bail them out. "Waiting for the U.S. recovery is an easy course of action for a corporation to take. Wait for the cyclical recovery. Wait for higher commodity prices. Wait for lower interest rates. Wait for a pick-up in the order book, and so forth. And hold off on the type of action that would result in increased business independent of what might happen with the recovery. Business in Canada tends not to be particularly effective in terms of anticipated strategic changes. Canadian businessmen tend to be cautious by nature, and not aggressive in assessing the changes needed to compete in the new type of environment we are living in. They are playing the rules as though the world really hasn't changed much in the last couple of cycles."

Where will growth come from? That is the central question facing most of the CEOs we interviewed. In the past, through most of their early business careers, growth moved at a fairly quick and predictable rate. An expanding post-war population, increasing demand for Canadian commodities, and a healthy capital market seemed like the normal conditions of business, marred only here and there by a temporary recession.

"With money at three percent, a capital intensive strategy seemed like a sure winner. Money was cheap, everyone needed metals, and prices were relatively stable. From time to time we had to close the mines, but not often. Engineers were in demand, and in those days, we didn't need to pay much attention to politics—it was, after all, more predictable. Now, long-term money is expensive, and we aren't sure of the payback timetable on the investment—there is just too much uncertainty in the planning horizon. And I am under pressure to produce results quarterly to keep our institutional shareholders happy," says another harried CEO, who preferred not to be named.

Question: *"When did you first notice that things were changing?"*

"When oil prices were no longer being managed by London and New York," said the CEO of a multinational energy company.

"When my husband and I advertised for part-time child care assistance and got twenty-three replies, most from young people who not only had graduated, but who had advanced degrees," said the chief legal advisor for a crown corporation.

"When I went to buy a car for my daughter's graduation, and realized what inflation was doing to the market," said a corporate economist.

"When I came to Canada, my first experience with a small market," recalls the CEO of a manufacturing company.

"When my son, just out of Queen's, came back home to live with us—temporarily—until he could find a good corporate job, without leaning on me, . . ." muses the head of a forest products company. *"By the way, he is still here; he decided to go back to school."*

Most of those we talked to expected to see their companies grow only by acquisition, "anything else is too risky." They expressed concern that the pressures on them to perform quarterly in the stock market was preventing them from taking risks. All the uncertainties in the environment are combining to make us far more conservative, we were told. "You just can't afford to have a bad quarter, even if you are sacrificing one or two quarters for a good strategic reason."

Another contributing pressure is the high interest rates. Saskatchewan's Dick Pinder: "In the retail business, if you are aggressive in terms of expansion and in building inventories, you are very interest rate sensitive. If the forecasters are off in their timing, and recently they have missed by more than six months in their predictions, that kind of misreading can put a real squeeze on a retailer. Even if the high rates last only six months or a year, if they weren't anticipated, it is still pretty damaging. We know how much it can hurt."

Most of those interviewed acknowledge the risk-averse behavior of big public companies, and they expect this to continue until the environment "settles down." As a consequence, they are particularly unwilling to expand their payrolls. They expect their labor force will be stable or declining. They mention the pressure to compete, not just in a North American environment, but in the world market. "Don't forget that their labor cost is cheaper than ours, . . ." and harken back to an earlier time when productivity gains were easily achieved.

In only one area did those we interviewed slide back into the industrial-age argument about economies of scale; in only one area did they feel free to stress that "bigger is better." For some of the large firms it is clear that developing "world class" capacity is a key element of their strategy; a bulwark against a declining certainty about the manifest destiny of big business.

World Class Markets   Northern Telecom's CEO, Walter Light, says thinking in world-class terms is crucial: "Unless we think first of the North American market, and then the world market, we're never going to have a base big enough to succeed."

Pierre Lortie, president of the Montreal Exchange, agrees. "What we're seeing across the world, be it in Europe, the U.S. or Asia, is a very rapid integration of stock, bond, commodity and money markets, so that basically they will be functioning 24 hours a day. Montreal can play a significant role; we have an explicit strategy to integrate ourselves into this emerging network. We decided to position ourselves to be the dominant exchange in Canada. My deep conviction is that the major exchange in the nineties will be the one which is best integrated into the international networks."

Ironically, when Pierre Lortie took on this job in 1980, his first decision was whether or not to close Canada's oldest stock-trading institution. Lortie believes survival comes with world trade: "We are a trading nation, but for some reason, we seem to lack the preoccupation that other trading-nations have with what's happening worldwide." Lortie's focus is clearly on laying the foundations for the future, but he has seen some great results in the present. Propelled by next-economy computer technology and a deep understanding of Canada's place in the world economy, the Montreal Exchange is trading more volume than it has in years.

74

World class is a constant theme among Canadian giants. One good expression of that strategy came from Frank Tyaack, chief executive officer of Westinghouse Canada, an American-owned subsidiary that has operated successfully in this country since the turn of the century. We'll take an extended look at the Westinghouse story as a classic profile of an Ontario manufacturer. Not only have they faced up effectively to a decline, but their CEO had the most thoughtful responses we encountered on strategies for coping with the next economy.

"Can you describe the job you lost?"

Uluschak

Case Study: The Future of Manufacturing   Westinghouse Canada thrived in the tariff-protected Canadian market, and turned in year after year of great performance and good returns until about 1954, John Kettle's estimated peak year in the manufacturing sector. The company slid to a loss in 1961, and then spent a decade and a half pruning, recovering to achieve a fairly steady stream of modest profits.

75

By the late seventies, Westinghouse management concluded that their options boiled down, quite simply, to "oblivion versus some modest growth." Tyaack observes, "Given our position inside the Canadian market, the only conclusion I can reach is that growth has got to come from the world market. We had a clear choice: either downsize ourselves out of existence, or find a new mission to export and grow in world markets. We have to trade because we're a mature industry—100 years old. The heyday is gone even in the big developed countries, but particularly in small ones like Canada."

We were struck many times during the course of writing this book with the importance of longer time frames among business leaders who have thought about the transition and what they must do to survive. "Some business executives behave as if the future were just a bunch of quarters strung together," remarked George Beal, vice-president of General Foods. "Good CEOs are bifocal leaders. They have two time horizons: today and ten years from today. Everything in-between should be left to the professionals in the organization to manage in depth."

Trimac's Don Jackson, who candidly admits to having bet on the wrong future, now looks for two levels of skill in senior managers. "To the chief operating officer we say, 'You're responsible for this year's budget. It's yours to prepare, but it's yours to accomplish.' And that means it's not some grand scheme, it's looking after the nickels and dimes. After that, you try to see a little further out: where you're going, your key businesses, which geographic areas are important . . . setting the direction for the longer term."

Like the money managers whom you'll meet in Chapter 8, business leaders define time frames quite differently. Frank Tyaack: "The short term I talk about is two years; medium term, anything from your typical strategic planning cycle of five to ten; and beyond ten, the long term. When you ask about structural change, that's long term.

"Right now my time frame is 25 years. Over that span, we're going to lose a lot of jobs. At the managerial level, we will lose five for every one we retain. On the shop floor, the ratio will be three to one. In white collar jobs, it will be two to one. Now we will get some of those jobs back at the professional level. In a company like mine, you start as a professional, and just as you are hitting your peak, if you're any good, you get pushed into management where you learn measurement and control. Fortunately, we won't need to do that anymore. In the next economy, most people in our company will be able to spend their lives as professionals."

If job loss and downsizing are facts of life for the next economy, the possibilities for growth and development must be sought in different arenas. Tyaack suggests we look first at the workplace itself.

76

"We have a production system that we have hung onto dearly for many decades—the Taylor system—which was based on the precept 'take the brains out of the shop.' That is a flagrant waste of intellectual capital. The notion of comparative advantage leads you to believe that in a developed country such as Canada one of our comparative advantages over the rest of the world is intellectual capital—providing we keep feeding it. We have to get into the new software of production where we can utilize this brain power.

"We're not brain surgeons. Workers think. But we have set up our factories so that their brains are not involved in the system. About 30 percent of our factory work force is producing waste for us. So there's a lot of energetic intellectual capital now being wasted on beating the system. How much improvement in quality or reduction in labor costs might we get if we restructured production to capture this?"

Manufacturing in the last economy was set up to employ relatively unschooled workers. Management set the task, slotted somebody into it, defined the standards of performance, and then measured every employee. Management control meant "inspiring" workers who fell short to either measure up or get out. That type of system was great for the last economy. It is now a very, very expensive control system which only works if you assume you're going to "take the brains out of the shop."

> "In one U.S. steel plant I visited they had low quality control, they were making pretzels, not parts. But management thought they were in good touch with the workers because they phoned once a day to get production numbers. The workers knew better but they told me: 'We know we're making scrap, but if all they care about is the numbers, if those bastards want tons, we'll give them tons!' "

If we decide to put the brains back into the shop, we will no longer need those simple numerical controls; we will have better jobs, and more delegation of responsibility. Says Tyaack, "About 90 percent of my managers are now tied up with measurement and control. So if I can cut the control system, we will to get a five to one reduction in managers over the long term."

In addition to more effective management, these new work structures will permit us to handle the shorter, more profitable production runs that will be a key to success in the next economy. One chief executive officer who is well aware of the need to alter the production system in the direction of flexibility, targeting and maximizing short-run lines is Tom Smyth, president of Heinz Canada. "At Heinz when we decided we were serious about introducing these new technologies, the first thing we did was to see to it that every one of our senior managers got some hands-on experience with these technologies. Talking about the information age is one thing, living it is quite a different story. Therefore we saw to it that each executive had a microcomputer to experiment with at home, with the family." That kind of leadership style is what is so often missing in our approach to the transition. Tom Smyth's direct approach and his understanding of the difference between "talking about" vs. "doing it" is quite distinctive.

Market Seekers vs. Efficiency Seekers   Thinkers in the big business community are looking at the structure of the market itself for clues to help them (and us) through the transition. That means completely re-examining the fundamentals of trading strategies.

Market-seeking strategists were the winners in the last economy. Trade in the industrial world that is now breaking down was conducted largely within the context of tariff-protected economies. Multinationals made investments in other countries because that was the way to reach the host country's market.

A contrasting strategy treats the whole world as a market, and home base as a region. Management decisions are then made on the basis of getting the best cost across the world, and not just on the basis of what will sell in any one market.

Frank Tyaack understands this strategy, and provides examples on a moment's notice. "A vice-president of corporate planning did a hot study. First, he looked at product lines within Westinghouse; then, he extended it to a lot of other firms. He discovered that there was a 70 percent correlation between the profitability of a product line at home base and the profitability of the product in other regions.

"The conclusion of the old style *market seeker* is that if the parent can't succeed, the subsidiary won't. The lesson to them is 'if you're weak at home, don't go international.' By contrast, the newer *efficiency seeker* would conclude those results only mean that there's a 70 percent chance that the subsidiary is a carbon copy of the parent with all its strengths and weaknesses. Their conclusion: *don't clone the sub,* let it find its own operating style, appropriate to its own operating environment."

Even IBM understands this efficiency seeking strategy now, perhaps because it made so many early mistakes. Tyaack recalls with amusement the meeting at which an IBM quality-control VP was asked, "Does IBM Japan have better quality than IBM world wide?" and he said, "No." Tyaack points out that the old-fashioned manager would misinterpret the IBM executive's

78

answer to mean "Super, IBM world-wide quality is as good as Japan." But that was *not* IBM's conclusion. IBM concluded that they had forced their Japanese subsidiary to lower quality to fit IBM's world-wide model. "IBM cut them loose to be Japanese. They are convinced that they will have a teacher in their midst to bring the quality of the rest up to those standards."

There was consensus that world trade and a different measure of productivity go hand-in-hand. The traditional measure of productivity is output per man-hour. We used it in the last economy because we knew how to count it, even though we also knew it was only a proxy for a lot of other inputs we couldn't count. Says Tyaack, "It is foolish to spend 80 percent of our time on just one productivity variable, and ignore the cost creep from poor management in other areas.

"But we know that for most of this century, 80 percent of our capital projects were dedicated to driving down direct labor content in the product. When, about 15 years ago, we stopped getting productivity gains as they were measured, we accepted that as a normal occurrence in a 'mature economy' where demand had slowed to the point of diminishing returns.

"We never thought that a change in the structure of labor on the factory floor might be the key to productivity gains. But the Japanese tried it. They 'undivisionalized' labor, elevated management control, abandoned the simplistic concept of worker efficiency, and concentrated on the question of where waste really was. They found it in inventory, in capital investment, in quality, and in cycle time."

"Cycle time" provides a clear example of how efficiency can be improved. Cycle time refers to the period of time it takes to deliver a product to a customer from the moment the customer orders to the moment he receives it. Frank Tyaack believes that people who concentrate on inventory control focus primarily on the factory, whereas in fact, if you use a concept like cycle time, it becomes clear that the sales force and the white collar worker in the office know of the order long before the factory floor gets the word.

"Half the cycle time's down the drain before the factory even knows there's an order. And there's a complex set of things you must do from the time the customer defines what he wants in his complicated, customized machinery order, that has to be translated into specifics the shop can understand. Here's an example: the process of designing a governor for a steam turbine depends on the customer's steam conditions, which in turn depend on what he's going to use the turbine for. That process used to take six weeks. Now we've got expert systems to make that translation, and we're getting through the process in *less than a day*. That's a huge productivity improvement."

(By the way, it took Westinghouse Canada less than three months in cycle time from making the decision to install expert systems, to start delivery of the product.)

Frank Tyaack believes this kind of restructuring can become Canada's long suit. "Our comparative advantage is our intellectual capital. That's what we have to exploit. The LDCs [Less Developed Countries] have cheap manual labor—we're not going to beat them there by keeping our labor manual. And the NICs [Newly Industrialized Countries]—many of them have already gone the step of putting heavy capital leverage to that manual labor.

"The only place left where we can head-on compete—not that we beat out all other nations arriving at this point—is in that sphere of intellectual capital. The kind of production system that we arrive at with these structural changes now becomes one that can give us efficient small-lot production."

This is downsizing in another context. This kind of production system is not a slave to long production runs. It can yet transform the economy into one in which efficiency and good value can be achieved with small lots. Consumers will not have to sacrifice their preferences and join together with other consumers and other users in order to afford the economies of long production runs.

There is good reason to believe Canadians could benefit from a restructuring that involves short production runs. Aside from more easily accommodating our domestic market, the United States is moving in the same direction. As a result of these simultaneous developments, Canada will benefit.

Multinationals Tyaack, who runs one of the biggest subsidiaries in Canada, distinguishes between the old tariff-protected, market-seeking operation of the last economy and the situation today.

" 'Branch plantism' was appropriate to that world, because the only way you could trade was for the parent to get a piece of the action in Canada. The only way you did that was by manufacturing here. And Canada welcomed it, and provided incentives for it—Canadians weren't pushing them off, they were drawing them in at the time. That was at the turn of the century, and the early 1900s. Once having established the subsidiary, the 'sub' then became autonomous. There was no need for parent policy. Each 'sub' was in its trundle bed—one's in Canada, one's in England, one's in France. No coordination required.

"The lowest-cost way to control the subsidiary was to let them control themselves. But in that kind of world, where the tariff wall goes as high as it must to cover your inefficiencies, no smart subsidiary manager would have done his own research and development, unless his competitors did. But they all fell into this description, because most of his competitors were also branch plants. Even if they weren't branch plants, they were still confined by this local market.

"Given the rules of the day, there was no one outside of Canada that you could trade with. So it was a wise choice for him to buy his technology through licence, and it was a wise choice for him not to move too fast to new technology—let the parent go through the labor pains giving birth to this—the factory start-up, the mistakes you make when you try to put a new product through a whole new manufacturing process.

"But in a trading world, and if you're going to be an *efficiency* seeker, all bets are off. You're not going to have the protection from inefficiency and therefore you cannot afford diffusion lags, and you cannot summarily dismiss R & D. If I'm going for comparative advantage, and if I'm also in the efficiency-seeking culture, all centres of excellence are not 'at home' but are decentralized. Then for Canada to thrive, I must also, here in Canada, be a centre of excellence for something.

"So when we talk advanced technology, that strategy for the longer time period—I'm talking about R & D for Canada, and particularly R & D applied on products and for markets the parent is not entering. *The relationship between the parent and the sub must now parallel the kind of relationship that world trade is supposed to bring—an economic interdependence between sovereigns.* Each nation retains its sovereignty, but is interdependent economically with the rest of the world."

Downsizing can be used in yet another context. It is the context of appropriate scale as opposed to small-scale or mega-projects. Westinghouse Canada, for example, sells turbines to LDCs—small, packaged electrical plants that can be incremented in small doses. They are sold as self-contained units, and have lower maintenance so that local labor can be trained to operate them with no need for highly skilled, expensive ex-patriot management.

Says Tyaack, "We've been selling too much at the high end—the steel mill that has been carefully designed to minimize labor, but maximizes capital. The LDC not only borrows, but we ensure that they borrow far more than they should. And their surplus labor is wasted, because they spend capital that they don't have as a substitute for labor that they have plenty of. They should be using the surplus labor and minimizing the capital they have to lay out. My little packaged electrical plant is more appropriate than anything our competitors have to offer. That's where Canada can compete—

81

we have a comparative advantage in intellectual capital. We're going to get the order if we can figure out a technology that's more appropriate for the customer than our competitors have figured out."

In the next Canadian economy, interdependence means less autonomy for big business than it did in the last economy. But the promise of world trade is better productivity, a better allocation of resources around the world. Says Tyaack, "In a world-wide network of interdependence, all the units are orchestrated and dependent on each other. We have to plan together with our parent. But the sacrifice of autonomy for mutual strength gives us a better trading future."

Productivity improvement today does not necessarily involve job displacement through robots. In factories now, efficiency is being improved by the rearrangement of machines, by involving workers in the search for better quality, reduced cycle times and lower inventory, and by adding software and modifying machines for quick changeover. Says Tyaack, "We're getting payback periods in some of our incremental projects in terms of weeks, not years. The capital going up front is very low. We're talking about micro-computers, independent stations that can talk to master stations, nothing very expensive. I've got a factory manager who has a ten-year plan with a lot of robots out in year ten, but there's none in the first five years at all."

In the white collar area, investments for the transition are lacking because the whole production system will have to change. Tyaack continues, "The problem with the clerk's job is that all the brains are in the procedure; we did that through the typewriter and the carbon paper and all the different colors for copies. You know—the pink one goes here and the green one goes there. Now we've got to drastically redefine those jobs because they're over-specialized."

Says Roy Cottier, senior vice-president, Northern Telecom, "Canada is an interdependent country. We have the essential resources to be independent as well. We have a latent brain-power pool comparable to any in the world. But if you look at the speed with which technology has moved in the last decade, my inclination is to say we don't have a lot of time to make decisions. We need to make a national commitment—not just to government, but industry, the universities—the Canadian people have got to commit to the fact that we have to generate a brain centre in Canada which will permit us to occupy a position of prominence and profitability in the brain industries."

The penalty for failure? Cottier warns, "We're going to be *dependent*, not independent or interdependent. And we're going to be nobody, because no one can afford to buy or obtain all their technology from other sources. When you do, in the world of the future, you become an economic vassal of your supplier, because he isn't selling you the technology he's using, he's selling you the technology he used yesterday. What you want is the technology he's going to use tomorrow."

Big business is struggling for its place in the next economy. It grew big when the cost of capital was low. It doesn't have that option now. It grew big when it was profitable to take risks on new products and new production techniques. Today, the enormous debt that was incurred in the boom times has made business increasingly cautious and conservative. The need to appear profitable on a quarter-to-quarter basis puts further pressure on corporations not to take risks.

Big business may still be creating wealth, but it is no longer creating jobs. What does that do to its political clout? With jobless growth what poker chips does it bring to the table?

Finally, the big business community is struggling to find its place in a world in which production is increasingly international and interdependent. It is not an easy position for people whose values were formed in an era when big was always beautiful, always a competitive edge.

For Canadian big business, the challenge is to think in ways which are unfamiliar because they never seemed necessary in the last economy. In the last economy, it was sufficient, even profitable, to supply the domestic market. Where it made economic sense to have long production runs, people—intellectual capital—could safely be ignored because productivity and efficiency had been built into the system.

The vice-president for planning of B.C. Tel, Ewout Van Dishoeck, points out: "We are endowed with a great natural wealth, which we have been able to develop to date, and will continue to take advantage of. There's one asset that we have tended to underrate and you'll probably find that there are tremendous gains to be had there, and that's in our people. We've just reaped our natural resources and done whatever it took to nurture those assets, and have done a lousy job in nurturing our people assets."

The transition to the next economy has turned our attitudes upside down. Now we are in an era when short runs are profitable, even necessary, and it is time to "put the brains back into the jobs." Large enterprises must think in world market terms. If the Japanese enjoyed an advantage in recent decades it was due to an early recognition of their weakness; they accepted the idea that they had no choice but to be internationally oriented.

If there was one dominant concern of those we talked with it was the need to eliminate the big bureaucratic trappings of the last economy and to learn how to utilize the brains of the people who are the newly recognized wealth of the next economy. Knowledge capital is on a par with other forms of capital. A romantic fascination with the freedom of the small independent businesses carries with it a wistful recognition of how much effort will be required to manage the transition. The world these big business leaders knew will not return; now it is time to get on with the job.

Chapter 7

THE MANDARINS

I f big business is being forced into thinking small, the same pressures go double for government: the public sector is going to have to shrink. Downsizing is the key activity for both big business and big government in the transition to the next economy. The giant government bureaucracies that grew up over the last forty years will be reduced in scale, if not in influence, as we move into the next economy. Not many people will be sorry to see the bureaucrats go.

While public servants are regarded as a necessity, they are universally disliked as a class, becoming natural scapegoats for abuses within the bureaucracy and easy targets for politicians, members of the opposition, and the press. Government bureaucracies grew too fat, too fast, and worst of all, bureaucrats seem too secure in their jobs when all the rest of us are worried about ours.

"The service sector has grown enormously in recent years, with the policies of the state supporting this expansion . . . in education, health care delivery, unemployment benefit schemes and the like. . . . The great bureaucracies which have resulted are likely to be amongst the early candidates for automation and are, in any case, generally unpopular with the public, being regarded as cold, impersonal and inefficient. They are likely to be replaced by smaller, partially automated units of greater efficiency," says Club of Rome forecaster Alexander King.

This is not simply a Canadian attitude; bureaucracies are universally disliked across the tax-paying world. Yet some of the leaders within the public service are likely to have pivotal roles in the transition to the next economy. In addition to the task of cleaning house and reforming the structure of the public service itself, they will be the ones who have to streamline the social service delivery system, suggest budget cuts, and make fairly drastic program changes if we are going to service the squeeze on revenues. They are the first line of defence against a growing deficit.

It may come as news to some that Canadian public servants are regarded elsewhere as among some of the best in the world. Often at international events, Canadian mandarins are asked to chair the committees, mediate in delicate disputes, and head the staff in international organizations. One building block in the transition to the next economy is the group of senior public servants who have been through a difficult but very important learning curve in the last decade. They are a valuable resource in the transition.

The top group of senior public servants has acquired the nickname of "mandarins." The label comes from the ancient Chinese court—"mandarin" was the name given to those skilled public administrators who were quite often also known as clever politicians. Most of the senior Canadian mandarins are by tradition, and in fact, apolitical. There are some high profile exceptions and they are rewarded by being moved out of the public service. Michael Kirby and Michael Pitfield, for example, were appointed to the Senate.

The role of the mandarins in the governing process has undergone, and will continue to undergo, a rapid transformation as we move into the next economy. Most of the senior mandarins, like their counterparts in business, grew up in an era of rapid growth. Their biggest responsibility was to preside over the distribution of Canada's wealth.

They have subsequently had to wrestle with a decade of oil price shocks, constitutional reforms, declining tax revenues, and a constant escalation of social service costs. Now they have to preside over the downsizing of the public service. Not unlike economists and businessmen, the mandarins have been forced to start learning the limits of their financial resources, and the limits of management "sciences." These realities shocked even some of the mandarins most in love with centralized "macro-planning." In the words of the former head of the Prime Minister's Office, Tom Axworthy, they are now faced with the need to "redistribute scarcity."

Slowly, too, the public service and its political masters have become aware of another change in their approach: their attitude towards public sector management. Just as the bureaucracies of big business are learning to be more entrepreneurial, more flexible and adaptive, the management style of government must also change.

"Remember, the public service was created in an atmosphere of defensiveness, to prevent patronage, to prevent dishonesty. It was a fundamentally negative posture. Now we need to learn to manage in a more positive style. There are some talented people in government, really good managers—but we tie their hands with unnecessarily complicated control procedures left over from that old defensive attitude," points out Jacques Guérin, deputy minister, Department of Environment.

"For example, hiring procedures are very rigid, and consequently very costly. Suppose we know we have a short-term program to conduct. Ideally, you should give a good manager a budget and let him decide whether to use five part-time students, or to hire a career civil servant. But with the system we have now, you can't do that very easily. A central agency gets involved. This doubling up of controls reduces productivity, reduces the efficiency you can get when you increase people's responsibility and autonomy. No one wants a return of the old patronage system, but neither do we want to lose the opportunity to mature, and to improve. That means opening up the system so there is room for creativity."

Another senior mandarin, who has perhaps the best track record in developing young managers, points out: "A tremendous amount of waste in the system is there because we don't give managers room to either succeed or fail. While the auditor general's office is a good idea because it may evolve into a way to test our effectiveness, it is quite a different matter with overlapping central agency controls. If we need to move in the direction of becoming decentralized, with smaller more efficient units, then we have to find a way to have our good managers operate and think like small businessmen. That means they have to fail once in awhile, and learn something from it. Our present system may prevent failure, but it also prevents excellence."

In the transition to the next economy it is clear that the mandarins' role must change from simply "redistribution" to clearing a path for wealth generation, and from a public service attitude of defensiveness to a more positive posture. Those who understand this have been quietly pressing for reforms in the system. Some argued against indexation, for example, but were outvoted by the politicians. After all, we had a budget surplus at the time.

Other reforms initiated by the mandarins were designed to try to force cabinet ministers to think about trade-offs when they were making budget decisions, as opposed to just "adding" one more expensive program. Politicians tend to get off the hook easily when mandarins lose these contests for reform; mandarins do not go public with their concerns. This charming old tradition may have to change in the transition to the next economy. While it supports the goal of staying apolitical, it handicaps us in knowing what the fight was all about. After all, it's our money they are spending.

It was a mandarin plan, for example, to install the envelope system for which the Clark government was credited. The envelope system was

87

designed to make the role of the government in the economy more clear by dividing all government spending into nine budgetary "envelopes," not just for the coming year, but for three years into the future. The purpose of the envelope system is to force cabinet to make large policy choices between, for example, the social affairs envelope and the economic development enve-lope. Although not a completely effective barrier, it does act as a curb on the ministerial tendency to simply invent programs and instruct the man-darins to "go find the money."

Although the idea was first suggested in 1972, and recommended virtually every year thereafter, the envelope system wasn't picked up until Clark took office. The new government, looking for something to put its stamp on, took it up; that is often how reforms happen.

We occasionally hear from the mandarins indirectly, through public inquiries such as the Lambert Commission. The 1979 Lambert Report rein-forced the mandarin determination to get Cabinet to make fiscal choices: "Planning is effective only in an environment in which there are real and finite limits to resources. Planning will never be successful if it is conducted on the assumption that resources are inexhaustible." The reason the enve-lope system hasn't worked better is that there has still been too much "loose" money in the system.

Another mandarin innovation, finally implemented by the politi-cians, has been the disclosure of *tax expenditures*. This allows Canadians to evaluate the costs of tax breaks. Even though the current figures do not reveal the full cost of these tax incentive programs, they do give us a better idea of the price. More importantly, the publication of a price tag on tax expenditures reminds us that such spending is not free.

Both of these improvements to the system make it tougher to take certain "add-on" decisions quietly, and without examining the trade-offs. They also enable those outside the system to get a better idea of costs, and to review the policy gaps more critically. Therefore, when the opposition says it is "completely in the dark," be wary.

Similarly, when the press fails to do the arithmetic on the cost of campaign promises, for example, it is not that they couldn't do better if they tried. They just haven't bothered, or they only report on the comments of the opposition. The coverage was so poor in the last election in this regard that *The Globe and Mail* had to formally apologize for a misleading headline on the cost of election promises. The retraction said the *Globe* "disregarded the fact that the Liberal estimate covered three and a half years, while the Conservative estimate covered only two and a half years." The sad part is that neither estimate was complete and the paper accepted the candidates' stories rather than doing its own investigative work.

In the wake of the Tory landslide election, the task of sorting out the mandate for the new government is more difficult than usual. The huge cabinet, the wide range of perspectives to be accommodated as the PCs struggle to define themselves as a truly national party, and the prime minister's campaign promises to keep universality, for example, will combine to make structural changes difficult. If mandarins had a hard time pressing even seasoned ministers to make cuts, they may have even more difficulty with a new crop, some of whom enter government with little experience and a pronounced suspicion of the advice they might receive from senior civil servants. "It is always a delicate task to explain to ministers that life is a little more complicated than they would like to believe. Now, given the structural changes in the economy, it will be an even greater challenge. The answers are not cut and dried for the next Canadian economy. We didn't even learn how to 'fine tune' things in the last one," says an assistant deputy minister.

The large number of new players also contributes to communications snags and makes the system even more unwieldy. "Large cabinets are particulary handicapped when they try to make budget cuts. There is no discipline; it is easy to let a proposal from one minister go by, after all, the cabinet minister across the table has his proposal to put forward next," points out one veteran of the priorties and planning process.

"I have always been in favor of the British system of tiered cabinets—with senior ministers in charge, and junior ministers reporting to them. You stand a much better chance at getting some control in the system and at resisting the politics of distribution which usually goes 'you get yours, I'll get mine.' But it has been hard to introduce this system here. Canadian cabinets have been far too large and unwieldy in the past, and the most recent federal election results, with the need to spread the win so widely, may have made matters worse in trying to control spending," says a senior public servant who prefers not to be named.

Contrary to popular belief, mandarins are in favor of new governments because that is the best opportunity for sweeping changes and reforms in the system. "The only time you get anything done is in the first year of a new government," says another veteran. Briefing books presented to a new government are designed not only to help the new ministers catch up with their responsibilities, but to press the departments to set priorities with more care. It is housecleaning time. Briefing books prepared for the Mulroney government stressed the need not only for careful budget cutting, but for some changes in the way the system is managed. The briefings recommended that the new prime minister focus on collaborating with the provincial premiers and consulting widely with the private sector—advice constructed to encourage the government to stop and reconsider the billions of dollars of campaign promises.

89

The message that was delivered loud and clear by the most experienced: "Consult all you want, but for God's sake, don't try to spend your way into being seen as 'active' and in 'control' . . . take a few months to learn the ropes and to find out what such sacred cows as 'universality' really cost!" Great concern has been expressed by senior deputy ministers that in the rush to be seen to be "in charge," the new ministers would move too quickly to take costly actions to prove their credibility with respect to election promises.

"For example, the promise to deliver equal pay for work of equal value made during the women's issues debate by Brian Mulroney could cost in the neighborhood of one billion dollars a year! Just figure it this way, and for simplicity I am rounding off: 500,000 federal workers, 300,000 or so are women, fully one-third of them by our estimate would need a pay increase of up to $10,000 apiece per year. I hope they decide to put a commission in place—with a reporting date in the year 1990—rather than just send down directives to execute this promise without checking on the $4 billion that it would cost in four years! And that cost does not even take into account the cost of doing the same things in Crown corporations, and of requiring suppliers to the government to follow similar guidelines!"

In short, the arithmetic done behind the heavy wooden doors in Ottawa costing out the campaign promises has drawn shudders of concern from the most knowledgeable of those who administer the government. "The good news for us with the new government is that at least some people out there seem to be watching and counting this time . . . maybe all the publicity about the deficit is having a useful effect on the ministers."

Fortunately, the new finance minister, Michael Wilson, expressed his belief that the election promises should be tied to the performance of the economy before taking office. In addition, the new energy minister from B.C. and former finance critic, Pat Carney, has cautioned that successful economic management is not just a matter of saying a few nice words to the Americans, re-naming FIRA, and stepping back to get out of the way of the flood of capital. Before the election, both were actively trying to get the other caucus members up to speed on economic matters, especially on the issue of facing the transition to the next Canadian economy.

Decisions about what to cut and what to keep are clearly different if you are waiting for a return to the good old days, or if you are looking to the demands of the next economy. For example, if you believe that Canada should compete with Korea by putting up automated textile factories, that means one kind of policy. But if you believe that "human capital" or "knowledge capital" is the critical component in the next economy, then that suggests increased funding for education, and serious attention to putting a retraining system together that goes deeper than political rhetoric. Amongst those who administer the system, there is a lot of respect for Don Johnston's analysis that "we don't yet even know what to retrain people for!"

But it takes a long time to put serious changes into effect. Russell Robinson, Consumer and Corporate Affairs: "We have some mental blocks to get over in order to confront the transition to the next economy. These include wishful thinking about returning to past simplicity, or that somehow an invisible hand will allow us to muddle through. The consequences of being wrong about things are enormous. We can't risk just sitting back and letting things happen; we're too close to the flashpoint. We have to be brave enough to confront the possibilities, armed with the knowledge that we'll have to ask difficult questions, that we'll make mistakes, that there are many areas where we won't have all the data. The worst thing we can do is fall back and wait for someone else to do it for us."

There is room for dramatic new directions in the first months of a new government. But if the fundamental assumptions aren't addressed in that period, if the questions aren't asked because the government is engaged in mood management to get "confidence " going in the country again, then another whole cycle of government gets lost in maintaining the status quo. The new government runs the risk of failing to critically examine the ways old assumptions from the last economy are blocking any effective transition to the next.

Here are some of the issues the mandarins would like to see closely, and openly, explored:

"We have several kinds of rigidities in the system—people can't move easily to where the jobs may be developed; it is difficult to retrain workers across sectors. To move a former factory worker into a service job, for example, may take a long time. And we also have rigidities in the wage system, and in our definition of the job itself—we are far too tied to a forty-hour-week-at-the-factory model.

"All these rigidities must yield to achieve a transition to the next economy. But you cannot get people to let go of those things unless they feel safe enough to experiment; what that implies is that we might have to strengthen the safety net for awhile, so that flexibility can be introduced to the system. Unfortunately, just at the time we might need to strengthen the net to provide a bridge to the next economy, we are short of funds," explains a senior mandarin.

Interesting notion—that one way to help loosen up the system, and speed the adaptation process, is to strengthen the safety net for awhile during the transition.

Another concern of the mandarins is how to pull away from the elements of the tax system that were designed for the last economy. There is a growing belief in their ranks, for example, that serious tax simplification—which would help introduce more flexibility into the system, and broaden the tax base, should be considered. But there is little confidence that these issues will be addressed at this stage. "With such a diffuse vote in the last election, virtually every interest group feels itself to be a contributor to the majority government win. That is, regrettably, the worst possible environment to try to get simplification or base-broadening." Former principal secretary Tom Axworthy agrees: "Tax reform brings out the special interest groups like nothing else."

Income Distribution   One of the biggest and most politically awkward issues that the Mulroney government faces is the problem of getting better use out of the funds tied up in providing unemployment insurance and welfare benefits. It is not just a "mechanical problem in delivery," but goes much deeper, to a fundamental assumption implicit in the way job loss is labelled. Calling unemployment a "temporary" problem for such a large chunk of the population contributes to a less than optimal program design. The UIC and welfare systems are designed to be a safety net to handle short-term stresses on the system brought about by relatively short downturns in the business cycle.

Deputy Minister Mark Daniels, a veteran of Finance, Labor and other government departments: "Haven't we learned anything in 80 years? Those who would argue that 'We made it through the last transition and we'll be able to muddle through the next' choose to overlook the human waste and terrible cost of the transition between the agricultural and industrial era. Let's be frank. *It is not without cost to our society to displace a worker.* If we've learned one thing, it is that everybody is part of the system; sooner or later we have to face up to the income distribution issue. This is a mutual problem, we should not waste the legacy of knowledge and mutual respect we've built up—solutions should be imaginative, flexible and responsive—but we need to approach this together."

How much do you think it really costs to put someone on the shuttle-bus between federal and provincial coffers? First the unemployed person goes on UIC (federally funded), then he goes on welfare (provincially funded), then he goes on "make work" (sometimes federally and provincially funded) just long enough to qualify to return to the federally financed UIC. For the governments, the object is to get the guy out of your budget, and into "theirs."

92

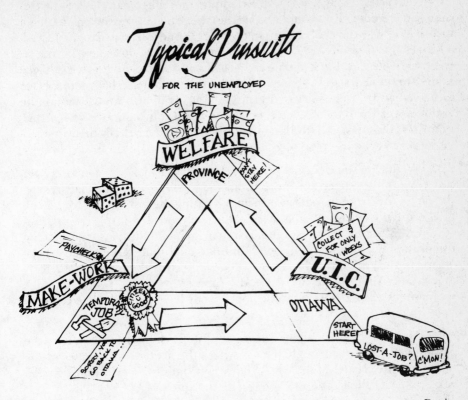

Davis

This UIC-welfare-makework-UIC shuttlebus may salve our consciences because it allows the shuttlebus passengers to put on their "good citizen" caps for part of the ride, but it costs us a lot to play this game. The fuel which keeps this shuttlebus on the road is the belief that (or the pretense that) unemployment is temporary. A mere momentary problem, until the next upswing of the business cycle, or until the recovery comes.

Once we admit that unemployment is a long-term, structural situation, we must bluntly face the reality that our welfare, unemployment insurance and job retraining schemes were designed to serve the last economy. We cannot afford, year after year, to hand out a billion dollars a month from a program that was designed as a "temporary" response to a "temporary" problem.

93

Tackling this scale of problem implies not only a far greater level of candor but tremendous cooperation from the provincial governments. This means a reduced level of tension in the internecine warfare that often characterizes the relations between federal and provincial bureaucrats—not to mention politicians. But it also means a willingness to explore massive changes in the fundamentals of the income distribution system. That requires tact and trust, and a framework for at least talking about income distribution. It also requires some political courage. For example, two ministers who tried to address those issues in the last government were muzzled by their worried cabinet colleagues.

Reducing the deficit by striking the right balance between safety net concerns and the need for more room for wealth-generating activity is at the top of the list of mandarin priorities. Getting the system in place for the next economy by downsizing, eliminating outmoded control systems, creating room for more entrepreneurial management attitudes, and making use of the new technologies is part and parcel of that. "One of the crucial effects of the computer revolution will be to destroy the bureaucratic hierarchy . . . technically we now have the capacity to enable people to make semi-autonomous decisions at the appropriate level and eliminate layers of management," suggests Jacques Guérin.

But the biggest challenge in accomplishing those things is to have the *political will* to see it through. This is where the leadership qualities of the politicians are crucial. Mandarins can propose options, but the final decision resides with Cabinet, and ultimately with the voter.

In the next chapter we'll see how those who must evaluate both big business and big government view the challenges they face in the transition to the next Canadian economy.

Chapter 8

THE MONEY
MANAGERS

The dramatic turmoil of the transition to the next economy is seen clearly in the industry which invests the wealth and savings of the nation. In addition to the private accounts which they manage, professional money managers control over $100 billion of Canadian pension fund money.

Their daily decisions can sway the confidence we have in the Canadian dollar, influence which companies will be subject to takeover, shape how many jobs might be available for our children, and affect how well we live in our retirement years.

As powerful and influential as they may seem to us, money managers, too, are being buffetted by the transitional winds. They are in the center of the maelstrom of the information revolution and can afford to buy and use the whole panoply of new communications technologies. But they use these advanced tools largely within the framework of the old structures. While each day they apply the techniques of the next economy, they are still managing the assets of the last one.

Changes caused by the speedy new information systems have altered not only the way the game is played, but the nature of the game itself. For example, the original trust function of money managers was pretty conservative. Their job was to place savings in investments that would grow and create wealth over the long term. That long-term trust function has been slowly undermined by escalating pressure to out-perform their competitors over a shorter and shorter time frame.

Money managers are in the spotlight. People keep a close watch on what they do. After all, they are controlling vast sums of other people's money and other people's assets. One positive consequence of the tough and frequent performance reviews is that money managers can't afford to hang onto dogma. They can't hold their audience just by telling a good story. Sooner or later, they have to justify their story by reference to "the bottom line." Did they, in fact, make money for their clients? How did they do up against the other guys? They get a report card on their performance quarterly, if not more often.

Says Salomon Brothers' senior economist Brian Fabbri: "The inter-quarter performance becomes the most important part of a portfolio manager's strategy, not only because of the need to achieve top yields, but also because of the need to maintain the investment base. The investment game has become far more competitive. And so the game is no longer just to beat some actuarial (yield curve) requirement, but also to achieve market prominence and attract funds from competitors. Therefore, the emphasis on interquarterly transactions now dominates the market."

In the industrial economy, there were fairly clear links between value, wealth, economic growth and jobs. The economy built on things we all valued; land, labor and money were combined with entrepreneurial talent to create wealth. When the process works, more jobs are created, more people are drawn into the economy, and all of us are drawn up the ladder of affluence.

While the intent is still there, in practice, the game is changing. It is no longer clear that so-called long-term money is invested for the long haul, nor that money managers struggle to find underlying, long-term value. Nor is it clear that all investments automatically create jobs. There is a big mismatch between the length of time that those billions of dollars of pension funds could be held, and the time frame within which those funds are presently managed. While these funds could be put to work over the long term, in practice, much of these pension fund monies are in short-term placements.

It used to be easy to distinguish between investment and speculation. Serious investors were supposed to be committed over the long haul. By contrast, speculators were just taking a short ride. Now that the performance pressures on money managers are so fierce, it is having an impact on the link between value, wealth, economic growth and jobs. In the process of finding their feet in the transition to the next economy, these powerful money managers may be contributing to a distortion in the traditional role of investors.

This is how the distortion happens. Because money managers are increasingly judged on their short-term performance, they seek high yields, even in the short run. The publicly listed corporations they invest in are in turn forced to set their sights on improving their quarterly reports lest the money managers dump their stock because of poor short-term performance.

As was noted in Chapter 6, corporations forced to focus on short-term performance are discouraged from taking risks to develop new products or services. They are hesitant to sacrifice a few quarters' performance to shore up a longer-term strategy; they wind up "investing" in safe acquisitions, rather than new start-ups. But that type of investment generates no new jobs—it is merely an exchange of ownership.

Chief executives have also been spending more time and energy looking for short-term fixes while trying to avoid takeover bids as larger companies, who are also using the strategy of growing by acquisition, go grazing in the market.

These activities have little to do with creating future wealth or jobs. Indeed, acquiring other companies or buying back their own stock simply recycles money that might otherwise be available to new companies just starting up. Petro-Canada's buyout of Petrofina and BP produced not a barrel more of oil; neither did Dome's takeover of Hudson Bay Oil and Gas.

The longer-term implications of these very conservative, risk-averse corporate decisions are worrisome. Fewer startups and less development of new products or oil fields add up to less wealth and fewer jobs. While knowledgeable people who run the Canadian investment houses, such as Jack Lawrence, CEO at Burns Fry, would caution against overstating the case, pointing out that the market does seek value, they also express concern about the conservative trend in investing.

Many Canadians do not even know where their pension funds are invested. This chapter looks at the world of the money managers and the problems that the transition to the next economy has created for them and for us, since we are the "other people" whose money they manage.

Our exploration of the heady world of the money managers takes us to two lofty offices, one overlooking New York harbor, the other high over Vancouver harbor. They share mountaintop vantage points of the economics of production, investment, and value creation despite differences in business philosophy and in personal and management style.

Vancouver   In Vancouver are the offices of M.K. Wong & Associates, one of Canada's newest, and most successful, entrants in the pension fund management field. Not only does the firm have an excellent track record, but in only four short years M. K. Wong & Associates has grown to

THE NEXT CANADIAN ECONOMY

control over a billion dollars, about 1 percent of the total Canadian pension fund portfolio. While the trading room bustles with activity, lined with flashing computer screens, Chinese tea is served in the pleasant meeting room. Milton Wong responds to the visitor's question about the beautiful collection of modern art works: "All these pictures were done by my sister, she's a very talented and creative person. But she would be the first to agree that business is equally creative."

His soft-spoken manner belies the fast pace and rigors of his day, which starts at 7 a.m. in the office. "During the morning we gather and exchange information with various people in the capital markets. We have telephone calls from London, New York, Toronto . . . and we talk amongst ourselves . . . maintaining a continuous update on what we consider to be important, and which enables us to adjust our portfolios. We don't have formal morning meetings like many of the Bay Street firms because we have a wide open room, and a constant exchange. That's one thing that's somewhat unique about our company, we have an open agenda.

"I don't even have a personal office. We all sit out there, unless we need to come in here to talk with a guest. This also says that we have a team with a high regard for one another. There is a lot of mutual understanding about our weaknesses, as well as our strengths. The choice of people in our company is very important, so that we can stand that kind of openness and the pressure. Other organizations have one man, one office. That to us creates unnecessary hidden agendas, and that's just not our style.

"All dreams must begin with a sound foundation. So that's basically where we begin in our choice of investments for the pension funds we manage. One has to be an observer of society, to explore where demands are increasing, what are the demographic factors, the changing values that create a demand pull. We were just talking about soft contact lenses, for example. That business recognizes both an aging population and the values of that group; they don't want to wear devices in front of their eyes; they prize intimacy and spontaneity. So 24-hour soft lenses work for them. That business will grow because of a combination of demography and *values*.

"That type of approach to the marketplace provides a strong foundation. So that when one does perceive a uniqueness of a product, you are actually assured of a final demand for that product. In other words, you could have a unique product, but if no one wants it, you might as well leave it in a drawer.

"In measuring a risk, when I call us aggressively conservative, I guess it's our way of suggesting that one should be mindful of the basics, such as assessing management. You can have a good idea, a unique product. But if the group or the individuals involved with it do not have the administrative or financial capability of carrying through, all is lost.

"Whether you're in the forest industry or mining industry, sometimes final demand for products in itself will carry the day. But when it really gets tough, then sensitive management could be the difference between making a profit or not making a profit. So we evaluate management's ability and discipline. That makes a big difference between a company you would buy, and one you would not."

Evaluation is one of the tasks money managers perform for us in putting discipline in the economy. Wong's philosophy regarding the investment of pension fund monies sounds much closer to what might be described as the traditional trust function; he spent seventeen years in the trust department of a bank before he left to form his own company. But in addition to evaluating companies one-by-one, he devotes much of his energy to forecasting the international investment climate. Central to his analysis is how the world of politics affects business options.

"So far in this business cycle the U.S. has not bailed us out. I think what has happened is that two or three years ago, our political and economic philosophy diverged from that of the United States. We both want and do enjoy a high standard of living. Both live on the same continent. But what has happened is that in Canada we have taken the liberty of diverging in political and economic philosophy, thereby causing a grave dislocation in this country. It has to do with the built-up political and social structures that we have here, where, rightly or wrongly, the political system intervenes in the private sector so much that many opportunities are no longer here.

"What that means, for example, is that we have a more difficult time attracting capital. Last year, over $6.6 billion left the country unidentified, according to the Bank of Canada. And that's a lot of money. Perhaps it is a reflection of Canadians' lack of confidence in the Canadian economy.

"In 1981 we had to go offshore, buying over $26 billion outside of the country, in large measure, to facilitate the Canadianization program. That's one source of the poor Canadian balance sheet. If you're in a resource-based country, the government sector should not expect to have the ability to regulate international commodities. I think that lesson is well-learned in the area of energy, where they attempted to regulate crude oil prices in the last few years, just to find out that oil, for example, is an international commodity.

"I think they misread the whole scene. I think we should look at the whole period of nationalism as a period in which the government sector

99

wanted to gain a bigger share of the revenue streams from the private sector, and in that way attempted to interfere in the private sector. You might recall, in terms of the mega-projects, I think there was a $13 billion mega-project in heavy oil. There was a little argument, I believe, with the private sector as to what was the price they should receive. When the price of oil was just actually beginning to go down, they were still arguing about what price it should be. The government sector also pre-spent a lot of their anticipated revenues. Herein lie our current problems. Now, we have to dismantle all the structural things that ought not to be there.

"Our domestic interest rates, relative to the economic activity that we have in this country, are too high. The cost of capital is much too high; this affects profit margins. We know labor costs are pretty well under control and material costs are pretty well under control. But interest costs are soaring."

Question: Now, by law, you have to invest most of your money in Canada?

Wong: Yes, we are limited to 10 percent non-Canadian investments. There has been talk of relinquishing that 10 percent or raising it. If we ever raised the amount that we could take out of the country, it would all go out of the country. And I don't think the government sector will, or should do that.

Question: Do you find yourself torn between being a patriot and wanting to get the best returns for your clients?

Wong: I don't personalize my investments. We have certain rules to follow, and within those rules we will do due diligence. And if they change the laws, we will adjust.

Since Wong's investment criteria include looking for fundamental values he has some very definite views about how to improve the Canadian economy. One of the first items on his agenda is the deficit. He emphasizes that reducing the deficit must be a gradual task, paring it down, not shocking the economy. He suggests we begin by restructuring:

"Cost savings could start with better coordination among all government levels. Then there is the dismantling process; we talked about one, the privatization of Crown corporations. Crown corporations' demands for funds in a capital market are now very, very high. On the other side, though, you must make it attractive for someone to buy a Crown corporation."

Milton Wong also looks with hope towards the impact of the new technologies on the shape of government bureaucracies. "The information revolution, with efficiencies gained through use of technology in the government sector, can be construed as a process of rationalizing which will perhaps over time, improve the government's effectiveness in delivering social services. That's something we should never underestimate. There are several other ways to reduce and rationalize government, but it will take time. Indexation could be phased out in many areas, for example. And we may need to review universality. All I'm suggesting is that this area should be re-evaluated in it's totality, so that perhaps we become a little more sensitive as to where to target social programs.

"I know that if the government sector is downsized, it is axiomatic that there will be a positive multiplier in the private sector. The body politic is demanding it, and will continue to demand it over the next ten years. I think there's a natural process of what I call, the 'creative disintegration of monolithic organizations.' There's a natural tendency now, given the new technologies, for these huge bureaucracies to disintegrate so that individuals can become more creative.

"It's a question of scale. It's not just government that's too big; you have banks, and major mining companies. And what happens is, the organic nature of these huge bureaucratic organizations is lost and they are no longer organic. They become archaic, rigid, and not able to respond to market demands.

"Solving the deficit problem perhaps isn't the end all, but if you do develop a gradual four- or five-year program to reduce the deficit, then confidence will begin to be restored. There will be less likelihood of Canadians leaving the country, voting with their feet.

"Within that broad framework, we should begin to establish priorities in terms of jobs and so forth. But, it's going to be a long, sticky road. I think the players in Canada are too used to a certain method of thinking and their head space has to be redirected before they can really solve the problem. It's more than just 'do this' and the problem will be solved. It has to do with our attitude.

"I feel that the unemployment levels will remain high. I would say that new jobs will grow in the small-business sector, where people can find little niches of activity. These small businesses are finding it very difficult, however, to get capital. And they have to have shooters to do it. Unfortunately, a lot of shooters have lost their money in the real estate market. . . . During an inflationary period, those who made money through real estate were really very venturesome. Now, it's completely gone the other way, so that a very important source of funding for new ventures has disappeared.

101

"We find in pension fund management that we cannot and should not be involved to a high degree in terms of venture capital because much of the money we manage is 'trust' money, rather than our own. I just don't really see where employment growth is going to come from. We may have to look forward to seeing our children moving to New York or Los Angeles . . . we may have to accept that.

"In Canada we're obviously very embryonic in terms of high technology. I don't think we should use 'high technology' as the savior of mankind, so to speak. But there are niches that can develop. We aren't going to become Silicon Valley North overnight. They have too much of a lead time on us.

"To be realistic, you have to look at Canada's relationship to the total world. So, if we're hurting now, you can imagine what's happening in Argentina and Chile. It's really something. To restore confidence is a long, arduous task, and it has to do with prudence. It seems to me that people will begin to spend only if they feel that there is a future for themselves."

Milton Wong is straddling the last and the next economies with a philosophy developed, in part, through his years of volunteer work. "I learned a lot from working with individuals who were volunteering . . . continually assessing why one person reacts one way versus the other way. You begin to learn behavior patterns. I often said that if I didn't go into investment, my second choice would be social work. Both fields have a commonality. Our job is to measure human behavior. We're there in one instance to make money for our clients, and in the other to help the individual out in his own personal life. They're not that far apart really.

"In a *voluntary* organization if someone is there for an ego trip, or for recognition, they get weeded out automatically by the volunteer process. It teaches you a lot of patience too, because whenever you deal with new volunteers, and they have to go through the same learning process. It may be old hat for you or me, but new to him. I think what you learn from all that volunteer work, is how to deal with people with patience and respect."

New York   On the other side of the continent we interviewed Brian Fabbri, senior economist and vice-president of Salomon Brothers. The hectic flavor of a huge New York office stands in sharp contrast with the smaller-scale, quiet efficiency of Milton Wong's offices. Fabbri's private office is on the 41st floor.

Salomon Brothers is one of the largest underwriters of publicly issued securities in the world, trading $2 trillion worth of securities last year. This New York giant is the American investment banker for seven out of ten provinces. Among its Canadian clients are the Bank of Montreal, the Royal

"I understand your economic model has broken down, but that's not my line of work."

Davis

Bank of Canada, Seagrams, and Ontario Hydro. Last year, Salomon Brothers represented three-quarters of all Canadian issues in the U.S.

Salomon Brothers clearly is an opinion maker. When Salomon Brothers comments on the market, the market responds. Brian Fabbri provides deep background material for the key financial writers around the world. Canadian money managers often look to American sources to make their own decisions about where to invest funds in Canada.

His is an information rich environment. Near his desk, there is a persistent hum from the three computer video screens which run simultaneously, almost like a video arcade. Those who master video games begin after a while to respond to them neurally, sensing patterns and predicting shifts in information flows—or star invaders—almost without conscious thought. In a similar way, but for stakes somewhat higher than most of the 25 cents-a-throw arcade games, Fabbri is poised while he writes, or even while he is on the phone, to keep track of several financial data streams flowing across the screens. When his body alerts him to a shift in the pattern of information, he glances up at one of the screens to see if he needs to give any special attention to the readout.

"The first terminal is a Quotron machine, which provides current quotes on the equity markets and all of the futures markets, including foreign exchange, as well as whatever stocks that you particularly want to monitor on a minute-by-minute basis. It also has a running Dow Jones commentary, so that you can find out what's going on in Washington. Since it's an internal system, it also has a number of computer programs built into it that enable users to do some of the bond and equity math that is required to make some quick judgments. There is also an enormous amount of information stored on stock price history and individual stock company data.

"The next machine, perhaps even more important these days, is called Telerate. I've always got a current screen on what's going on. It provides an up-to-the-minute market picture on all the financial markets, futures, governments, money markets and foreign exchange, and secondly, it also provides another input, a very important input, I might add, in that the Telerate stores information on Federal Reserve activity and market activity. It stores current news events, including the entire story, so that on any given day you can find out what made the headlines.

"And finally, there is the terminal that connects me to both in-house computer systems as well as external vendor services, both directly and also by telephone."

One of the first things that is reflected in the information flows that Fabbri monitors is the critical attention paid to the effect of politics on the financial markets. The interaction between government and economics from the financial market participant's point of view today has changed from that of fifteen or twenty years ago, when the markets were far less volatile. Today, market participants are in a position to react almost instantly to the latest political economic decisions. Twenty years ago, with the information stream moving more slowly, portfolio managers had more time to evolve a sense of direction.

The information that Fabbri checks regularly, almost at ten-minute intervals, would have taken a researcher days, or even weeks to compile twenty years ago. Yet a large, well-integrated firm such as Salomon Brothers now relies on the speed of its reaction time to move in and out of markets, even before others have a chance to assess the implications of the news.

An ordinary day in the office for Brian Fabbri starts at 7:30. He first prepares a batch of notes covering economic events that will develop during the day, summarizing yesterday's trading activity, ideas about "where the market might open this morning on the basis not only of yesterday's close, but what else might have transpired in the news media."

A TOP WALL STREET ECONOMIST'S INFORMATION RESOURCES

"The first thing that I review after being away is the Federal Reserve Board releases which show the condition of the banking system, the loan growth by business corporations in the paper market and at the banks, the balance sheet of the Federal Reserve, which gives some indication as to what and why the funds rate behaved as it did. Shifting from those monetary pieces of information, a quick look at the yield curve and how it changed a little bit over the last couple of days, a further quick look at the equity markets to see what sectors were most affected by the recent sell-off.

And then I turn to the economic inputs that have been recently released. Including those on inflation, on machine tool orders, on . . . and then finally to take a look at some of the underlying values that will be used in the forecast for this week's and next week's economic data. That's short-term and mid term.

A check of Congress to see what they've been doing with respect to the major tax bills that have been in conference, a check to determine whether or not spending provisions have been negotiated and hammered out to satisfactory compromises.

I check on who is testifying in Washington; and evaluate whether or not that might bring about some important news release that could affect the market. For example, testimony from the chairman of the Federal Reserve, Paul Volcker. I always look to that for clues to any change in his thinking, any reordering of his priorities, or a new emphasis on certain values, which the markets might try to translate as a cue to the next direction that the Fed might take.

Then I check to see what state my projects are in. (Currently, I'm working on a paper having to do with the impact of adjustable rate mortgages on the economy over the next couple of years. I'm currently working on a piece that will investigate the relationship, or the reasons behind the, well, a cyclical look at inflation and why it's likely to accelerate later this year and early next year, and why it hasn't so far.) And finally, a look at my own monthly monitor of economic conditions."

"All these factors will bear on how the market might respond that day. Preparing the market for its own expectations is probably one way of judging it. I transmit this briefing to various senior traders, both in the equity and the fixed income markets. And then once that's through, one has to be generally prepared to absorb the blows as the day comes on and some of these expectations don't materialize. That brings us to about 8:30. And the start of a new day.

"The day progresses with a series of phone calls from people within the firm, which could include Hong Kong, London, and all the domestic branches. We exchange outlooks, updates and reaffirmations of what has gone on and how it's affected the markets. A series of client meetings usually begins early, lasts through lunch, and many times, through dinner. The clients might be from corporate finance, or they could be portfolio managers. In the midst of all of this, scattered between various meetings and telephone calls, are meetings within the department to design and develop the next bit of research that needs to be done. And hopefully some time left over in this schedule to do some writing and/or editing for the various publications that we have, and the intermittent reports we produce. I also spend a lot of time answering phone calls from reporters around the world, providing deep background on the strength and shape of various markets."

No wonder Fabbri takes the time to work out on Nautilus equipment. You have to be a first-class athelete to manage that schedule and those performance pressures.

The pressure is enormous. And so, usually, are the rewards. The theory says competition is good in the marketplace; the theory says competition permits the most competent to rise to the top. That competitive environment is itself the first distorting factor. While they control and manage assets that are supposed to be preserved over decades, they find themselves investing in shorter and shorter time frames, in order to pile up a better "intraquarter record." They are constantly measured on a daily and weekly basis against the performance of their competitors. When asked, "What is your time frame for investments?" we hear: "Short-term is day-trading, medium-term is three weeks, and long-term, well, that's three months, or more, . . . perhaps up to three quarters."

Naturally, the money managers on Wall Street and Bay Street have developed some interesting defensive moves to protect themselves. First, they huddle. They take great issue with each other on small points, but they stay close to the median when they publish their views. And despite what they forecast for publication, they hedge—in their investment actions, they put in place counter-strategies, and, whenever possible, fail safes.

106

"The investor population, unfortunately, has found it necessary to condense activities and economic and social influences to only those things that can affect an investment decision within a year. They basically disregard those longer-term dimensions as being outside their decision-making sphere," says Fabbri.

"People who have longer-term position points of view are those that presumably can afford to have that point of view, either because they're not running up against quarterly performance standards, such as extremely wealthy individuals, or some of the state and local funds. Family money and even some small venture capitalists may have a longer-term perspective and a greater interest in the intrinsic quality of the investment than some of the so-called professional money managers.

"The new entrants into the investment field appear to be better trained in mathematics. To a large extent, because of the infusion of computerization into most investment decisions, they've got to be more technically responsive."

Question: These are the elves, in common parlance?

Fabbri: Mathematical wizards. For example, the mathematics department has multiplied enormously in our own firm. And it's been duplicated and matched in most other major institutions, not just competitors, who must compete with us in these fields, but clients, so they can understand the relevance of this approach. So indeed we've got a whole new generation of relatively young and highly mathematically-oriented people who are searching out performance from the yield curve. Which may or may not include some basic underlying trends in the economy and society at large.

Question: Well they're almost looking at it as if it were some kind of ATARI game, rather than dealing with the intrinsic value or quality of the businesses that they are involved with. They don't even have to look at the businesses, do they?

Fabbri: On the surface, it does look like the most masterful ATARI game ever conceived by man.

Question: It's almost fantasy?

Fabbri: Much of the trading that takes place for itself, on a micro basis, is indeed fanciful, in that it's designed to take advantage of the latest, pure mathematical concept to heighten yield by some fraction of a percentage point.

107

Question: Over a short period of time . . . just a few days?

Fabbri: Over a *very* short period of time. They could be putting on day trades. The interesting thing about all that, in some grander scheme, is that the summation of all of these decisions to induce yield, or performance out of the yield curve, presumably makes the markets more efficient. And that's the rule of thumb and the guiding light, I think, that all investment managers and all financial people sort of run under.

Question: We all learn that as a religious principle.

Fabbri: And we adhere to it. It is the principle that we rely on.

Question: Even though it creates myopia about quality?

Fabbri: Well, quality, I think in this regard, is dependent upon the institution and the time frame in which the investment is being made. The quality aspect of the investment, presumably is swallowed up under the name and guise of hedging.

Brian Fabbri is accurately describing an abstract world, and one that in many ways is remote from the experience of the man-on-the-street. Yet it's *his* pension fund. We get a picture of younger and younger, mathematically schooled technical experts, with a fancier battery of computers, who may in fact know less and less about business, and more and more about the rarified art of managing yields on short-term highly volatile markets, where the longest time they can think about is from here to Christmas. They do not even have to know how to read a balance sheet. They have a strong performance drive to manage money, but may not be directly concerned with long-term value.

Each day Brian Fabbri scans a wide and complex world. He understands his place in this economy, and the next one, very well. "Our firm is essentially involved in the *dissemination of information*. That's perhaps the principal product that we sell. It's synthesis."

Money managers are synthesizers of the raw data of politics, as well as economics, which in their hands become useful intelligence. Their primary role, however, is to evaluate the economic activities of our culture for their immediate financial value. As evaluators they have a heavy impact on choices made by our wealth-generating institutions, and sometimes it is not a positive effect. The pressure to focus on the short term is creating distortions on the management choices of some of our large publically held companies.

How do we define "value" in the next economy in such a way that the money managers are creating real wealth through their investment choices?

Chapter 9

THE SIREN SONG OF SMALL BUSINESS

In the last economy, big business was where it was at. It was our chosen route to solving all our problems. It's where jobs were created, where we got our experience, where we invested our savings, where we got our sense of self-worth, and the source of our security in our retirement years.

But the siren song now comes from small business. *That's* where we are told the jobs are being created. *That's* how we are told we will ensure our financial independence. In the transition, small business is touted as our savior and our salvation.

If big business backed the wrong future of ever-upward growth, small business "bucked a generally hostile environment with an act of extraordinary will," says Pat Johnston-Lavigueur, former executive vice-president of the Canadian Federation for Independent Business (CFIB), now a consultant, long a spokesman for small business in Canada. "Starting a small business is a creative act—just as creative as art, just as creative as music. It's putting things together, and building a dream."

That dream has become an infatuation: more than a million Canadians are now self-employed—up 30 percent from a decade ago. Much of the net new job creation in Canada in the past several years has come from businesses with fewer than fifty employees.

"I think there are a number of studies that have shown that the major corporations have their own problems and mythologies. . . . But small businesses are the real engine of growth and they've been highly successful.

109

There's more recognition being accorded them lately. You've seen people quoting statistics that 70 percent of new jobs are in small business. We've said that for several years, and we've been working with small business quite successfully," says Reg MacDonald, senior vice-president, Royal Bank of Canada.

Everybody wants to be their own boss. There's an appeal to being self-employed that most Canadians can identify with. Says Jim Bennett, vice-president of the Canadian Federation for Independent Business, "Sure, you look at small-business people working seventy hours a week, and that looks pretty tough, but you don't have a boss. The freedom to close down on Wednesday afternoon and go fishing has a certain appeal. People are willing to work hard for that kind of freedom." Not to mention the freedom not to be fired, not to be laid off, not to be an IBM card, not to be punching a time clock.

Jim Fleck, head of Fleck Industries, thinks a small-business man has more bosses, not fewer: "People want to be their own bosses," he says. "But what they often don't recognize is when you go into your own business, you're working for everyone. You're so conscious of having to keep everyone motivated . . . you can't slack on the job, you have to set an example, you have to respond immediately to your customers, so you're working for all of them."

"The history of entrepreneurship shows that people often start businesses when they're desperate. We have a lot of desperate people, and they're starting a lot of businesses. But there's a positive thrust as well in that desperation," says Pat Johnston-Lavigueur. "Maybe it's a legacy of Woodstock to distrust bigness and bureaucracy. A lot of people just don't want to work in big places anymore. They don't want to be just a number. They have a different value system." These people no longer look to the state to resolve all of Canada's economic problems. The state, however, has turned specifically to business to pull the economy out of the hole in which we find ourselves.

There is a small-business revolution going on both in Canada and the United States. In the U.S., 42 percent of those in business call themselves "self-employed." The American 1983 data also show that the self-employed are creating proportionately more jobs than the traditional sectors. The entrepreneurial revolution in the States is so visible that it is being watched worldwide. Even the Japanese are suddenly worried about adapting their huge corporations to the next economy and are busy sending delegations to North America to find out how we encourage entrepreneurial attitudes. Michael Phillips and other small business specialists are being asked to teach the Japanese how to set up small business networks there that are more

110

appropriate to the next economy.[5] Confides Bennett, "We also had the president of our British affiliate in here this week. They're trying to see what they can do to foster an entrepreneurial revolution at home."

"Any small-business man who's successful, who has total dedication, who has tremendous self-confidence—they are prepared to go out and challenge the system and they're terribly innovative. If you have those things, then you look at the individual and say, 'Hey, am I going to play with this person, can I back them?' Now, that's a judgment call that comes from experience, and we've got some marvellous success stories there," says Reg MacDonald.

Small business activity is growing in Canada, although the evidence is not as well-recorded. Bennett: "Government here doesn't even have a good register of firms that are starting up. We have an institutional attitude—from government and from labor too—that small businesses are messy. They can't benefit from the structures that are in place." Johnston-Lavigueur: "It's like irresistible force meeting immoveable object. There's a tremendous entrepreneurial explosion going on, but running up against all the barriers created in the fifties and sixties when we thought we were so damn affluent."

Those barriers are driving Canadians not only out of small business, but out of the country. Last year, a Canadian Federation questionnaire to 300 manufacturers in Ontario showed that 40 percent of them are shopping for locations in the States. Sixteen percent have already relocated. Not only are small manufacturers going, so are the new software and services businesses.

BARRIER 1: Respect. The biggest barrier, say the irresistible forces, is the general feeling that entrepreneurship is not valued—that it's being stifled. Bennett: "Our guidance counsellors, and the people who are forming the expectations and the outlook of a lot of the students, have not yet begun to think of starting a business as a career choice for the students who are in schools. We've got a full-time guy here who does nothing but work on the educational institutions, trying to get guidance counsellors to use the business games in their programs, trying to get them to go to these various small-business trade shows and learn a little bit about the opportunities there are in starting your own business.

"The Canadian attitude is very different from the American or the German model. Germany has basically the same area and same population as the U.K., but in Germany, where they have a whole trade and craft apprenticeship system, they learn entrepreneurship as they are learning their technical skills. Once you get your master ticket, you basically go out

111

and start your own business. They have eight times as many businesses in any given sector as in the U.K. The U.K. has been dominated by big businesses and very large unions and a very sick economy for a long time, and we, unfortunately, look like the U.K.

"Models are a big part of it. The authority figures, in this case the schools, talk about big business and traditional jobs. We've got a long way to go in terms of changing attitudes. And there is the cumulative feeling that our government has been anti-business or anti-free enterprise for the last six, eight, ten years; the last term in government, in particular."

Bennett may be giving voice to similar feelings among a much wider segment of the population. In the last federal election, forty of the members from Ontario elected to the House of Commons were from independent business. Only seventeen were lawyers, a big change in the professional pattern in politics.

BARRIER 2: Fear of Failure. Getting in (and out) of small business ventures smoothly is an art. There are both attitude problems and legal barriers to learning-by-doing in small-scale ventures.

A lot of the people who start businesses will fail by definition. But a lot of them will start again. The only way they can start again is if the bankruptcy laws and the regulatory and financial environment are appropriate. Many of the mistakes that enterpreneurs will make can be tolerated if they have enough money. If they have a strong balance sheet and an environment in which people are prepared to take chances on their next round of success, then they can afford to make mistakes.

While most of the studies on small business focus on entry barriers, the problems of leaving a certain sector, both personally and from the perspective of national pride, present a difficult hurdle.

While James Fleck cannot be described as a "small-business man," he certainly enjoys start-ups and has made a study of entrepreneurial attitudes. He is one of those new breed of Canadians who has worn several hats in his lifetime. He has been a businessman, an academic at the University of Toronto, and even a mandarin: deputy minister of industry in Ontario. His firm, Fleck Industries, supplies wiring cables and harnesses to other manufacturers—of cars, computers, washers, fridges. The success of that enterprise has enabled Fleck to develop his entrepreneurial talents: a cable TV network, a multilingual TV station, a microwave station, and other high-growth areas.

"I think a lot of jobs are going to come out of small firms. I don't know which ones, but I do know that we have to provide a climate that encourages the development of those jobs, and that doesn't inhibit the exit of firms. For example, it isn't right that the government is pouring large sums of money into the textile or shoe industry. If there are some specialized textile or shoe companies, they'll survive anyway.

"One of the big differences between Canada and Japan is that the Japanese have a very active transition strategy. They've moved quickly into industries that are growing, but they also have very consciously let industries that were dying, die. We're afraid to do that. The Japanese used to be big exporters of textiles. Now they import textiles from Taiwan and Korea. They recognize first that it's not a growth area, and second, that it's not an area where they have any particular advantage, nor want to have. Our exit barriers for industries are too high."

In Québec, they say the furniture industry is dying, the textile industry is dying. But you go to the craft shows in Montreal and you'll see an explosion of manufacturing in textiles, leather, furniture, footwear. High quality, high design component. There's a little shop on Laurier that sells Québec-made furniture for kids. It starts out as a crib and then collapses into a two-year-old's bed when the child is two, and the same furniture builds itself into a desk when the child is six. That comes from native woodworking skills developed in a traditional wood industry, translated into creative craft by an individual who had those skills, married to modern designs, and communications and new ideas about retailing.

—Johnston-Lavigueur.

BARRIER 3: Political Attitudes. Bennett: "Both major parties now are scrambling to try to figure out what they should do about the small business revolution—these eight or nine hundred thousand little pygmies out there that actually are creating jobs. And they're no fun. You can't go in and give them a cheque for $50 million, and have a well-publicized ribbon cutting or something. They are hiring these people one at a time, or half a person at a time. All these part-time workers. How can you get any profile? That's what our politicians run on: profile.

"We tell them, 'Sorry guys, you're not going to be able to deal with me. You'll have to close down half of the department of regional industrial expansion, because it's not necessary. Our guys don't want your program money.' "

If more small business programs are not the answer, what is? Fleck: "What we need is a national goal of becoming better over a period of time.

Most of our findings about Canadian business have a good-news, bad-news component. What we can't do from studies is say, 'Put your money into that industry.' What we can show is that growth industries change. What was a high growth industry fifteen years ago, no longer is. That reinforces the bias that you can't pick winners." Again, the implication is that we need to foster a better overall climate for the development of small business, and make our exit and entry barriers more flexible.

One of the important elements of the business climate that politicians can influence is to keep our markets within Canada wide open, and not protectionist. Fleck points out: "We should have at least as much free trade of goods and labor and capital among the provinces of Canada as they have between the countries in Europe. And we don't. One of the biggest barriers to movement in Canada is local government purchasing practices—either ten percent preference pricing, or others simply aren't allowed to compete. Some barriers are in the movement of labor—Newfoundland and the oil rigs, Quebec and the construction industry. Some in the movement of capital—remember when Canadian Pacific wanted to buy MacMillan Bloedel? The point is, we've only got 25 million people. If you break that up into even smaller markets, we're in serious trouble in terms of efficiency."

BARRIER 4: Labor Codes and Benefits. Many small-business people are resentful of the fact that labor legislation is geared to big businesses that have administrative staffs equipped to deal with the massive amounts of paperwork that accompany the legislation. "They could exempt firms with less than twenty employees from some of the labor relations legislation that was designed for an Air Canada, or for an Inco. When you have 11 employees, all this adversarial gobbledygook in labor relations just doesn't make any sense. We have people who get so frustrated by it, they'll close down their business rather than deal with it.

"On the other hand, we do need to find a way to deal with the equity problem for the part-time people. That is not just a problem of red tape, it is a more sensitive and difficult structural issue," says Bennett.

We need more flexibility, they keep telling us. Johnston-Lavigueur: "Small businesses hire more women. They hire more aged people. They hire more young people. They don't have the same kind of 'credentialism' that pervades the rest of modern society—large corporations and government. They believe strongly in the capacity of someone to do the job if they show they can do the job. They value hard work more than anything else."

While this is true, it is also true that people who are old, young, women, or without credentials can be hired for lower wages. Many we interviewed were equally concerned about the lack of sufficient social coverage for small-business employees; for example, the need for portable pension provisions for people who work in small businesses and for some way to deal equitably with part-time employees. "Our safety net systems are all aimed at big business, full-time work," they told us. "We need more coherence in a policy for the more volatile smaller businesses, especially in the expanding service sector which uses part-time workers."

BARRIER 5: The Tax System. Small business experts are concerned that the tax system as it is presently constituted is a patchwork that does not deal adequately with the needs of a growing small business community. The tax environment with which small business must deal includes regulations from three levels of government.

Bennett: "Almost every province has a lower small business tax rate, so it's not so much even corporate taxes. It's municipal and property taxes. The states have tax-free zones. There are payroll taxes in Quebec, with its so called health levy, and Manitoba has a similar one. Our people see those as anti-job creation. They are employment disincentives. The more people you hire, the more of these payroll taxes you're paying."

Tax simplification is the goal of every small business person we interviewed. Small businessmen, by definition, do not have the administrative resources to deal with new regulations two or three times a year, at federal and provincial budget times; neither are they enthusiastic about having to cope with tax incentives designed to encourage or discourage market behavior—even when encouragement in the form of development bonds for example, is directed at them. Basically, what this group of entrepreneurs is saying is "Give us some rules that are easy to understand and comply with, and some guarantees that they will be in place for a while, and then get out of our way."

In addition to a plea for tax simplification, the small business community is concerned that governments, in using the tax system to encourage specific kinds of behavior (for example, saving for retirement), have inadvertently reduced the ability of small business to attract capital.

BARRIER 6: Financing. It's tough to get money for start-ups and even for expansion. Bennett: "You can get all the loans you want as long as you've got 300 percent collateral. But to get equity is very difficult. The primary source of equity, the informal source of capital, is from friends and family."

> *Question*: "Why do all the surveys show that women are more successful in starting and succeeding in small businesses?"
>
> *Answer*: "Women don't have delusions of grandeur. They plan better, they do it more slowly, they don't get easy bank credit so they have to build incrementally on their own cash flow. They don't really take a lot of flyers. They're used to dealing with nickels and dimes. They know how to economize."
>
> —Johnston-Lavigueur.

"Let's use the tax system so that the 45-year-old who was laid off at Chrysler, Stelco, Inco, Massey can take his or her pension money and roll that into equity in starting his or her own business. Take some of the $30-35 billion in RRSP money. Get that invested in these small firms," argues Jim Bennett.

"Right now, people have to de-register their RRSPs and go through a lot of hassle. They only get half the money, because they've lost that tax deferral and they've somehow done violence to the nest egg that they think they have. If they could just put a portion of that into a self-administered RRSP, put it through a trust company or whatever, and have it invested in their daughter's or their niece's or their nephew's firm, business would get the equity it needs to be able to survive what we see is another rollercoaster on interest rates. Over the long term, those people would get a good return on their money."

> *Question*: "Where is that RRSP money going now?"
>
> *Answer*: "That money is going into 90-day paper. Ninety percent of it's placed here in Toronto; commercial paper, largely government bonds, of course, doing practically nothing, but paying interest on interest. And it's not creating any jobs."
>
> *Question*: "And how much do we have?"
>
> *Answer*: "There's about $30 billion there. Government has already deferred the taxes on it, so it's not going to cost them another nickel."
>
> *Question*: "What about the pension funds?"
>
> *Answer*: "We have $100 billion in pension funds, mainly in mortgages, stock market and short-term paper. Between mortgages and stocks and short-term paper, it's not doing much. It's been a good source of funding for big businesses and for government, but it isn't creating any jobs."

Says Scott McCreath, senior vice-president, Canadian Commercial Bank: "As long as interest rates are high worldwide, that money will move to institutional rather than individual holdings. In other words, the people today with large pockets of money are the large institutions: worldwide pension funds, financial institutions, wealthy corporations and countries or individuals. A persistent lack of willingness to take risks is not good for the worldwide economy. We see all those things here in Canada. The money has moved to a risk-averse environment. We're seeing a flight to quality in the banking system, to the larger banks. But there is some concern as to the quality of even some of the larger banks."

"Small business is not just lending. There are hundreds of thousands of small businesses in this country who do not borrow from banks but who are depositors, and use other services, such as payroll services. I think that's something that has been totally overlooked. Most banks have finally realized that now. I think you're starting to see it in most of the new banks coming in and there is far more focus on the whole area of independent business," points out Reg MacDonald.

It has taken the banks a long time to recognize that it might be profitable for them to lend to small business. Nicholas Deutsch, principal, McKinsey and Company, says banks have a hard time "identifying with any degree of precision where and how they make money." The high status among bankers has been in loans to big business, multinationals and foreign governments. In Canada, that's where 40 percent of their new business came from in the seventies.

But even "with a profit growth of 18 percent a year compounded for the decade ending in 1981, return on equity increased only a third of a percentage point," says Deutsch. The value of bank stocks declined sharply. What this means is that investors believe the Big Five chartered banks are carrying about $3 billion in unproductive assets. Deutsch discounts the "quick and easy answer" that these are non-performing Third World or domestic oil company loans. "Over the last five or six years, profit margins on loans to multinational corporations has been insufficient to cover normal marketing expenses, corporate overhead and loan loss provisions," says Deutsch. In the face of a belated recognition that they don't make much money on some of the large, flashy deals, small business lending is looking more attractive to our bankers.

BARRIER 7: The Deficit. "If you have the best small-business policy in the world, that is to say, a wonderful tax system and wonderful support systems and an entrepreneurial education environment and lots of skills training for your kids—and you have an interest rate policy determined because of a $30 billion deficit, it will all be for naught. You can't just look at small business, you have to get the whole machine working. In Canada, a big part of getting the machine working is getting the deficit down," points out Johnston-Lavigueur.

Concern over the deficit is a kind of shorthand for saying that small business experts don't believe that those in charge of the economy are taking a long-term view, or a coordinated approach. This type of narrow approach threatens to create a poor climate for personal investment in Canada. After all, small businesses are much more mobile than Chrysler or the multinational oil companies, and far less politically visible.

BARRIER 8: Employee Participation. Bennett: "Traditionally, the owner-manager has been a closely-held private-family thing. We asked members of the CFIB [Canadian Federation of Independent Business] whether they were prepared to let their employees buy into their company. Just under half of them said yes, they were prepared to let their employees buy in. And this has been a group that has traditionally resisted going to venture capital or letting the Federal Business Development Bank buy a piece of the equity.

"The majority of those who were prepared to let their employees buy in were prepared to let them have some degree of say in the direction and the management. They didn't just want the equity. They were prepared to really go into employee participation in terms of management as well as money. That's got to be one of the things that we look at.

"For example, one company here has a product branch that's just marginal, and they're thinking about closing it down. Instead of just laying those people off, if they could give them a subcontract, let them set up their own firm, and let them go out and start selling specialized products—that subcontracting venture lets them get the financing they need. They use the credit—the major's credit—they use the technical expertise for a while until they develop their own. But, because they're dealing with all these other firms, they pick up a specialized knowledge. Before long, the company will have a cheaper source, a better quality component or whatever of that particular product. Because these people have gained an expertise through their interaction with others. We've got to do it as a bridging mechanism. It's a foreign concept here. We've got to do more of it."

BARRIER 9: Federal Money—Grants Vs. Policies. Bennett: "When we send our material off to the government, we say, 'Give us some policies. Don't give us programs. We don't want you coming out and cutting ribbons and the rest of it.' Nobody can even remember the names of the programs anyway. We're looking at some of this youth employment stuff, for example. There are dozens of provincial programs on top of the dozens of federal programs. Our federal structure is not serving us well in this area, because everybody wants to do their own thing for their own political credit.

"One of the major challenges for the government is to start cooperating with the provinces on a whole development package that takes training and the educational system, and the tax system, federal and provincial, and starts almost a crusade.

"We're spending a billion dollars a month on unemployment insurance. That billion dollars a month does nothing except keep those people alive; it pays them not to work. It's not productive. Let's get some of that money involved in skills training and attitude training. In depressed areas where it doesn't look like there are going to be any opportunities, let's look at more imaginative ways of using that money. How do we change attitudes? How do we get people creating their own jobs? How do we set the climate for entrepreneurship?"

New Opportunities   Despite the barriers, the experts are enthusiastic. "For small business, the opportunities are there because what is facing the economy is a structural situation. The collapse of a lot of our corporate giants, although lamentable if you happen to be a shareholder or a senior executive, is basically an opportunity for an awful lot of entrepreneurs.

"I think about half the government officials are starting to realize that we are going through something that's fundamental, structural. It's pervading the whole western economy. I think that a number of current civil servants went through the transformation that I went through. Coming out of the university, thinking, 'Go into government and help save the world. If we've got a problem, we'll create a ministry or a secretary of state or you name it, we'll solve it.'

"I think people are saying, 'You've had 16 years of trying to let government solve it for us, and maybe it's time we did it for ourselves.' I think it's too bad we've had to go through what we've gone through in the last couple of years to get there. But I think it's healthy that a lot of people are now starting to look at doing it for themselves." says Bennett.

Pierre Laurin, former director of Montreal's Hautes Etudes Commerciales, now a vice-president of Alcan, concurs: "Now, more and more, you will see successes where you have smaller units responsible for their own things. Look at what we're experiencing at Alcan: we used to have very big plants and we discovered that it's much more difficult to manage and have the people feel that they have an identity. So now we have concluded that we will have smaller plants than in the past. We think that people can identify more with their work and also that it will be easier for them to

119

interface with the people who, in the final analysis, are responsible for what they are doing. The old law of increasing return per unit when you increase volume is now very much challenged."

While all of us are willing, indeed even eager, to let the small-business option lead the transition to the next economy, there are, objectively, some nagging doubts. Small-business entrepreneurs may be very, very good at making money, but do we really believe small businesses have a life of their own? Are they not just appendages to big businesses, able to exist because of the trickle down of big business demands? As usual, there is no Canadian evidence we can call upon to show definitively that small businesses can stand on their own two feet.

American studies have looked at the linkages between big and small businesses. Says Pat Johnston-Lavigueur, "A very small fraction of small businesses are linked in that fundamental way with big business. They are linked more to the consumer market. Even manufacturers—most of them start out life as a distributor and then decide that the product that they are distributing could be better made by them.

"I think we're moving more in the direction of more innovation and design going into the creation of manufacturing companies that are 'stand-alone,' that haven't been reliant on large companies for initial supply contracts. The movement toward that has to do with a couple of things. First, the market is full of things which can be imitated. Second, communications. Third, computers and skill levels. A lot of that growth is attributable to stand-alone, young companies."

"Stand-alone, young companies"—the phrase typifies what is so attractive about the small-business option, and why the siren song is being sung with increasing fervor. Canadians identify small-business people as those who have the characteristics that will let them more easily withstand the buffeting of the transition to the next economy.

Small-business people are adaptive, flexible and mobile; they can move quickly to take advantage of rapidly changing times and newly-emerging opportunities. They are less encumbered by the rigid rules and regulations that make it so difficult for big business, big government, and big unions to change. Small-business people are more like ordinary Canadians, who themselves are seeking ways to cope with the transition to the next economy.

120

Chapter 10

VOTING WITH THEIR FEET: THE TAXPAYER REVOLT

C anadians have decided how to get to the next economy—
they are walking there, by themselves. Tired of waiting
for the business and government leaders to describe what's coming next,
impatient with the soothing assurances that Reaganomics will bail us out, if
it ever crosses the border, Canadians are voting with their feet, digging in
their heels and seeking their own personal solutions to the uneasiness they
feel in the transition to the next economy.

Canadians have long been recognized around the world as good followers, lovers of peace and authority, and perhaps overly respectful of their
government: "What is clearly absent from Canadian political consciousness,
is the conviction that the state and its apparatus are the natural enemies of
freedom. . . . Peace, order and good government in Canada depend ultimately on the deep acquiescence of the people in the idea that they have no
inalienable rights." [6]

But in one short decade, all of those descriptions have begun to
change. Complacency is being replaced by anger and annoyance, and, even
more shocking, by evidence of a determination to be more self-reliant, less
dependent on government. As the authority figures of the past crumble
before this onslaught, Canadians are wasting little time on grumbling and
have turned to putting their own houses in order. Although media columnists waste a lot of time sniffing about the "lack of leadership," Canadians
seem to have found their own direction.

121

They are voting with their feet. Canadians are simply, but steadily, walking away from the institutions they have sustained and which, in turn, were supposed to sustain them. For decades, for example, Canadians have been good tax payers. Canada is still a relatively new country; people throughout this century have chosen to emigrate here. New hope, curiosity, and support for the adopted country were very high. "It wasn't too long ago that paying taxes was a privilege. Not any more," points out Milton Wong who is concerned about the increasing deficits and the declining tax base— but even more worried about the values that reflects. "There's an attitudinal problem now towards taxes. We don't mind giving for our health services, we don't mind giving for education. On the other hand, when the servants of the country become our masters, then we do become very negative towards giving to the government."

The middle income earner, whose lifestyle has been hardest hit by unemployment and the recession, is starting to fight back; at the politician, at the retail "middleman" and especially, at the taxman. "I see the middle income people, the great base of our mass democracy, beginning to lose that optimism and beginning to start to rip off the system, which they never used to do before," observes Tom Axworthy, former principal secretary to the prime minister, and now a Harvard professor. "Once that begins to unravel, a lot of things begin to unravel. . . . They're getting squeezed everywhere. People aren't listening to them. They want to have a stake, they want to have control of their own destiny."

These changes have come swiftly and decisively. The roots of this turnabout in our national psyche may be traced back to the early seventies, when a majority of Canadians made the harsh discovery that many of the rules they had learned in non-inflationary times—*"save"*—*"live within your means"*— *"only buy on credit when you have no other choice"*—had become personally damaging in an inflation cycle.

Their disillusionment was heightened by the realization that their leaders couldn't tell them anything to help them cope with a world in which they could no longer trust prices to reflect value. What *should* a steak cost? What *should* the price of a pair of shoes be?

Where the average Canadian really began to lose out to inflation was through the tax system when wage increases couldn't keep up with inflation; real purchasing power declined. Indexing the personal income tax system in 1974 was a partial response to this problem. But, while it comforted us briefly to know that the government was aware of our dilemma, the psychological sense of gain was minimal. The brief sense of relief was quickly dissipated the following year when wage and price controls were imposed.

By the mid-seventies, everybody was getting smarter and more cynical. "Borrow as much as you can and pay back with cheaper dollars" became the goal, as both corporations and individuals realized that the rules of the game had been turned upside down. While the savers were losing ground, the borrowers were gaining.

An inflation psychology began to take hold. Meanwhile, faith in the ability of economists and politicians to enforce traditional economic remedies declined. Consumers came up with three coping strategies to protect themselves: invest in inflation, invest in tangibles, or invest in independence.

Invest in inflation. Those who chose the strategy of investing in inflation most closely resemble the traditional consumers of the industrial age—they are good and faithful spenders and borrowers, without much thought for the long-term future. Generally, they trust the system to provide for them. Those who decided to invest in inflation assumed that the economic system would continue to be indexed to inflation, and that the government would not or could not interrupt the upward spiral of costs and wages. Although they believed prices would go up, there was not much pressure to control prices because they were sure that wages would keep pace. They also believed that if there was a sharp economic downturn it would affect everyone, and therefore the government would be forced to act to prevent a depression. This hope was not entirely sustained.

Invest in tangibles. This strategy, investing in tangible goods such as real estate, gold, silver, antiques and art, rather than stocks or other "paper assets," was an option pursued by those who remained convinced that although we were going through tough times when values were volatile, "stability" would eventually return. They therefore sought investments they hoped would appreciate, or at least retain their value, despite inflation. Couples who used this strategy would, for example, decide to remain childless longer—using one income for daily expenses keeping the other to invest. In an era of sharp devaluations, especially in real estate, the strategy of investing in tangibles caught many short. As interest rates rose, those who had borrowed too much were caught in the squeeze. That is the downside risk of this strategy.

While both of the above strategies reflect a desire to "take matters into one's own hands," to counter inflation's erosion of capital and purchasing power, they still relied on a return to stability in the money-based economy. Many Canadians began to feel that a more certain way to gain control was to retreat from the mainstream economy and the values associated with the affluent consumer society of the fifties and sixties. A third strategy emerged.

Invest in independence. A growing number of consumers decided to insulate themselves from a "system" that is unpredictable and therefore untrustworthy as support for their personal security. They learned to reduce their costs; to become more frugal, less impulsive spenders. They developed additional sources of income either to supplement their wages, or moved entirely outside the money system and into the barter networks. These consumers set their sights on acquiring practical skills and independent technologies (breaking their dependence on B.C. Hydro by installing solar collectors or methane converters, for example) to reduce their dependence on retail purchases. They emphasize conservation: the repair, re-use and recycling of possessions.

Rural and urban versions of "investing in independence" differ—one is "back to the land" while the other stresses redesigned social systems such as cooperative buying, communal or multi-family living arrangements, and shared child-care. These individuals were early candidates for the invisible economy: besides seeking a cash income, they barter goods, swap skills and trade time on projects.

One thing all three strategies have in common is a declining faith in the value of money. Even if inflation is, in fact, being squeezed out of the system—and some say we are entering an era of deflation—it has left a legacy of distrust in the money economy.

While a national attitude of "respectful compliance" and faith in order and authority may have slowed the awakening to quietly declining prospects, Canadians learned the lessons of inflation well. While a good number learned to turn inflation to their advantage and to "work the system," most came to view inflation as an *unfair* redistribution of wealth and income.

The recession/depression of the late seventies drove home the lesson. What started as an instinctive response to stem the erosion of household incomes became a "survival psychology" aimed at safeguarding the future. And this time it was not the marginal groups or the outsiders who were feeling wounded by the recession, but the backbone of Canadian society—the middle class.

In Canada we have come to believe that "all of us are entitled to share in society's bounty if we want it badly enough, if we're prepared to work. As a credo, it has proved its worth. It is a dynamic engine. It is a political stabilizer," *Financial Post* writer John Lownsbrough reminds us. Ravaged first by inflation, then by recession, the values and shared assumptions of a better tomorrow that cemented this layer of trust are crumbling.

124

The effects are being felt across the whole range of our social, political and economic systems. A "soft revolution" is in progress—in social attitudes and mores, in assumptions about the economy and the relationship between leader and led, in symbols of success and rewards, in goals and the means to achieve them.

Middle-class Canadians have been forced to alter their behavior and their values to fit diminishing expectations; the growing mismatch between expectations learned in school that "tomorrow will always be better," and the reality of hard times has been a source of shame, anger and strong dissatisfaction with the politicians, expressed vigorously in the rout of the federal Liberals in the last election. Feelings of frustration run high, the sense of unfairness is sharpening, and an element of the social glue which binds us to conventional behavior is melting.

Nowadays, very few Canadians still assume that saving money automatically leads to financial security, or that a university education guarantees employment, or that today's steady job will ensure a secure old age. Most expect a prolonged period of slow growth, disposable income to remain flat, and unemployment to remain high. This mood is underlined by polls showing that this generation of middle-class Canadians is the first since the war who do not expect their children to be more successful than themselves.

New Status Symbols   Values and status symbols are changing along with our assumptions about our future prospects. For example there is more emphasis on forms of personal satisfaction and achievement that are less tied to big government and big business, less tied to symbols of success marked by medals or titles. The status symbols of the eighties reflect a strong desire for financial independence and the values of mobility, adaptability, and self-sufficiency, and to a more self-determined sense of place, in the community, and in history. In Trudeau's last months in office his peace initiatives, for example, captured some of these emotions and were therefore highly regarded.

New value is being placed on such achievements as starting your own *independent* business, acquiring a new adaptive skill, even a manual skill that contributes to household *survival*, such as planting a garden or building a wind generator. At the community level, points are given for leading a battle against pollution of a local waterway in an attempt to reduce risks for your children and your children's children. At the personal level, winning a marathon (or even participating) is a symbol of health and *control* over your physical condition. In this context, even the fitness boom becomes part of an "I can do it myself" political expression.

125

As material values become less trustworthy and predictable, the desire to appreciate more non-material satisfactions has grown. Personal fulfillment is sought through greater immersion in family life or through a variety of transpersonal and more conventional Western religious disciplines. Nearly everyone is studying Zen, meditating, learning the "relaxation response" or buying self-help books on how to better organize their time and energy.

Struggling to come to grips with uncertainty, middle-class Canadians are increasingly experimenting with their values and their lifestyles, aiming to maintain maximum flexibility, husbanding their personal and household resources with care, and weighing their financial options carefully. As parents, Canadians are determined that their children learn adaptive skills and master the technologies of independence. They are demanding greater input to curricula in the schools and chafing at the educational system's sluggish response to integrating computer learning techniques. They are working hard to supplement the lessons of the formal classroom at home. *Sensing a long-term social adjustment, they are trying to ensure that their children overcome their own handicaps.*

Shoppers are "cherry-picking" for the best deals in town, trying for the best price and the best credit terms, examining the lifecycle and energy costs of their purchases, not merely the initial purchase cost. They are insisting on ample warranties and are much more demanding about service and maintenance. They spend selectively on both durable and non-durable goods and services, often timing purchases to take advantage of tax incentives, rate cuts and other discounts or "creative financing" schemes. To a surprising degree, household purchases are now being treated as "investments" not just expenses. "Personal-security" spending for the long-term has begun to replace credit expansion, a trend reinforced by demographic shifts as the baby boom generation approaches middle age.

As Paul Paré, chairman of Imasco, a major retailer of consumer goods, puts it: "A lot of Canadians are expressing the [need to know] when they're winning." One way that more and more Canadians are choosing: entering the cash economy and joining barter networks to ease the tax bite and keep a lid on the costs of basic necessities by keeping out the "middle man."

Replacement of the Money Economy   Canadians are seeking to reduce their dependence on purchased goods and skills by trading time on projects, bartering or swapping goods and services, and acquiring practical skills that they can use to eliminate the need to spend hard-won cash. These "informal" economic activities, though unmeasured for the most part by the GNP, are growing in importance along with middle-class Canada's sense of frustration.

One key indication of the growing size of this alternative economy—and of its increasing social acceptability—is the subtle shift in the language used to describe it. Only a short decade ago we used the phrase "the black market" and used it mostly to describe events offshore. Then as these activities became more common here we started to call it the "underground" economy. Shortly, even that connotation was dropped and we started saying the "invisible" economy. Now this expression, too, is in decline. Non-monetary forms of economic activity are now so pervasive in Canada that we have simply switched to referring to it as the "informal" economy.

The household is at the center of much of this informal economic activity. Russell Robinson, assistant deputy minister, Policy, of Consumer and Corporate Affairs points to an important shift that this implies: "It reverses nearly half a century of our industrial-age socialization process; it is a kind of broadening of what used to be only a social relationship. A household is becoming more and more a locus of an economic partnership."

Within this redefined concept of the household, new tools scaled for home use are proving a boon in tapping sources of flexible employment and alternative incomes. Russell Robinson: "The new technologies, on the plus side, are going to permit new flexible life and work styles, especially more income opportunities for those who are in smaller units. While this may happen over a decade or so, it is not likely to happen fast enough to deal with the unmet needs for traditional, full-time jobs. And we don't know yet how to count this type of employment; *our current tax policy, and social policy even works against these changes happening naturally.*"

A whole range of institutional constraints on Canadians' ability to be flexible and adaptable are becoming a nasty source of irritation. For example, there are zoning bylaws that prevent the use of buildings for both residential and professional purposes. There are also outdated "guild laws" that could land you a fine for a swap arranged with your neighbor—you paint his house, he fixes your car. Other regulations are forcing homeowners in Quebec to go out-of-province to buy those plastic plumbing parts that make it a snap to do-it-yourself. But it is the tax system that is prompting the greatest outcry.

Voting With Their Feet   Perhaps the most telling sign of the overall lack of confidence with government, can be measured by the distaste for tax policy. There is a strong link in a democracy between support for government and compliance with the voluntary income tax system. And so the real vote of support for the government is reflected less in support for a new majority government and more in what Canadians are doing with their taxable income.

One thing is crystal clear—we are not willingly handing over hard-earned income to Revenue Canada with either the consistency or the willingness of the past. Some officials estimate that even if there were a recovery tomorrow, Revenue Canada would *not* receive the same volume of tax revenues that they might have gained only five years earlier.

"Sure — take the easy way out!"

Uluschak

Research suggests that we are in the midst of a strong and stubborn tax revolt. Attitudes in Canada today are similar to those measured in California several years ago that triggered a spate of tax reform measures. Official Ottawa seems determined to ignore or underestimate the force of these feelings. By contrast, in Washington, the head of the Federal Reserve Board, Paul Volcker, is actively speaking out on the subject, saying that the government had better get serious about two things—controlling spending, but most importantly, broadening the tax base.

The Canadian tax rebellion has emerged at the grass roots level, in parallel with the development of a determination to be more self-reliant. Self-reliance implies the need to have something to spend, and much less interest in seeing the income vanish, especially if the belief in the social contract has been shaken. The revolt that has broken out was not led by the media, or by either of the major political parties. In fact, it took the Tories a very long time to jump on the bandwagon.

Paul Paré, CEO of Imasco: "We should be looking to create an environment which encourages freedom of the individual to prosper, which of course we've had the opposite of for the last twenty years. . . . People want to do their own thing. As for tax reform, . . . I certainly would support a thrust that clarified the rules, encouraged people to (a) take risks and (b) be the beneficiaries of the risks that they're prepared to take."

Most of those who raised the tax reform issue with us agreed that the current system discourages risk-taking and diverts much of our creative intellectual capital to the pursuit of tax loopholes and incentives—to our collective loss. And a surprising number of CEOs who potentially could benefit from those loopholes expressed irritation at what they considered almost an insult to the intelligence in the way Canadian "tax dodges" are set up.

David Culver, president of Alcan: "It's upsetting to see so much effort going into avoiding taxes. . . . Simplify the tax system and get rid of the loopholes and they'll all go back to productive ways of investing money rather than doing the wrong thing for the right tax reason."

Arthur Drache, tax consultant and former assistant deputy minister for Finance Canada: "I find it quite fascinating the extent to which people will tie themselves in knots to save a point or two in tax. Invest in things they shouldn't invest in, arrange their affairs to get, in many cases, very marginal benefits through a very complex rearrangement of their money. Creating an acceptable tax system is as much an exercise in psychology as in economics."

The delicate psychology that shapes our voluntary compliance with the system has been shattered. Fed up with a tax system widely seen to serve as a substitute for policy and to be inequitable and unproductive, many Canadians are walking away, into the informal economy, and also offshore. Drache: "Let's say I have a client who wants to put money in an annuity, a single-premium annuity. He's 40 years old, he's just inherited $100,000, he doesn't need the money right now. He goes and he takes the money to a Canadian insurance company, puts it in there and it'll compound unbelievably and he'll get it when he's 65 and he'll pay the tax then. The government will collect the tax because they know where it is. That is, he could, before the MacEachen budget.

"Now instead, they take away the deferred annuity. The same guy then goes offshore. Have you ever heard of anything that's so stupid in economic terms? The offshore funds are invested in Canada Savings Bonds, in government of Canada debt, and they're running it out through Bahamas or somewhere, in a complex corporate structure and then they bring it back. But now Revenue Canada doesn't know who my client is. People who were investing out in the open in Canada suddenly are investing surreptitiously."

Lack of continuity in the rules of the game is another crucial factor behind the broad consensus we found that the system is unfair and unproductive. Scott McCreath: "Tax reform would be best answered if you could just tell me what the rules are. Give me some permanence to the rules. Let me plan. If I can create money, let me take my risk. My risk was in looking at the rules that existed, then constantly seeing them change. Whether it's my self-directed RRSP, whether it's indexing or the amount of tax I pay. The fact that many try to shelter tax is just one small part. All the real estate, all the oil and gas, and all the movie tax shelters; those rules have all been bent, twisted changed, manipulated, destroyed, gone out of practice, brought in. It's poor management. No more, no less."

Virtually all those we interviewed in the process of preparing this book mentioned problems with the tax system as one of the issues that must be addressed as Canada tackles the difficult transition to the next economy. While few of them had any hard ideas about the direction tax reform should take, all agreed that reform is inevitable. Most pointed to shrinking government revenues as the main reason for change.

The recommended objectives were to clarify, simplify, and stabilize the tax rules to ensure that the system is not only fair, but seen to be fair. The good consequence of achieving those objectives, it was argued, would be to broaden the tax base and improve the incentives for voluntary compliance. Failure to do so will likely lead to either increased consumption taxes (more sales taxes) or to the imposition of value added taxes (taxes paid by producers at each step in the manufacturing chain).

By far the most popular suggestion was that we should seriously consider some form of a flat tax to smooth the transition to the next economy. The complex web of rules and regulations now in place, even if they were stabilized, are severely hampering the transition. Most of the "carrots and sticks" in our present system were built up in an attempt to achieve not only revenue goals, but to try to force a specific set of economic decisions. Tax expenditures and incentives accumulated over the years to try to aid the government in "managing" the economy towards certain ends.

Aside from the question of whether we ever knew enough to do that effectively even for the last economy, it is certain that no one knows enough about the shape of the next economy, or the length of the transition period, to design tax policies to guide it in detail. The first thing that has to be done is to "unblock" the adaptive capacity of the transition economy. The rigid and outmoded tax system left over from the last economy is hamstringing the transition.

The overriding policy question to be addressed is: Do we adjust the tax system to go with the tide, to encourage personal coping strategies, to increase small investor flexibility, fit with new producer/consumer ("pro-sumer") households, and better align tax policies with new lifestyle alternatives? Or, do we tinker with the existing tax system and watch revenues decline? A smooth transition to the next economy will require something beyond a cosmetic approach to this issue.

While, as Tom Axworthy points out, no government wants to step into the quicksand of tax reform, few will have again the unprecedented majority of the present prime minister. "Tax simplification has the potential to be an enormous issue. Tax reform brings out the special interest groups like nothing else. Everybody, everywhere, every constituency. To take that on is mind-numbing in its intensity. To stand up to the hordes of lobbyists you would have to come out and say, 'We were elected on this, we're going to have to do it.' You can make great changes, but only if you have the force of popular will. And you almost always have that will only with an election campaign, with a mandate, and about a year after. After that the engine begins to lose steam. . . ."

The penalty if we don't take the risk is that Canadians will continue to vote with their feet, to walk south across the border with their business, their investment capital, and their hopes. Without exception, those we interviewed said they would prefer to fight long and hard to change this system that they love, rather than to let opportunity walk away.

THE
SOFT
REVOLUTION

Chapter 11

STAR WARS

Finding an approach to the new technologies that are emerging at an ever-increasing pace around the world provides one of the most critical challenges in the transition to the next economy. Headlines greet us the triumphs of science, the latest discovery, the most recent scare from the biotech labs. We are dazzled by the space race, and the new quicker computer which weighs only three pounds and works on batteries. Brand new phrases casually enter our vocabulary and get tossed around by nine-year-olds: *"Did you see the satellite pictures of the Canadian arm?" "Does your dad's PC have a mouse?" "What did you do with your down-time last weekend?"*

Along with all these shiny new toys, which both frighten and intrigue us, there is a different sense of time sliding into the language: "real time," the time spent "on-line" talking with the computer, and "down-time," time unconnected from the computer. A whole new breed of metaphors racing by on their way to school. We have become much more conscious of the passage of time, and the shortage of time we have to get things done. "What did you do with your down-time?" means not only that the only time that counts is while you were "on line," but asks also "How did you structure your play time?" No wonder the explosion of books on how to better manage your time is accompanied by a few hundred more on how to relax.[7]

Although it all seems to have sped up lately, we really had quite a long time to get ready for computers, and a long time to get ready for robots and space flights. Books, magazines, newspapers and movies have helpfully conjured up images of a science-fiction future, preparing us for what is to come.

"With the means of almost instantaneous communication of intelligence between the most distant points of the country, space will be, to all practical purposes of information, completely annihilated. The citizen will

133

be [almost ubiquitous] to a degree that the human mind, until recently, has hardly dared to contemplate seriously as belonging to human agency, from an instinctive feeling of religious reverence [for] a power of such awful grandeur."

These visions of the future give us courage, and give us pause. The above passage, for example, was written in 1838, about Samual Morse's telegraph by the Commerce Committee of the U.S. House of Representatives. From the telegraph to the telephone to the computers talking not across lines but through satellites, the revolution in communications has just continued to speed up.[8]

Perhaps the wave of changes that caught us least prepared comes from the new biotechnologies. We've known for centuries about selective breeding on the farm, but test-tube babies and controversies over sperm banks caught us seemingly by surprise. We knew something about germ warfare. We saw films about strange creatures rising from the depths of the pond, or the sea, suddenly swollen or twisted because they had been struck by radiation, or grown from a spore on an alien planet. But we seem unready to cope with the notion that a common garden variety organism, "E-coli," is a good carrier for our emerging science of genetic engineering—we keep speculating about what happens if it gets out of the lab . . . too soon.

Of all the dramatic scientific advances, the new biotechnologies seem to have grabbed our imaginations the most forcefully. We hear a lilting description of the dreams emerging along with the new biotechnologies. A siren song of freedom from hunger, freedom from disease, and perhaps even freedom from the sad side-effects of old age.

"We'll be able to grow crops without petrochemicals; they'll fertilize themselves," a high-school student told us. *"With biotech our forests will be totally regenerated,"* said a logger in B.C. *"We'll grow our own fish in a tub inside the house,"* rattled off an eight-year-old who drew for us a crayon drawing of what the house of the future would look like. But her stoney-eyed older brother, almost twelve, had another idea: *"It won't matter because I won't be there and you won't be there,"* meaning the nuclear holocaust would wipe out everyone.

All across Canada, sometimes in the same families, we found these conflicting visions of the future; bright pictures of the far-away time, dark pictures of "What will happen to us if we don't pay attention to the things that really matter?" The in-between parts are masked and muted with a grey uncertainly, a hesitancy about the next steps.

These pictures of a ragged staircase leading to two sealed doors to the future found in conversations with children and their parents, were mirrored by the specialists who are supposed to be in the know, although they used a different, almost foreign tongue of science in describing their images of Canadian choices for the next economy. They used longer words, like "megaprojects" and "electro-optical technologies."

The shorter, more familiar words were "lasers," "computers," and "gene machines." Everyone knows what lasers look like; they used them in "Star Wars." The use of lasers not just for warfare, but in health and communications is stimulating some pretty interesting debates. Lasers make possible delicate operations on genetic material, or more subtle manipulation of tissue, for medical purposes.

DATELINE VANCOUVER. "The medical community cannot obtain the human organs it needs for transplants because it depends on the wrong incentive for donation, a Simon Fraser University professor says. His research shows that depending on voluntary donations at the time of death—what he refers to as the spot market—is inadequate to the demand for human organs. In the United States last year, there were more than 12,000 people on waiting lists for hearts, kidneys, livers and corneas.

Professor Vining argues that "whenever you try to negotiate this kind of thing in the spot market it's going to be traumatic because it's going to be at a very trying time." In Canada it is illegal to buy or sell organs. [A man in Alberta, however, recently advertised for a kidney, offering $5,000.] In the United States, only the state of Virginia specifically forbids the practise."

—*Globe & Mail*, September 1, 1984

DATELINE NEW YORK. "Already men and women with kidney disease had been saved by a kidney transplanted from an identical twin. A doctor in Paris used transplants from close relatives, classifying up to one hundred points of incompatibility to judge in advance how successful the transplant would be. Eye transplants were common. An eye donor could wait until he died before he saved another man's sight.

By 1990 it was possible to store any living human organ for any reasonable length of time. Transplants had become routine, helped along by the "scalpel of infinite thinness," the laser. The dying regularly willed their remains to organ banks. The mortuary lobbies couldn't stop it. But such gifts from the dead were not always useful.

> In l993 Vermont passed the first of the organ bank laws. Vermont has always had the death penalty. Now a condemned man could know that his death would save lives. It was no longer true that execution served no good purpose. . . ."
>
> —*The Jigsaw Man*, Harlan Ellison 1967

Biotech   The expression "gene machines" is pretty easy to figure out, too-that's the technology part of the rapidly-evolving science of biology that may keep away hunger, keep away disease, and maybe, just maybe, in that ocean of health and plenitude, keep away war. We can even use microbes to reduce pollution.

The first Canadian patent for a living organism was filed in 1976 by Abitibi-Price. The company patented a natural yeast strain which could break down pollutants in the discharge from sulphite mills. It took seven years to win the patent appeal. Although they subsequently found a cheaper method, it was a landmark decision that helped to stimulate Canada's fledgling biotechnology industry.

Our logger was certainly hopeful that biotechnology would help restore the economy of B.C. The scientist's picture of the full growth of regenerated forests, however, is slightly different from the logger's: "We can look forward to improving the quality of the forest resource. It will probably be pretty expensive, but we can now engineer clonal forests, with virtually identical trees—tall, straight, suitable for harvesting by machine. We can get clear boards with bioengineering, get rid of the finger joints, the knotty wood. The trees will be uniform and predictable."

"We are learning how to shorten the generational interval; with hormones, we can induce early flowering and shorten the growth cycle," reports a specialist in forestry working for a large, west-coast forest products company. "Of course these uniform stands are somewhat less stable, less resistant to disease, but when you mix a few other types in, . . ."

"And then there are exciting new bacterial strains being developed to control spruce budworm. But you have to contend with public reaction to spraying genetically engineered bacteria all over the countryside. Wouldn't want a panic, like that guy Jeremy Rifkin started in the States—getting an injunction against spraying until the procedures for an environmental impact statement had been followed. It's so easy to panic people about the idea of a doctored gene on the loose."

So we asked around. What are the dangers of spraying genetically engineered material over the countryside? A high-ranking science-policy expert acknowledged that there was a lot to learn, but calmed the questioner with an accurate, if slightly bitter rejoinder: "There is not too much to worry about because in Canada, we're always likely to be second to try anything like that. It will probably be safe because someone else will have already tested it out by the time we get around to committing any serious resources to doing anything here."

One of the most knowledgeable persons in the country on this subject is Dr. Lewis Slotin, director of programs, Medical Research Council, and former member of the task force on biotechnology. He has a series of very thoughtful questions on biotechnology:

Who decides which genetic resources are to be modified? On what basis—for the greatest good? For the most profit? What direction should we go towards—super cows? Square, easy to harvest tomatoes? Making everyone's IQ a full 200 points or more? Who should be granted exclusive ownership? How far up the evolutionary ladder does this control appropriately extend? Who will be held responsible for the mistakes, the accidents?

Yet can we afford not to enter such a promising field? Most of the other major countries in the world, both developed and developing, have set up policies and programs. Do we hold back because we lack the knowledge base to predict outcomes? Does Canada hesitate because those questions aren't answered?

Micro-Electronics Right after the biotechnologies, the public is most excited about the potentials of the micro-electronics field, expecially where it intersects advanced communications. Computers are easy to understand, too; they are the windows on the future. Younger and younger children are becoming comfortable with the possibilities:

"I remember my daughter's happy eyes when I told her she could type on the bright green display I used at home to send messages to friends all over the country. But I asked her to wait until the telephone connection was no longer in use, because I didn't want to pay the communication and computer rates while she learned the keyboard. She was very disappointed, and with all the authority of her five years, she told me she didn't want just to type on the pretty screen. 'I WANT TO TYPE AT SOMEBODY!' she insisted. She had already associated the idea of the terminal with that of a window on the outside world, a window through which she could see her friends and exchange bright, joyful greetings."[9]

The specialists are excited too. These industry spokesmen are also optimistic about Canada's comparative advantage, assuming, of course, the government gets some consistency into its policy and strengthens tax credits for research and development—a constant refrain from the telecommunications lobby. The dean of that group reminds us:

"Electronic systems cover a whole gamut of industries," says Northern Telecom Vice-President Roy Cottier. "Computer software, semi-conductors, telecommunications . . . these are the industries of the future; these are going to be the basic industries that will create the dynamic and winning industrial infrastructure. If we do not get a part of this world business and create these industrial infrastructures, we're going to be in a tough situation ten or twenty years from now."

Although the government may be slow to develop an overall policy, Canadians are determined that their children become "computer literate" so that they will have a chance at the emerging professions. But the issue is much broader than access to computers—concern for education has moved up the ladder of national issues rapidly in the last two years. Two of the last Liberal leadership candidates—Jean Chrétien and Don Johnston—understood this well and startled the provinces, which have been quietly decreasing their support for costly educational programs, by offering more federal support in this sensitive area.

While families are searching in their own ways to see that their children are prepared, academics and corporate executives are busy conducting their own version of Star Wars with Ottawa. They worry that Canada should not hesitate too long to get into these new technologies with a fuller commitment lest we be left out of the game. John Evans, a medical doctor, formerly president of the University of Toronto, now head of Allelix Corporation, sees some of these possibilities: "These technologies are crucial to Canada, especially in the development of our renewable resources and in the health sciences. We have the talent, the question is do we have the will to commit the financial resources?"

Scientists and academics speak of "windows of opportunity" and "getting into the networks," meaning that you have to have something to trade—fresh knowledge for fresh insight: "It is our only ticket to staying up with the fields internationally," says one of Canada's top laser technology experts. On the corporate side, we are forcefully reminded, again by Roy Cottier, that if we have nothing to trade we wind up buying their old technology on the world market. The head of the Science Council, Dr. Stuart Smith puts it this way:

"A lot will happen in the next little while and Canada has to be a part of it. The rate of new development and fundamental discoveries is very high in the new technologies and they cascade one upon the other. The lag period between a discovery and the time that it's marketed is very short and seems to be getting shorter. We should bring in the best technology we can get from abroad, but we should bring it in under the best terms possible. And the best terms possible usually require a good licencing arrangement, a joint venture of some kind and usually that *you have something to bring to the partnership as well.*

"If you just wait for them to sell it to you 'off the shelf,' they have a much more advanced model back home which they're already using. So it's not just a simple matter to import more technology. Of course we should import more technology; the point is that we've got to be in a position to import it under good terms, and it's the terms that are a serious concern."

All the experts agree on the idea that we should be doing more, and that there are some windows in some fields that might close down as other countries decide to focus on the military utility of, for example, lasers and biotechnology. They all convey an urgency, a pressure to come to grips with Canada's position on these technologies, as understanding of, and access to, the technologies will determine much of our international role in the next economy. Says Bill Hamilton, former Tory cabinet member, now a Macdonald commissioner: "How can we expect to write a report on the future of the economy without having a far better understanding of the emerging technologies? We need at least to spell out the trade-offs for a thorough public debate."

There is another key area of agreement. The experts do not believe that these technologies will generate new employment. All the experts interviewed felt that we should not count on any net job gain associated with the emerging hi-tech areas. Rather, they cautioned that for the next decade *we should anticipate a net job loss* because the technology spillover—through higher productivity—into the traditional sectors of the economy will further reduce the labor force.

All the arguments about "appropriate scale" and "comparative advantage" come to a head when you talk about picking winners and losers in these technology areas, or even, minimally, defining some umbrella policy priorities: "Biotech is a very attractive area. Look how well small firms have done, and it isn't very capital intensive—three professors can spin off from a university and start up a firm. And, they have a chance to succeed! Besides, with our economy being so dependent on renewable resources, we can hardly afford not to jump into this in a big way.

"And what about materials substitution—we count so much on metals, can we afford not to pursue research on the superplastics? After all, cars

139

are getting lighter and smarter. . . . I read somewhere the Japanese are working on a prototype all-plastic car, with a ceramic engine, . . .

"I hear the Japanese are going all out for creating smart computers, smart thinking machines. They intend to be the best in the world in artificial intelligence. We don't want to get stuck buying all our smart machines from them, do we? After all, that is how we lost our share of the small electronics industry."

Deciding where to invest our relatively scarce capital, and that includes knowledge capital as well as financial capital, is a difficult task. All the hardware-versus-software decisions, the question of whether to invest in physical plant or to put it into people—these are stubborn issues that refuse to go away. Not even a new resurgence of growth would begin to mask the traumas associated with these trade-offs.

Let's take a look at a couple of contrasting proposals to illustrate the kinds of trade-offs in dollars, materials, energy, and values, that are being debated in Ottawa and the boardrooms. Most of the time the value issues are hidden, or just politely submerged. Four years ago a good example would have been the conflict between the so-called "hard" energy megaprojects (extracting fossil fuels) and the "soft" energy path (solar and wind power) described by philosopher-physicist Amory Lovins.

That debate has been muted by the cyclical crash of the "hard" megaproject-style energy industries. Of the myriad projects dealt with in the megaprojects task force report of just a few years ago, only a few are on their way to reality.

Let's take a short look at the kinds of large-scale technology projects that still may be in our future. They suggest the fierce Star Wars battleground of science policy in the eighties. The first is one of the largest water resource engineering projects ever conceived, called the Grand Canal. The second, the Canadian Software Bank, emphasizes the development of our knowledge capital.

The Grand Canal Project   One of the most ambitious, dynamic, and downright colossal megaprojects ever conceived in Canada is known as the Grand Canal project. The central feature is a canal designed to link James Bay with the Great Lakes, creating the largest dam on the planet, carrying a sufficient volume of water to refresh and replenish the water table in the Great Lakes and the midwestern United States. According to the vice-president of the National Research Council, Keith Glegg, this project could cost $100 billion, employ 350,000 people a year, and take 15 years to complete.

Politically, it is attractive because of the high job content (enough to get us through a transition to the next economy) and the potential joint sponsorship with the United States. Aside from the influx of capital, the gratitude of our southern neighbor is claimed to be guaranteed for the next several centuries, thereby cementing the continental strategy and finally, irrevocably, guaranteeing us unlimited (non-tariff) access to the huge market just across the border.

Keith Glegg: "We take the position that we don't know if the project is good. But we do know that it's interesting. The NRC thinks that instead of being paralyzed and terrified at the thought of a Grand Canal, we should spend enough money to see whether it's intrinsically good or could be made so."

The Grand Canal is the largest macro-engineering project ever conceived in Canada, and stands in sharp contrast to another major project making the rounds. The Canadian Software Bank is designed to create a rapid learning environment across the whole culture; this "software" project assumes that people are the wealth of the next economy.

The Canadian Software Bank   Building on our existing strengths in communications, satellite transmission, the trans-Canada telephone system and the technology leadership of Northern Tel in fibre-optics, this project is designed to make available to every citizen of Canada access to the best of the current software with one local phone call.[10]

The idea is simple. The government of Canada would license or purchase from those software creators and publishers the unlimited rights to re-publish their products within Canada. These would be "banked" and then could be drawn down over the telephone lines, at the request of any interested user.

The software in the bank would range from educational programs to accounting, to more specialized-applications software. This access to learning systems and management systems would, in effect, subsidize a very rapid national learning curve. People would be able to experiment, make mistakes, self-select areas of interest, and of course, suggest modifications and improvements in the overall network. In fact, thousands of small networks would be started.

The total cost of installing the system might be $10 billion, with an annual software library budget of $500 million for the first few years. As Don Chisholm, vice-president of Northern Telecom puts it: "The sex is in the hi-tech, but the cost is in the ditch," referring to the rapidly declining costs of the fibre-optic technology, contrasted with the high cost of labor required to lay the cable.

Right now it can cost close to half a million dollars to get a piece of software into the Canadian marketplace, and unless the item is "copy protected" against duplication, it will not sell enough copies to cover the costs. One consequence of the high cost of getting products to market is that many software developers don't even try for the Canadian market, they just go straight to the U.S. Similarly, products coming from offshore don't even bother to enter the small Canadian market: "it's just too much risk for too little return."

The software bank would be coupled with the installation of a fibre-optic network, making Canada the first country to be able to handle high quality data and voice transmission in every neighborhood—giving us a several-years head start on everyone else. Although the French government is moving in this direction, here, the relative concentration of our population is a real advantage.

Another add-on might be a tax incentive to purchase the equipment at the household level. The provincial government side of the investment would be to change the configuration of local libraries to provide access to the software bank through these and other community institutions. One community group rapidly gaining experience with this is the YMCA. The head of the Y, Sol Kasimir, finds "a tremendous excitement with even the beginning programs. It goes far beyond what people are learning; perhaps the most important thing that they are getting from our programs is a sense of their own self-worth, that they can get into the world of computers, and through that, expand their skills in many other areas."

A nation-wide "freeware" system drawn from a Canadian software bank can build upon some experience elsewhere. The most extensive system pioneering some of these concepts was the ARPA network that linked universities and research institutions across the United States. And the most recent experiment with setting up open networks have produced literally thousands of more specialized information exchanges. One recent guide, *The Computer Data and Database Source Book* has nearly 900 pages, listing free public sources in 500 categories as well as over 1000 commercial databases.[11]

Andrew Fluggleman, editor of *PC World*, who pioneered the concept of "freeware" in California, finds that he gets paid for a greater percentage of the copies of his free software programs (each program has a little notice in it which says if you like it, send a donation to the author) around than do his competitors, who want $300 up front. "They may charge more, but they also have a greater proportion of unauthorized copies than we do. The best part about freeware is that you can test it and see if you like it and spread it around to your friends without guilt or an outrageously high price tag. A remarkable number of people read the notice, and send a check. That's one of the best parts of the new networks that have started—it brings out the best in people. There are no authority figures, you have to be a responsible contributor."

These are two projects that could be in Canada's future, both utilizing macro-engineering but with very different byproducts. These two mega-projects give an indication of the type of national goals that are being explored. The values that underly these decisions must be responsive to all of our needs and perceptions.

The politicians who have to decide about these large resource allocation possibilities don't know much more than we do. Regrettably, our political system is poorly equipped to make these complex, long-term decisions. Fortunately, quite a bit of the access to the new technologies is no longer controllable "from the top." You can already get a three-pound computer for $500, and then all you need is a phone.

Chapter 12

THE POLITICS OF TRANSITION

I f our old political institutions evolved to fit the demands of mass markets for ideas in an industrializing world, what will our new ones look like? How are we going to manage in the transition to the next economy?

Do our politicians know how to govern when their budgets can't expand? Do they know how to fund new programs when Canadians are beginning to back out of the income tax system? Do they know how to design a social security system for a world in which personal identity and income may no longer be tied to a job? Would they know the windows of opportunity for the new technologies if they were staring right through them? Do they know how to avert a nuclear war?

This desire for a new approach to politics found its expression in the landslide majority given to the Progressive Conservatives by Canadians in the 1984 election. The pundits and politicians, in the wake of that election, are hunting for the meaning of that mandate for "change." But they are handicapped by trying to find that mandate in conventional, industrial age language of "left" or "right." One thing is very clear: it was not an endorsement of traditional conservative ideology.

Political research conducted in recent years supports a different interpretation.[12] What Canadians elected in 1984 was a government that reflects a "new conservatism." Canadians remain committed to the objective of a society characterized by social equity. What they have begun to question is the scale, the powers, and the role of government in defining and meeting that objective.

145

There are three elements of the new-style conservatism that are to be kept in balance, if the political agenda is to reflect the emerging political will. The key words are "rights," "access" and "limits."

The clear delineation of *rights* is the first requirement. Canadians are seeking reassurance that their basic entitlements are in place: medicare, the economic safety net, for example. We have been making increasing use of new instruments in recent years—the Charter, for example, and locally-sponsored referenda—in an attempt to determine the extent of an appropriate government role. Privacy and independence are tied up with these issues as the potentially invasive technologies of the next economy lead more people to be concerned about the line that divides legitimate state power from interference in private life.

Access to government decision-making is a crucial ingredient. This is the expectation that lies behind so much of the language that has crept into politics in recent years—"prior notification," "cooperation," "consultation," "openness" and even that awkward phrase, "multipartitism." Traditions of secrecy in parliament, in caucus, and especially in budget preparations no longer fit gracefully with our relentless need to know in this new economy. We can no longer tolerate the finance minister saying "Surprise—gotcha again," as he announces yet another change in the tax system on a budget night. So many of the most crucial issues in the transition to the next economy cannot be settled by the backroom boys dividing up the pie—the diversifying interest groups in the Canadian public want to hear about those trade-offs, and get in on the decisions. They don't want to wait for a *fait accompli*.

Finally, as the problem of structural deficits grows more dramatic and more difficult to reverse, Canadians seek ways to *limit* government size. In the "Mandarins" chapter we looked at this issue, and in the next chapter, we'll explore it in more detail. Worry about the deficits does not mean support for drastic across-the-board cutbacks, but rather, pressure to have the trade-offs clearly outlined. In addition to rationalizing the scale of government, the push is to define better what we want from government and a fair way to pay for it.

Although most of our politicians continue to talk and act as if the good old days are just around the bend, if only we are have confidence in the economy, a few political figures have finally begun to question their own assumptions about what it means to be a politician nowadays. They know that the "good guys" are consultative, while the "bad guys" manufacture crises. They admit that life has just not turned out to be what they thought it would be when they embarked on their careers. Two of the most interesting and frank perspectives came from individuals who would have been described in traditional terms as being at opposite ends of the political spectrum; one, an experienced Liberal Ottawa political advisor, and the other, a staunch provincial Conservative from a farming community in Saskatchewan.

One of the politicians who has thought a lot about new political realities—and about the forces shaping them—is Bob Andrew. At times he is even willing to take off his hat as finance minister of Saskatchewan's Conservative government and think about them aloud. "We need to be more blunt about our choices if we are going to confront the issues of the next economy. And time is getting short—we need to start talking about those choices right now."

Tom Axworthy, principal secretary to former prime minister Pierre Trudeau, presently teaching at the Kennedy School of Government at Harvard, is another political figure who has realized just how much the politician's job has changed in recent years, and how much more it will have to change if the politician of the future is to remain an effective leader.

"In the sixties and seventies, when resources were abundant," he says, "it was satisfying to redistribute incomes—a lot more satisfying then to redistribute scarcity, which is what we now face. Then it was in some ways easier to be prime minister—a lot more fun ten years ago than it will be for the next decade. The world has changed in crucial ways."

Andrew just shakes his head. "You know," he says, "once I got into politics I started to get very frustrated because nobody wanted to listen to new ideas, nobody wanted to think about how and why things were changing."

The times were indeed "achanging," but no politician wanted to be the first to talk about it. One legacy of the economic and political uncertainty caused by the economic dislocations of the late seventies and early eighties is some deep social scars. There is a growing public distrust of leadership—public and private—and a strong sense of discomfort among Canadians about the adequacy and appropriateness of many of the nation's institutions.

Very often political analysts and politicians themselves characterize this distrust of leadership as a "problem of confidence." The lack of confidence is put down to the usual "personality" or "popularity" problems that all politicians must occasionally face. Worse yet, it is treated as "an image problem." Many have argued that the problem of confidence is a temporary one that will disappear with a change of names.

Unfortunately, this facile view ignores a decade of steady decline in institutional legitimacy, particularly for public-sector institutions. People no

147

longer believe that all you need to do to solve a problem is change leaders or throw money at it.

There is a growing belief among Canadians that many of the country's most intractable problems—unemployment, for instance, or interest rates or health care—may not even be decided by domestic politicians, that their solutions lie elsewhere, if indeed they can be resolved at all. It's also clear that Canadians now doubt that any one political party has more or better "answers" to the issues, or, that once elected to office, any one leader can untangle "the problems with the system."

"You'll have to speak up, John."

Uluschak

The End of Ideology   In the last federal election campaign Canadians saw little substantive basis for a choice between the leaders of the major national parties. "The Bobbsey Twins of Bay Street"—the label given to Liberal leader Turner and Conservative leader Mulroney by NDP leader Broadbent—was picked up across the country by humorists and columnists.

The "Bobbsey Twins" label stuck, not because Canadians believe what the NDP leader said, but because the phrase so aptly captured what millions of Canadians had privately come to believe: "They're all the same, anyway," goes the conventional wisdom. "You can't tell what a politician will do by reading his party label—or even by reading his lips."

Canadians feel that there is little utility in ideological labels—"left," "right," particularly party labels. "The so-called Conservatives made more

148

Gable

costly campaign promises than the Liberals!" During the last election campaign voters could "choose" between a Liberal leader who promised to halve the deficit in seven years, although never on the backs of the disadvantaged, and a PC leader who promised to pay down the deficit, while insisting the principle of universality was "inviolate."

The political party leaders themselves contributed to the confusion. John Turner called Brian Mulroney a "me-too Liberal." Tories warned that "a vote for the NDP is a vote for the Liberals." John Crosbie dubbed the NDP "the little red rump of the Liberal party." New Democrats responded with attacks against what they called the "Liberal-Conservative" party. The NDP further warned that both were "fake" socialists, and given a fair chance, the real ones would stand up.

Meanwhile, everyone was accusing everyone else of "stealing" his ideas or programs. The overall result was a sense that there was no difference between the parties on grounds of traditional left-right policy criteria, the differences were style. In the politics of the new conservatism, however, an open and consultative style, for example, is very important. And Prime Minister Mulroney won that battle decisively.

Many of the business decision makers we interviewed underscored the increasing convergence of Canada's political parties. "It's an interesting time in Canadian politics," says Don Jackson of Trimac. "Decisions about economics and commerce, as well as about Canada's role on a broader scale, are going to be made more pragmatically, less nationalistically—whether you backed Turner or Mulroney."

"If you look at all three parties in this country and add up their policy similarities, versus their policy differences, the balance is tremendously tilted in favor of what they all agree on," Bob Andrew points out. "And yet we insist on confining ourselves to the 'Jonathan-Swift-model' of arguing among ourselves about the thickness of the shell of an egg in Canadian politics."

At the provincial level, for example, Conservative governments have been just as likely as their Liberal brethren to tighten environmental regulations if they had a poll which showed that to do so would be popular. In Alberta, mandarins in a Conservative government manage a $17 billion Heritage Fund. In Saskatchewan, a Conservative government keeps alive the legacy of its NDP predecessor in the form of the Crown corporations, making no move to "privatize" organizations that Saskatchewan voters like just the way they are.

The average politician is in a double bind. He faces a rock-solid baseline of public distrust each time he speaks or acts. He faces a public that increasingly perceives him to be little different from the guy he's competing with for votes. Because Canadians believe that the established political parties won't or can't distinguish themselves, debates and disagreements are often characterized as more apparent than real. Increasingly, such stand-offs are seen as counter-productive, if not deceitful.

Bob Andrew says, "If the biggest news coming out of Parliament last year was on procedural blockages of legislation, that doesn't tell us much about what the system is doing for us. There are a lot of politicians rubbing their hands and nudging each other, thinking, 'Great! We rang the bells for six days!' But how can we think that's a great system? It has ceased to be a debating forum, ceased to be a forum for creating compromises, creating agreements, and creating decisions. And that was what Parliament is supposed to do."

Thinkers like Bob Andrew understand that something far more fundamental than a change in one leader or a drop in another's popularity will shake things up politically in Canada. "Not only do we have to solve the country's economic problems—or at least try to solve them," he argues, "but we have to create a new political system in order to do it."

"I Must Catch Up To My People"   Andrew believes that a first step towards that new political system has to be a pretty dramatic change in attitude on the part of contemporary politicians themselves. "My view is that the general public is very skeptical and growing more skeptical of politicians all the time. What people really want, I believe, is for us to start being a lot more realistic—to try and sell that realism politically in a lot more ways. That's difficult at times, without question. Being realistic and being a modern politician are often not a good fit."

Tom Axworthy thinks so, too. "It's a balance of being able to say, 'We can still achieve much, but in order to do it we've got to be realistic. Here's a modest but real way we can go, and I'm not trying to fool you.'"

Clearly, the reluctance to be the bearers of bad news was a habit our politicians picked up in their teething days when the post-war economy was booming. The capacity of politicians to respond in the old ways—to "spend their way" to solutions—is now seriously constrained. "Many governments in this country don't have any discretionary income," Andrew points out. "The reality is, we're running out of room. If discretionary income is going to come from closing universities and closing hospitals, that's some discretion!"

Not only is the modern politician cash-strapped, but the public patience he could once count on is now wearing thin. Canadians themselves don't believe that tomorrow is necessarily going to be better than today— only that it will be quite different, and require some sizable adjustments. In

151

fact, the "good news" politicians—the ones who claim they can magically cut the deficit in half, reduce interest rates at will, or usher in a new era of prosperity, all without cost—are automatically discounted.

Bob Andrew talks thoughtfully about the attitudinal problem that politicians have to face: "Politicians get into the system, and suddenly—especially in Ottawa—you hear them say, 'Well, the people are too stupid to know what's good for them.' I've never had that view of people. I grew up with a genuine faith that people, by their nature, have an innate sense or an instinct about what has to be done. If you really study politics, you find there's a lot more to it than politicians tend to give the voting public credit for. Maybe they're not as articulate or they don't know the right words, but they sense things."

Tom Axworthy concurs: "I think you can talk realistically to a populace, because I think people understand and learn quickly. I think they quickly find out which of all the vast promises politicians make are BS, and which aren't."

On the whole, Canadians are less hopeful and willing followers than they were a decade ago. The principal legacy of the seventies is a deep sense of uncertainty, partly because the social and economic changes hammered at them too rapidly, and partly because they have lost a sense of where they are going.

"I think we went through a time when people became very reliant upon government. We saw the rise of the Crown sector and the massive growth of bureaucracy. It wasn't just the political parties doing it, it was the voters, whether they lived in British Columbia or Saskatchewan, whether they voted for Bill Bennett or Allan Blakeney. But now there is more willingness among people to rely on themselves. They're saying, 'I want to do it myself. I'm going to do it myself.' They want hints about how they can help themselves, not barriers that keep them from doing so," says Bob Andrew.

What has made many Canadians less willing followers is that we believe our institutions and leaders have failed to adequately protect us from economic uncertainty. Our response has been to begin doing it ourselves. We're starting our own independent businesses, growing and making our own food, engaging in volunteer activities, starting our own self-help groups—and more and more of us are sheltering our income from the tax man by joining the invisible economy.

All these behaviors and expectations mean that the typical Canadian's search for security and fulfillment is being pursued on a highly individualized, personal basis. People no longer automatically believe that delegating responsibility to large, traditional institutions—including political institutions—will guarantee them even security, not to mention fulfillment.

As we have become less reliant on our large institutions and less trusting of the decisions made by them, our stress on self-sufficiency and independence is fostering the creation of a much more pluralistic culture. Experimentation with alternative lifestyles used to be the preserve of fringe counterculture groups during the sixties. In the eighties it is a way of life for middle-class Canadians struggling to preserve their standard of living in the face of declining incomes and future uncertainty. As a consequence, there is a tremendous diversification in the lifestyles, values and expectations of average Canadians. It is becoming more and more difficult to define a "typical" Canadian these days.

Political leaders have historically assumed that there is a reliable "majority will." Social scientists have provided them with the technology to monitor this majority will and perhaps even anticipate it. But just when our polling methods have improved, just when our technology of testing is being enhanced by the computer, there is evidence that the hoped-for simple majority, who will vote predictably, is rapidly dissipating. In the face of uncertainty, not only are Canadians less willing followers, but a middle-of-the-road Canadian culture is giving way to a more diverse, pluralistic world.

Tom Axworthy is concerned about responding to these changes: "Middle-income people have traditionally been the bulwark of democratic societies. Certainly, they've paid most of the taxes. Now they're getting squeezed everywhere. They want to have a stake in things. They want to have some control over their destinies. But I don't think politicians have been paying much attention to them. Now I see middle-income people— the great base of our mass democracy—beginning to lose their optimism, beginning to rip off the system. That's something they never did before. Once that part of the system begins to unravel, a lot of things start to unravel."

Bob Andrew quickly puts his finger on one of the key political challenges involved in managing a pluralistic culture, one in which people are less willing to play "follow the leader." "We're going to have to go back to fundamental questions about how we care for ourselves, how we care for our fellow man, and reassess the whole thing. It's clear to me that we don't have the money to behave the way we used to, and we can't keep asking the people for more."

Other trends fuel this diversification process. Education, for example, leads to diversity. Canadians are increasingly well-educated, trying to improve their economic options by upgrading their skills. But a highly educated society is also a more pluralistic one, a society characterized by complex, multiple signals rather than simple ones. Improvements in education

153

are also coupled with a drive for more people to enter the mainstream. Diverse groups have won rights for women, the disadvantaged, racial, ethnic and linguistic minorities, and the elderly, propelling their new issues, agendas, values and aspirations into the centre of political decision-making.

As we saw in the "Star Wars" chapter, the new technologies, especially biotechnology, medical technology, nuclear technology and computer technology, have forced a whole new set of issues onto the political agenda. They are often issues that involve complex value choices and moral or ethical dilemmas. Abortion, euthanasia and nuclear disarmament are just a few issues on which it is increasingly difficult to generate majority agreement and middle-of-the-road positions.

Simple majorities—the mass market in political ideas—are becoming tougher to identify. The "normal" bell-shaped curve of political convictions that the politician once could easily manage is vanishing. The normal curve is flattening out. There is a much wider range of views in the political marketplace.

Much of the effective political pressure in Canada is now being generated by *ad hoc* coalitions of interest groups. Momentary majorities—usually "veto" majorities—form around single issues. But stable majorities, those that subscribe to consistent left-right philosophies of government or consistently argued positions on economic development have disappeared.

Bob Andrew is also concerned about the reactive, short-term nature of politics: "We have a classic cover-your-ass mentality in government. Very often the politician is driven by ulterior motives—by special interests, short-term payoffs, if you like. I try to never think short-term. On the other hand, the long-term is too far away for me to understand it very clearly. So I always think in the medium-term, anywhere from three to six years."

These emerging political sensibilities build on the Canadian experience with the "inflation psychology" of the seventies and the severe "middle-class" recession of the early eighties—periods when faith in the government's—any government's—ability to solve social and economic problems was severly eroded.

The Informal Polity   A new network of social and political activists is now emerging in response. It is less willing to grant a clear social and economic policy mandate to government. It is also more likely to support a *minimization* of government's prescriptive involvement in the economy.

Much of the emerging activisim occurs outside the political mainstream. It even takes the form of civil disobedience and mass protest—in the case of the B.C. restraint program, for instance. It increasingly takes the

154

form of legal challenges to government decisions, for example, high profile Charter cases over Cruise missile tests. Another form is of locally sponsored referenda—the Manitoba language issue, for instance.

It is an *informal polity* which draws constituents from the many fragmented, grass roots coalitions that have sprung up across the country over the past two decades. This informal polity includes environmentalists, right-to-lifers and freedom-of-choice groups, the community groups and self-help groups that sprang up due to the recession.

The informal polity has given rise to a number of strange bedfellow alliances on key political issues. We find, for instance, pro-life groups and freedom-of-choice groups are allies on the pornography issue. B.C.'s Operation Solidarity includes over thirty groups, from the Vancouver policemen's union to gay rights activists. Nuclear disarmament concerns brings together conservative religious leaders and fringe activists on what would once have been considered the far left.

Significantly, these groups are not composed of marginal participants in Canadian life who simply seek entry to the mainstream. They are middle-class Canadians who fear their hard-won place in the economy is threatened, and who are increasingly concerned about the security of their children and their grandchildren. They can't be easily pigeonholed in conventional demographic categories by sex, age, language, religious affiliation, or geography.

Finally, these groups are distinctly non-partisan. They are outside the traditional left-right party spectrum and prefer informal alignments with political parties, if any. One has only to look at the high profile new "parties" that are emerging in Canada to see how totally inappropriate it is to try to label their positions as left-right. The Greens, for example, proclaim themselves to be "neither left nor right," but "in front." Their spokespersons proclaim that if capitalism pollutes the Great Lakes, it is also true that socialism pollutes Lake Baikal.

No one seriously tries to pin down the position of the Rhinoceros Party as left or right, either. Yet there was a brief moment in the last election when a lot of Canadians were admitting that the Rhinos may have had their fingers on the right problems. Now, if only they could come up with the right solutions, . . . We haven't yet reached the point of New Zealand-style politics where there were no fewer than twenty-five parties on the last ballot. They included the Computer Party, the Cheer Up Party, the McGillicuddy Serious Party, and the Home Brewers United Front.

But the election race in Vancouver Quadra in 1984 came close. Mr. Turner faced no less than eight fringe candidates, including a young taxi driver, an engineer-turned-farmer running for the Green Party, and one so-called Gaetan Feuille d'Erable, running for the UIC (United Impoverished Canadian) Party. Laughter aside, these candidates reflect a search for political expression that is not being met within the framework of our existing political institutions.

The political vocabulary of the industrial age doesn't quite fit this informal polity, where alliances are based on a complex horizontal network of interests. Yet these patterns come very close to being more appropriate for the horizontal age of the next economy. And the networking technologies are making these roiling alliances far more feasible; they do not need to be organized, or controlled from such centers as Ottawa. By the next federal election, these technologies and political forms will have a potentially much stronger impact.

The influence can already be felt; members of the informal polity, rather than the politicians, are increasingly defining the national agenda. Tax reform, the integration of women's concerns into political decision-making, world peace, small-business development and environmental integrity were all defined and initiated *from the bottom up by informal polity alliances.*

Those that have been thinking seriously about the kinds of political changes occurring in Canada know that the challenge does not simply lie in changing the rank of five top issues on the national agenda or making a few adjustments to institutional responses. They understand that the challenge is to re-examine the basic purposes and procedures of political institutions and to re-assess their relevance for the next economy.

"The last thing people need is more tinkering with the system," says Bob Andrew. Tom Axworthy further questions government activism *per se*: "In the tradition of Keynes, Beveridge and Roosevelt, an activist government was the instrument by which Liberals sought to change society," he muses. "But has government now become part of the problem rather than the solution?"

Trimac's Don Jackson also senses the mismatch between our political institutions and the emerging priorities of the informal polity. "Our government systems are not very imaginative. They're not very entrepreneurial. They're not very risk-oriented. And they're not at all oriented to the individual's responsibility for his or her own behavior. It's a small-L liberal view that our governments continue to pursue. It's a problem in our political psyche."

How then will the politics of transition have to function if, as a nation, we are to move from the industrial economy to the newly emerging information economy?

156

Bob Andrew thinks a key step will be for politicians to begin facing the tough questions—even if they don't have all the answers. It won't be sufficient to talk about "turnarounds" or "recoveries"—we'll need to talk more about "changing structures." "We have to face up to the reality that unemployment is severe and will likely be at least as severe for the next decade," Andrew says. "There are two things that we're not going to be able to do. One is to create a lot of short-term jobs forever. The other is to create a lot of nice high-paying jobs forever.

"So how do we deal with it? How do we use the government sector? How do we use the private sector? Solving the employment problem means looking at all the ways we now spend our money—on education, on welfare, on unemployment insurance, and so on. We have to put all these questions into the boiler together."

Andrew stresses the need to bring a longer-term perspective to bear on these questions: "Given our demographics, our problems are likely to be a decade in length, at least," he argues. "In another decade, the baby boomers of the fifties will be middle-aged and will start shaking the safety net. They shook the school system; they're shaking the business system and the job system, *next they're going to shake the welfare system and the health care system.*"

Wall Street economist Brian Fabbri agrees: "The worst form of government is a government that literally does nothing. The next-to-worst form of government is a government that is driven by short-run dislocations and attempts to cure them without considering the long-run costs of the programs they impose. That will never lead us to any progress along a longer path of economic and social growth."

Fabbri, too, is worried about the deficits which are rising in industrialized countries around the world. He is disturbed not only about the immediate consequences for the economy, but about the long-term uncertainty. "The biggest of all the problems that the structural deficit poses for economists and politicians is uncertainty. We are beyond our ken in attempting to project what ever-larger deficits might do to financial markets, our own economy and the world economy."

To manage these tough questions both Bob Andrew and Tom Axworthy stress the need to drop the left-right ideological baggage of an earlier era of adversarial politics. Bob Andrew thinks that the management of the deficit will force a change in the way politics are conducted in Canada. "The only way Canadian governments can deal with it is to *collectively* identify the extent of the problem, define the necessary action, and *collectively* act."

"We've traditionally had two sets of believers in our society," Tom Axworthy points out. "There has been the 'let-the-market-do-it' side and

157

there has been the 'we-must-do-it-all' side. But now there are a lot more people trying for a synthesis of the two. They believe there is a role for market forces, but also a role for the state in providing direction and establishing incentive frameworks."

Bob Andrew points out: "In the parliamentary system of politics, we have a game once every four years. The winner takes all. I think that's unfortunate. If we're ever going to build alliances in this country, we have to start with the politicians. If we can't approach problems and issues collectively—as members of different parties, or as members of nine or ten governments—how the hell do we expect to get cooperation among government, business and labor on crucial issues?"

Andrew also believes that the "scapegoating" will have to stop. "Canadians are not prepared to stand for a government that blames everyone else—the feds, the provinces, the opposition parties, even Ronald Reagan. I think what people are fed up with is that they believe they elected a government to do something. I think what Canadians are saying is that we have to have the wherewithall to solve our problems, and that they'll go in search of the people who are prepared to provide the options and alternatives if we can't."

Politicians will need new ways to define and mediate amongst the complex array of demands being placed on them by the newly emerging informal polity. If a politician can be likened to a pianist, the challenge in dealing with the informal polity is in learning to play the right chords. "When are we politicians going to look at this as businessmen and say, 'Look, we've got a lot of people working for us and they all have legitimate aspirations. How do we maximize those things for the benefit of all of us?' I think we need to apply that kind of perspective to the whole country."

But not only politicians are involved. "We need more intelligent thought," argues Bob Andrew, "not only from academics, but from the media, from labor leaders, from businessmen and from the politicians. We all have to become more oriented toward synthesis and cooperation. It's the old baseball coach, asking if we're really not all part of a group working together."

"I think we have to look at new ways of achieving old ends," says Axworthy, and cites an example: "We had one experiment for the textile industry. We wanted to help displaced workers, retrain them. So we took government money and gave it to a business-labor board that wasn't operating in the usual advisory mode to the minister. We said, 'No, you make the decisions. Call your labor people in. You businessmen, volunteer your time. You make the decisions. You work it out. We'll give you the door under this mandate, but you take care of it. We don't think government departments can do it because we sure haven't done it in the past.'

"The bureaucrats, of course, hated it. A lot of the politicians, too. It took away some of their responsibilities. No patronage either! But I think it has worked exceedingly well—business and labor in a government post, delivering a service. But that means trusting the guys out there. No more custodial elite."

"The challenge to politicians," Bob Andrew concludes, "is whether we sit in the old system of government and let the big wave push us where it will—just trying to stay in power—or whether we try to get a head start on the wave so that we can ride down the front of it rather than get caught in the middle of the damned thing."

"I think it was Theodore Roosevelt who said we have to have the courage to dare to fail greatly," Tom Axworthy muses. "Well, we'll have to dare to fail greatly. Let's not be so afraid."

Chapter 13

THE CHALLENGE OF RESTRAINT: CONFRONTATION OR COOPERATION

The problem of restraint will be with us for the foreseeable future. How various Canadian governments respond, the climate they choose to set, and the choices they make with respect to "what gets cut" and "what gets protected" will either smooth the transition to the next economy, open up our options, or make an already difficult set of challenges more fraught with personal risk.

The transition to the next economy is going to be particularly difficult for government. Politicians are struggling to maintain the political expectations of the voters, and the mandarins are trying to preserve the institutions left over from the last economy. They are operating with substantially less revenue than they enjoyed in the past, and with no prospects for rapid growth on the horizon.

Maintaining political equilibrium while bridging to the programs of the future is a difficult challenge. Most governments now agree that they are likely to have an increasing strain on revenues, and a difficult fight to make budget cuts. They have few guidelines and little experience. After all, for two decades government revenues and government budgets simply went up.

Keeping peace while cutting back is essentially a conservative task. So many of the people who came into government during the sixties were stimulated by the creativity of government then; now, much of the "fun" has gone out of their jobs. Probably the turning point came in 1975, the last year that John Turner was finance minister. When Brian Mulroney first determined to become prime minister, it was certainly still a very pleasant prospect. After all, the biggest challenges were to *redistribute* wealth. Now, that has all changed.

So sure was the federal finance department that we were on a never-ending upward spiral that they were prepared to index the personal income tax system to the rate of inflation. Then finance minister John Turner announced that the government would no longer collect taxes on income increases that resulted from an inflationary bump up into a higher tax bracket. After all, in 1974 we had a budget *surplus* of 1.4 billion dollars! Since then, politicians, mandarins, and bureaucrats have had a lot of re-learning to do. Only some of them have managed to do so with grace.

"Who's at the door?"   "The federal deficit!"

Uluschak

Two provincial governments that have recently labored with the necessity of cutting back public sector outlays while preserving a sense of community, are British Columbia and Manitoba. Both the Social Credit government of Bill Bennett and the NDP government of Howard Pawley have been faced with the need to cut back shortly after being elected.

Although the deficit and unemployment problems were similar, both governments chose different styles of resolving it. They were well aware

162

that public-sector employees were handy scapegoats in the current political climate. One government was advised to take a high-profile "win-lose" confrontation route, while the other decided to try for a lower profile "win-win" collaborative strategy.

We invited spokesmen from both restraint efforts to talk about what they attempted, and what they learned; and found a further contrast in the way they wanted to talk about it. In both instances we sought the architects of the process both within the government and within the labor movement. For B.C., we interviewed Art Kube, head of the B.C. Federation of Labor, and Norman Spector, the person most widely credited as being Bennett's key advisor in the B.C. government strategy. In Manitoba, we talked with Gary Doer, head of the Manitoba Government Employees Union, and with Michael Decter, the secretary to the Cabinet, Clerk of Executive Council.

One striking difference in the legacy of the two approaches to restraint stood out as we sought to arrange the interviews: both Michael Decter and Gary Doer suggested that they would be pleased to arrange a joint interview. By contrast, in B.C., Norman Spector told us that he preferred to be interviewed separately. B.C. Fed president, Art Kube said he would be comfortable with doing it either way.

Almost two years after the initial confrontation in B.C., the two sides, clearly delineated, are still struggling with poor communications and the residue of political distrust. While in Manitoba, despite upcoming contract negotiations, the lines of communication, if wary, are still very much open.

The B.C. budget controversy was widely publicized outside the province. Residual difficulties continue to take the form of flare-ups in labor disputes and new government initiatives to "regulate," in Norman Spector's terms, the labor market in B.C. The following is a condensed version of the answers which Norman Spector and Art Kube provided to an identical set of questions. The responses have been paired so both views are side by side.

Question: What is your perspective on the need for restraint?

Spector: I think there are some governments that will have less spare money than others. The resource producing areas will likely be disadvantaged relative to the manufacturing areas. I accept the low growth forecast for British Columbia throughout the decade. I think we're not likely to see a return to the commodity boom; we'll see resource prices continue to be depressed on an international scale. And therefore, I think British Columbia, in particular, will be in a cash-hungry position.

Kube: Restraint is a legitimate goal, an important long-term goal in this era. But let's be very clear on one thing: we haven't experienced restraint. The first Bennett budget had a fairly hefty increase of 12.3 percent, the following budget also has a spending increase. But what we did see was major shifts in priorities. First, the shift was away from the social envelope to mega-projects; and again, $470 million in the second budget away from the social envelope. If you use money for social expenditures, the multiplier is much greater—it creates jobs.

The legislation that accompanied the Bennett budget created a psychology of fear amongst 250,000 workers. That psychology of fear changed spending patterns; instead of spending their money, they were so insecure about their employment prospects that they started to save. The business community felt the consequences. This had a negative effect on the provincial economy, and increased unemployment.

Question: Are the changes in the economy long-term and structural, or short-term and cyclical?

Spector: B.C. has gone from the top of the heap to the bottom of the heap since 1981. The recession has got a cyclical component, no doubt about it, but this problem is structural. Canada itself is a small, open economy, but in B.C. we're the quintessential small, open economy. Protectionism is not an option for British Columbia. There's no political, i.e., sovereign policy that can correct the terms of trade that we are subjected to: we don't have quotas, we can't have tariffs, we can't have any of that. And we have to sell two-thirds of our production on international markets. That's about double the national average.

Kube: We have some cyclical problems, and we have some structural problems, no question about that. The cyclical problems have to do with the reduced demand for our products. But there are also structural problems. For example, in British Columbia, *fewer* people are producing *more* things. Technological change has had a major impact: the forest industry employs 25 percent fewer people than it did 36 months ago, and these people produce as much as before. The structural problem is—what do you do with the 25 percent who have no jobs?

Question: What will we have to give up to cope with structural deficits?

Spector: Well, I don't know how much you look at public opinion polls, but here is the latest Goldfarb omnibus (he does an annual key trend where he interviews 800 people). His analysis says the trade-offs are between:

creating employment (69%)   vs.   decreasing the deficit (20%)

not raising taxes
to reduce the deficit (69%)   vs.   raising taxes (19%)

not cutting back on UIC to reduce the deficit (63%)	vs.	cutting back on UIC to reduce the deficit (26%)
controlling unemployment (69%)	vs.	controlling inflation (26%)

Personally, I'm not convinced these are trade-offs, but politicians are telling the public these are the trade-offs. There is only one that there's at least an even split on: means tests for social programs (46%) vs. universality (46%).

British Columbians have been asked to give up a lot, and that's what we went through, I think the only point I'm making, as Goldfarb concludes, is that 'no cut is politically palatable,' and there's such a contradiction in public opinion and lack of education that it's very difficult to sell any cut. But our deficit has gone from $1.6 billion last year (we've had two budgets in the same fiscal year) down to $670 million in the 84-85 budget. Now that, as you know, produced some violent shocks to the system, but the job has effectively been done.

Kube: If you're completely honest with people, and enlist their help in dealing with the long-term problems, and develop policies with a strong, broad consensus, then you can do a number of things, because people at least know what's at the end of the process. The other thing that's absolutely essential is that you recognize *who* can make a sacrifice, and who can't. Tightening your belt for somebody in a middle-income or upper-income group is one thing. For somebody who is already an outcast from the system, who has been unemployed for two years and has used up all his savings, sacrifice means something very different.

Question: How would you characterize the intent of the Bennett restraint budgets?

Spector: Well, I think to be fair, there was a mixture of motives. But I would say the primary motive, and it's been an article of faith in social credit as you know since 1952, is that budgets should balance. It may be a simplistic notion, and it's one that W.A.C. Bennett was derided on for many years, but it's virtually an article of faith. I would say that was and is the primary motivation.

Kube: The Bennett government decided that now's the time to take the bold step and veer off to the right. The finances of the province were not in such bad shape. Socred governments in British Columbia always underestimate revenues and overestimate expenditures. The whole thing was not done because the province was in bad financial condition; it was done very largely to appease the 20 percent of the electoral right.

Question: Was "restraint" used as an umbrella goal—was there a longer-term necessity to reduce the expectations of the B.C. labor force?

Spector: The B.C. labor force was the highest paid, there's no doubt about that. What's happening in B.C. is a structural adjustment to all values. By values, I mean both economic values and attitudes. Since 1981, share values in the forestry industry have declined by about 30 percent. For example, Macmillan Bloedel was taken over in the range of $62-63, now it's trading in the $40s. Property prices in Vancouver and Victoria have declined by 15 to 25 percent. Wages had been the highest in the country, but they're now approaching the national average. Public-sector wage settlements led the country—they're now about 30 percent below the national average.

In areas where the market works, politicians love the market. One of the reasons politicians love the market, I think, is that they don't have to do the dirty work, so it's always better to use the market. But there are areas where the market clearly wasn't working, and one of them was the public sector. There are different approaches that have been used across the country. Québec, for example, legislated rollbacks in existing contracts; the federal government and Ontario suspended collective-bargaining rights and in effect gave very handsome arbitrated awards.

B.C. chose an approach which I would characterize as "regulated" collective bargaining, which says that the market doesn't operate, and therefore, there are market imperfections. Just as we would legislate other non-functioning markets, we're going to regulate the public-sector labor market. . . . We're now regulating; we've got an independent commission set up, no contracts have been imposed, they've all been arrived at through free collective bargaining, and the average settlements are down in the range of 2, 2-1/2 percent.

Kube: The government is trying to create situations where they undermine union strength by, for example, massive changes to the labor code; the attack on labor has been consistent throughout. That's why I say the whole thing doesn't have anything to do with trying to improve the economy. They attacked human rights, the poor, the disabled. Anyone who tries to find an argument that the government did these things because they made economic sense is missing the point. *These things didn't save the province a single cent.*

Question: But the deficit is down, isn't it?

Kube: This province's income is cyclical. The cycle would have been okay over five years.

Question: Why do you think the programs, the budgets, the direction was so widely treated as "union baiting?"

Spector: The province is so polarized—and right down the middle, and has been for many years—that no interpretation is ridiculous. In other words, if you say "black," 50 percent of the people will believe you and 50 percent won't. But if you say "white," 50 percent of the people won't believe you and the other 50 percent will. It's the same thing with the restraint program. I believe *The Globe and Mail* had a large part to play in the misunderstanding of that budget. It continues to have a large part. And the *Toronto Star* as well, continues to have a large responsibility for how it's been misunderstood.

I think there was a great split between the public- and the private-sector unions, and essentially the Solidarity movement came to an end because of that split. The private-sector unions proved that they were just not willing to fight against the concept of layoffs in the public sector, and against the concept of wage controls in the public sector.

Kube: The so-called restraint budget was an attack on labor. There was tremendous anger generated when they brought in the budget and the accompanying legislation, because they felt completely betrayed.

Question: Why was there such a big public reaction to the budget, if the government was elected on that mandate? The voters were supposed to be for your government, and then there was just such a big public reaction, do you think that people saw what you were trying to do as being unfair?

Spector: The government was voted in with 50 percent of the popular vote—the opposition got 45 percent of the popular vote. Bill Bennett would lose 10 elections out of 10 with the percentage vote Pierre Trudeau generally got, or that Bill Davis gets. That's why I say here it's highly mobilized, highly politicized, and highly polarized. And therefore there were large numbers of people who voted against, and voted very strongly against the restraint policy that first was announced in February of 1982.

I think the *perception* of fairness is the key to the success of these programs. What is fair in a polarized society is sometimes difficult to reach a consensus on. I think it might be easier at the federal level, at the national level, to reach that kind of a perception, where politics tend to be more moderate, more civilized.

Question: What would you do differently?

Spector: I think in its heart of hearts the government feels there were probably a couple of elements there that need not have been done as they were, and elements where changes were made ultimately. For example, I think the use of the term "termination without cause" when what was really sought was layoffs, economic layoffs. The criteria that are in that act are identical to the criteria in the Ontario public service act, but the use of that term "without cause" was (a) unnecessary, and (b) unfortunate. And it was just poor legal advice the government took.

167

Kube: The whole thing happened so quickly, the anger was so strong, and we didn't have any blueprints on how to apply pressure on the government. We were after all, surprised; throughout the election campaign, both parties were hogging the centre so much, you didn't know which party was which. Barrett, for example, wanted to do away with the moderate restraint program then in place, and Bennett said he wanted to maintain it. The campaign didn't reflect at all what Bennett then did.

Question: What did the government learn?

Spector: Well, I shouldn't lead you astray on this. I think you should know that despite all the reaction, the support for the government was very strong. The support for Solidarity eventually eroded to about 15 percent and the support for the government actually increased.[13] That's something that people should understand about British Columbia too. I mean, British Columbia's got a lot of people for whom the issue of nuclear testing and nuclear-free zones and ecology are the most important issues. But there's also a lot of people here for whom taxes and bureaucracy and all kinds of other buzzwords are the issue as well.

Kube: I don't think that the government learned anything. I'm coming to the conclusion that the government is composed of people who are socially barbaric, economically incompetent, and in most instances utterly stupid.

Question: What do you think labor should have learned from this?

Spector: I think labor should have learned that parliament is sovereign. That governments are elected at the ballot box and not in the streets. And I think they have learned that there's a rather large gap between the public-sector unionist and the private-sector unionist, between the teacher and the logger.

Kube: We learned we need a wider array of responses, and that demonstrations only work if someone is listening. The Bennett government seemed to feel it was some kind of a contest instead of reacting by saying "we'd better stop and consult—try and work this out together."

Question: What is the environment now?

Spector: The current environment is still quite highly polarized. On the other hand it's always been a highly polarized society. The economy is in very poor shape, high degree of economic uncertainty—but I think a lot of the sharp edges of last fall have worn off.

I think that polarization was increased in intensity by the restraint program, but I think, properly charted, it was a temporary problem, a temporary phenomenon. In other words, B.C. has always been highly polarized

This advertisement paid for by funds saved by firing Rosalie Staplepicker, Class III provincial civil servant.

Peterson

and always will be. And on the question of the economic situation, my own view is that the failure to act would probably have produced more serious economic conditions than having acted.

Kube: The environment here is one of resignation and real anger; the support for the government continues to decline.

Question: Could the unpleasantness and the poor economic consequences have been avoided?

Spector: The real issue is, what are the alternatives and where can you point to an alternative strategy? It's clear in my experience that governments' willingness to do this sort of thing erodes as they get closer to the next election. And I think whatever the drawbacks, it's certain that the government achieved its objectives. They had the political will to stay the course, they had the political will to take a lot of heat, they had the political will to do two budgets in a year, and that phase is behind them. I think the polarization of this par-

169

THE NEXT CANADIAN ECONOMY

ticular society called British Columbia is such that that mistrust is there—it's an enduring situation—and on both sides.

Kube: The question everybody has to ask is, "Was the whole thing necessary?" If they had come out and said, "we find ourselves in some economic difficulty, and we have to, for instance, raise taxes," I think generally the population would have understood.

Art Kube and Norman Spector wound up frustrated over the deficit issue, Spector believing the province to be permanently "polarized," Kube believing the government was not acting in good faith, not "listening." The situation in Manitoba is very different; the key participants there believe the deficit is too important *not* to cooperate.

Here is a shortened version of the dialogue between the key adversaries in the Manitoba restraint efforts, Michael Decter, Clerk of the Executive Council, Province of Manitoba, and Gary Doer, the president of the Manitoba Government Employees Union. The first speaker is Gary Doer. Doer is a young, handsome and debonair fellow who, on appearances alone, could as easily fit into any one of the boardrooms of the nation's top hundred corporations as into his own modest offices on Portage Avenue in Winnipeg. Neither does Michael Decter fit the stereotype of a Cabinet secretary. His casual attitude and clothing belie both his sharpness of wit and the power he wields.

Doer: One of our first challenges, from a public-sector union leader's perspective, was to convince people that collective bargaining with an alleged labor government was not simply a matter of backing up a Brinks truck and telling them when to stop loading the money! In that situation, a labor leader's job changes from *increasing* expectations to *reducing* expectations.

With our parliamentary system of government, especially when we are confronting the difficult problem of restraint, the leader has to be the key, has to set the tone. The premier's style is crucial; it matters very much whether his approach is confrontational, or cooperative; manipulative, or open. I think Premier Pawley's style has been very, very open and cooperative. There's been no question about that. Not that we haven't had our disagreements, or that we won't continue to have them. But I respect his approach.

Decter: It's been a very difficult environment for dealing with the problem of restraint, because the pressures are very great on both sides: there is very great pressure on the government to manage a deficit, and to find and direct more resources to job creation, and very great pressure on the union not to be part of some general process of "give-backs."

170

Doer: We had some very frank and open discussions when we renegotiated the contract. Michael Decter sat in on some of the first meetings, before we got down to some very tough decisions on both sides in terms of what we were getting, and what we were giving up, and what we were prepared to sell to our membership.

Decter: And on our side, we had a lot of internal thinking to do. After all, the easiest group of unionized employees for a government to bash are the ones that are the least popular, and those happen to be, unfortunately, the public servants.

Fortunately we have ministers in the government who have an excellent sense of what the process of collective bargaining is about. They don't see it as something foreign. We have an interesting mix of cabinet ministers who come from the labor movement, including the finance minister, who was a fireman active in his union before he went back to take law, and a Treasury Board chairman who was a steel worker.

But that can also create difficulties as they tend to see the bargaining process as "adversarial" and to see themselves now in the role of management. Other ministers, who didn't have experience in labor relations, tend to see cooperation as very central, especially the premier.

Doer: I would agree, there are ministers that carry off the adversarial dimension very well, particularly those from the ranks of the trade union movement. The old saying is that the worst boss you can deal with is an ex-union leader. There is some truth to that.

Decter: I think it helped a great deal to have Dick Martin as head of the Federation of Labor. It helped to have someone quite innovative and forward-looking in that role. By contrast, if you don't, it sets a constraint. I won't point fingers, but if you had as head of the federation someone who sees everything in quite narrow bargaining terms, it makes it much more difficult for constituent leaders to move beyond simple "win-lose" confrontations.

Doer: Sometimes when you have a small, but important disagreement with the government that you must actually fight, it can get a little feisty and rhetorical. That's when we'll hear: "Where's Dick Martin?" The role of the fed leader is to keep the communication lines open. That's his job.

Decter: Last year, when Manitoba faced an escalating deficit and a shortage of jobs, it required labor leadership both within and without the public sector unions. After all, the members of Gary's union "gave back" $10 million in pay hikes, $600 per person.

171

Doer: Last year we voluntarily renegotiated our contract, with a net result that we put $10 million in the provincial jobs fund. We had seen the recession before the government had, in my opinion, and we were way too high in the second year of our collective agreement. To keep the settlement in the second year was immoral, and it was costly.

We said to the membership, "Yes, we got a great collective agreement, but we're going to have to look at this thing because you can't have your neighbors getting zero percent increases or being laid-off, while we get a 10 percent raise." So it was a voluntary decision. We renegotiated, and each member voted to give back $600 apiece, which took some work. But I think they felt that they could look the neighbors in the eye a little bit better, you know, having made that move.

I really believe that there is that kind of environment out there all across Canada, if people understand the trade-offs. I don't think it is just in Manitoba.

I think members in the public service want to have a say on public policy. They don't just want their employee organization to deal with agreements or whether they get ten cents an hour. They want to have a say, and we have proposed that our shop stewards be involved in the budget process as a way of getting information to the top that's often censored through the layers of government.

Decter: The impact of the voluntary reduction extended beyond just the government because the Pawley government was elected when certain bargaining patterns had already been set, and not by the direct provincial public service. And, the government faced an escalating deficit that moved alarmingly from 200 or 300 million to a forecast, at the worst point, of almost 600 million.

The government needed to do two things. First, we needed labor settlements that wouldn't worsen a structural deficit. We also needed to free up some money to reduce the number of unemployed below 50,000, an unprecedented figure in our lifetime. The innovative agreement with the public-sector union enabled us to achieve both goals; we were able to stretch out the funds we had and to put up some new money to create jobs. *That gave a positive signal to the whole Manitoba economy.*

I think it's very difficult to quantify how many other employers—and there were lots, both in the union sector and the non-union sector—that in one way or another tried something similar. They tried either to protect existing jobs, or to squeeze out some more money to create jobs. It was a never formalized process, just a signal of hope, just a good example.

172

Doer: On the job creation side, I think it's fair to say—well, by contrast with B.C., their unemployment figures went up. Our rate, and the actual numbers, have come down from the mid-50,000's to under 40,000 in a period of a year. A lot of psychology is involved in that, a lot of the feeling that Manitoba employers, with a little help from the government, had the confidence to pull together and hire people. The union-government efforts provided a demonstration that this kind of cooperative effort was viable. It wasn't just everybody hanging on to what they had and letting somebody else worry about what the net effects would be in terms of the overall system.

Decter: We now have the lowest unemployment rate in Canada. Not a bad number to have as part of an indicator of what has been accomplished. On the other side we still face the long-term mutual problem of a deficit.

Doer: In facing the deficit issue, there must be a longer-term agreement not only between our organization and the government, but also between the labor movement and the business community. The longer-term goal is employment security, as much as can be protected in a viable way versus compensation, standards of increase and improvements in the collective-bargaining process. And we look at it moving in tangible ways *with* the deficit. Rather than trying to knock half the deficit out in one year, we look at a four-or five-year cycle, and seek agreement that the deficit will move down in a way that's fair not only to groups in the public service, but to all other groups dependant upon government. That may mean agreeing to wage increases at the average industrial wage in the province or below for a period of time.

[Aside] I'm in a bad position here because I'm starting to bargain with a tape recorder going! [laughter] An informal agreement with the government, an explanation of a "social contract" that takes the long view, may not be to the liking of all my colleagues.

But we need to try together to establish some realistic projections of what revenues will be, where they will go, and where we can move that deficit balance, so we don't hit a wall. And I know with fairness, and an agreement on a longer-term plan, that we could get consensus within our own constituency. I feel that strongly with my own organization. As long as we don't get the feeling that somebody is not pulling their weight, I think there is a willingness in our membership to pull our weight on the mutual problem. I could see sitting down and working on a five-year plan.

Decter: I don't think management inside the provincial governments can get much leaner. We run a civil service that's much leaner than any other in the country. I think the starkest contrast is with the federal government. Now that the federal government is going into direct federal delivery, we often

173

have comparable operations. I can tell you when those exist side by side, the provincial ones, due in part to the efforts of Gary's membership, are certainly more efficient, as well as much smaller.

Doer: The bottom line is that our provincial public service is the leanest in western Canada per capita, both in cost and numbers. It's the second leanest in the country, and the only group that compares more favourably is Ontario, and they don't need many conservation officers on the 401.

Decter: I'm willing to venture a few speculative ideas. (I don't usually give interviews, so I'm not in any immediate danger of contradicting something I have on the public record.) The comparison between B.C. and Manitoba came home in an interesting discussion the other night when we had dinner with forty senior people from the largest Japanese securities and insurance firms in their respective fields. They'd been in Vancouver to look at investing there, but with the unsettled and distrustful labor-relations situation in B.C., they very candidly said they were dubious about investing in B.C. The Japanese investors see B.C. as having gone down the road of the conflict model; that suggested to them increasing instability. For them it was not a matter of the distribution of power, but rather that that whole question was not subject to anything resembling what I'd like to call conflict-resolution machinery. The old machinery was gone, and nothing had replaced it. There was no sense that anything *would* replace it other than appeals to the electorate, which in their minds would create continuing instability.

By contrast, Manitoba has had, historically, a very good labor-relations climate, and our recent experience of wrestling with the restraint issue has improved our faith in our capacity to tackle things, together. Those Japanese investors seemed to feel very comfortable with that approach.

Doer: The other contrast with Manitoba is that British Columbia has that absurd peak-and-valley situation, with 42 percent settlements a couple of years ago that came like a wave across Canada, especially in the health care field, and came like a wave back. Education people got 18 percent, absurd amounts of money, and now they're down to zero and minuses. While in Manitoba (we've done a study of the last ten years) it's been within 1.5 percent of the average industrial wage. The public-sector decisions are being made in the context of the greater marketplace, rather than just in isolation, with some university professor deciding what the value of the labor might be.

Decter: One of the real challenges I see is to work out some joint mechanisms for effective retraining. I think that the provincial civil service is likely to stay about the same size. Where we have the real difficulty is that priorities change, program needs change, therefore people's needs change. It used to

174

be, and maybe it was OK in a frontier economy, that you let the people go that you didn't need, and hired others with different skills. But I think we're now moving in a different direction. How, for example, do we plan for the people who have been freed up in one area, whether by technological change or structural change? For instance, there are fewer kids going to school, so we need fewer teachers. What are we going to do with all the teachers?

We are taking some halting steps. This is going to be a major challenge both for the government and the union, because it gets at the issue of how much planning, how much foresight you can have. Can you plan together, or do you have an annual kind of ritual where you do this dance about whether somebody's going to get laid off or not?

Doer: Well, if we can have an undertaker retrained to be Minister of Health, we can have almost anybody retrained to be anything. In the community colleges, for example, we have retrained hairdressers for data-processing instruction. We've had some good examples, but it is still a challenge, because we still have a lot of people saying: "I came on in this job because that's what I was hired to do and I'm going to be there forever and I want my union to protect me . . . ." Things like keeping park rangers in their saddles.

Decter: Eventually, we're going to have to move away from a rigid definition of jobs and we're going to have to redefine work. I think that's happening anyway, but we have a notion now that someone who goes to work for forty hours a week is employed and draws a paycheque. I think we're going to see a lot of pushing at the borders of that definition.

One direction is going to be, in fact it's already there, a great increase in part-time work. I think you're going to see some occupational push for things that might not have been mainstream occupations. For example, we signed last week a $23 million Cultural Enterprises agreement with the federal government. Culture, up until now, was seen as something that you subsidized. You didn't look to it as an engine of economic growth and activity. That will change as will other perceptions of which activities are "economic."

A similar issue is the make-work jobs or welfare vs. UIC issue—it may not be "economic" to leave these labels and links unexamined. Anticipating some changes here, we moved the employment services out of our labor department, and put it together with the income-securities side of community services, our welfare department. But that's just a start.

Question: When did you realize that the changes were long-term, structural, rather than short-lived?

Doer: The first time I walked around Lynn Lake, where houses were at one time worth around $75,000, and then you couldn't sell them for $6,000, and it hit me, when I was talking to a person who couldn't sell a house for $6,000, that this was just one part of a massive chain reaction. The Swifts plant going down and a number of other places. That was the summer of '81, I believe. It was the first time I'd gotten to walk around a lot of work places that I wouldn't normally get to. You could have looked at it in isolation as a one industry town, but I got the bloody feeling that it was much broader than that. I just got the feeling that it was world wide, and that it was totally different and that was reinforced in the next couple of weeks. And I haven't lost that feeling. I like to read about the signs of recovery, but I don't believe it.

Decter: I guess I realized how serious the changes were when I was in the estimates process. The first time I sat through the estimates process, I was a young civil servant in Ed Schreyer's government. After we'd got to the end of it—it was two weeks of debate over this and that—I guess you could say, all the reasonable demands, all the programs of the ministers had been met. There was still a hundred million dollars on the table, and there was then a big discussion as to whether to give that back, by way of tax cuts, or whether to put it into some form of investment or to do some major reprogramming. Keynesian theory would have said put it away for a rainy day. . . .

Ten years later I sat at the same table, not quite as young, and before the process even got started, before any of the reasonable demands were met, the cabinet was short $200 million! So the first decision was: do we raise taxes, or do we cut programs—we hadn't even talked about what they needed for the next year, we're simply talking about the same mix of programs as last year, at last year's dollar level. So no provision for reasonable increase in prices or wages. That to me said very much that something permanent had changed. In both cases there were five-year forward forecasts. In the case of a decade ago, the forecast was that "things were probably going to get somewhat worse." In the case of now, the forecast was the same, "that things are going to get somewhat worse." And to me that sums up a lot of difference in where we're at in the economy.

Doer: We're dealing with a permanent shift here, both a permanent change in the economy, from a structural point of view, and a permanent change in that share of the GNP that's readily accessible by governments through the tax system since the federal government brought in indexing. We're trying to deliver the same or more services with fewer resources.

Technology may offer one avenue, but technological change without a very cooperative labor relations situation is not going to lead in the right direction at all. So I guess I start from the premise that you need some creativity on both sides in terms of both the government and the union

176

saying "structural unemployment may be a permanent situation," and "We want to deal with it *within* the framework of labor relations."

Decter: Certainly there's been some hard bargaining here, I think both Manitoba ministers and Gary Doer would want to say that they felt that they bargained very hard in those situations where bargaining was what was called for. But I think what's been called for is some creative thinking and I would strongly agree with Gary's examples, that in the long term what's going to be the most interesting is the involvement of stewards and of non-management personnel in the resourcing decisions.

Doer: The idea is to get people at the line level, shop stewards, involved with the minister in terms of information, not in terms of decision-making, not pre-empting the Parliamentary or legislative process. And I think that will do two things. One is provide the minister with more data to make decisions; next is to keep the censored bureaucracy more honest. And third, it gives greater ownership to the people that are delivering the service to the public.

Decter: There is, at this level, an interesting anecdote about what one Ukrainian farmer believes to be the future shape of government revenues.

The Pope is coming to visit Bird's Hill Park in Manitoba. Right next to Bird's Hill Park, there is an old Ukrainian farmer who's in his nineties, who has stacked up on his mantlepiece every Canada pension-plan cheque they've ever sent him. He figures if he cashes them, someday, they'll want the money back. A very self-sufficient man who told me that he'd come to Bird's Hill Park just after World War I, had been there ever since then, never been to the city of Winnipeg—lives twenty miles from there, and never visits. I asked him how he likes living there? *He said it was a very nice place to live; there are no wars.*

Chapter 14

THE SOFT REVOLUTION

Institutions are more than just the buildings we live and work in; they are also the unwritten rules we live by. While we may not see the cracks or hear an audible rumble, the ground beneath them is shaking. Our proud pillars of permanence are caging us in, holding us back from a smooth transition to the next economy.

Forged by the iron of an industrial age, Canada's institutions both evolved from and reinforced the values of a materialistic age. It is not too surprising, therefore, that we are accustomed to visualizing institutions as "hardware" structures, as fixed three-dimensional "things," rooted firmly to the ground.

It is more difficult to see the "software" systems, customs and rules that make up our cultural institutions. Yet, these intangible, software institutions shape our present lives and our future choices. The tax system, the parliamentary system, the collective bargaining system, education, social welfare, the health care system, all grew up as part of the "rules of the game" for the industrial age. How we handle changes in these intangible institutions will be crucial in determining Canada's place internationally in the next economy.

The old rules of the game served us relatively well, evolving slowly and usually peacefully over more than a century. In an era of rapid growth, there was every confidence that virtually any problem could (would) eventually be solved. We could afford to be patient and trusting . . . after all, we all understood the rules of the game.

179

But the game is now rapidly changing—and the old rules we played by may be a poor guide for the new one. Tom Axworthy: "Our large institutions aren't very adaptive, and that's why I say that we'll likely try to muddle along. I don't think we have to, but we haven't gone through enough yet to face up to it. Our institutions, be they parliament, the party system or others, are pretty slow to adapt."

While some institutions are crumbling quietly in the rapid onslaught of the next economy, others resist any threat to their power or prominence, hard-won in the last economy. This stubbornness is often reinforced by fear that institutions will vanish leaving nothing to replace them; after all, they were created for a purpose.

> *If large collective-bargaining units dissolve, what will replace them to ensure fairness in the workplace?*
>
> *If our religions diversify, do we risk having Christian values "watered down"?*
>
> *What if the Third World loans are not repaid; will Canada's banking system absorb the shock?*
>
> *What if we cannot meet the pension plan premiums required to keep the system intact for the huge baby boom generation?*
>
> *What if tax rules become so out of step that entire communities stop supporting the system?*

The industrial age ushered in an era of highly-structured institutions. Virtually everything became associated with a formal institution, performed within the secure confines of the appropriate hallowed halls under the official auspices of the right specialist. Even birth and dying take place in sanctuaries; hospitals and funeral parlors, respectively presided over by medical experts and make-up artists.

Institutions of the industrial age are *place-, time- and manner-bound*, each one guarded by an established guild or priesthood. Everything has an exclusive place, a set time and a firm, sequenced series of rules and procedures. It is only recently, for example, that we even started planning homes with multi-purpose areas, family rooms, instead of parlors and bedrooms.

Education happens at school, healing at the hospital, lawyering at the courthouse, working at the office, negotiating at the bargaining table, legislating at the parliament buildings. . . .

Education is spooned out to children aged 5 to 18, between the rings of a bell at nine o'clock and at three o'clock, from September to June; medical care is rendered by appointment—only in an emergency at any time;

justice is administered when court is in session; work is done between nine and five by people from 18 to 65 years of age, Monday to Friday, except for bank holidays and a two-week shutdown in late July; negotiations take place according to the terms of the last contract; legislation is passed when the house is sitting—and the bells are *not* ringing. . . .

Each institution maintains its own select guild or priesthood that holds rank in the social order through exclusive access to a proprietary set of information. Teachers are listened to in classrooms since they provide the curriculum needed to pass final exams; doctors orders are followed because they hold a monopoly on medical information; lawyers are raised above contempt for their ability to comprehend legal documents; managers' directives are heeded because they read the latest sales report; campaign strategists are courted if they have the results of the latest public opinion poll. . . .

We play by the rules of the game established by the information holder, or we are simply "left out." But what happens if individuals gain direct access to the information that is now the exclusive custody of revered guilds and priesthoods? What happens to teachers and classrooms if videotaped lessons can be borrowed from the local library? Can we envision a generation reflecting nostalgically on an old computer-tutor instead of cherishing memories of ivy-covered walls? What happens to doctors and hospitals if computerized home diagnosis and treatment is made available? What happens to lawyers and courtrooms if computers are programmed to search legal precedents and predict case outcomes? What happens to business executives and boardrooms if pieces of a corporation are bought and sold five times in five minutes? What happens to parliamentarians and legislative assemblies if "instant referenda" are held?

These place-, time- and manner-bound restrictions that have so neatly shaped the contours of institutions in the industrial-age economy are being dissolved. Rather than patching up the cracks in the old institutions, let's look at some of the troubling questions about this transition period that are now beginning to emerge. The soft revolution in our institutions is not simply about what we *can* do, but about what we *choose* to do. For *families*, this soft revolution that has occurred in our homes over the last dozen years, for example, is very difficult to pin down. But we do know that women seeking a paycheque, jobless children in their 20s moving back in with their parents, marriages breaking down or being redefined, families mending, blending and extending, are all part of the transition.

In *business*, although Frank Tyaack outlines some exciting options, we don't know how to picture or respond to a sudden and silent transformation in the dominant means of production. We vacillate between fear of robots stealing our jobs and excitement about "putting the brains back in the shop." Some say we can do this for all jobs, others say that 80 percent of jobs will be de-skilled. One thing is sure: the questions from the tide of micro-electronic technologies are not just "technical," but generate a some-times frightening undertow of political, economic and social choices. No single invention since the steam engine will sweep over our lives as much as the integrated circuit and the thinking machines will.

Some telling clues to the secrets of the next economy are whispered in the new passwords that people who already dwell in the information age use in conversation: "to be interdependent," "to keyboard," "to network"—a vocabulary that would offend the sensitive ear of any English-grammar teacher, but a good indication of the values of the next economy.

This language signals the demise of a way of life that is harnessed to the formal, tightly structured, hierarchical, fixed requirements of industrial tasks: people with specialized duties, both at work and at home; employees concentrated around a central workplace; families oriented to a rigid division of time between the work world and their home life; an education system geared to producing able workers.

This language foreshadows a way of life that links up through informal, loosely-structured networks. There are new horizontal flows of information, new ways of structuring time. There will be people with a variety of income-earning skills; worker/owners running cottage industries at home; families operating like small businesses; educational systems doing more than just slotting people into career niches.

The pyramid, the vertical hierarchy, is no longer the shape for our institutions. In the next economy, authority, power and communication channels might look more like interlocking circles than tight boxes or straight lines. Authority, respect and loyalty will be collegial and earned rather than paternal or maternal and dutifully rendered. According to Jacques Vallée, author of *The Network Revolution*, "Computer conferencing is a first step toward the creation of such a medium: a revolutionary network where each node is equal in power to all the others."

The Structure of Work   The tightly-knotted concept of a "job," for example, the most basic bond of Canadians to the economy, is unravelling. It is very difficult now—especially after the last three years—for us as parents to justify telling our teenagers to "work hard and follow all the rules" when we (and particularly our children) know so many people who always did just that, but are currently without jobs.

"My biggest fear is what the people of the Big Generation, those born in the fifties and early sixties, are going to do with their lives," says John Kettle, editor of the *Futureletter*. Most of this generation will be forced to explore a wider range of options throughout their lives than did their parents and grandparents. Many will have to invent their work or create their own business, not just find a job.

Alternating between work and parenting and frequent career shifts are becoming commonplace, partly by choice, partly by necessity. The average family recognizes that this means a great deal more fluctuation in income as his and her paycheques vary over the years. But Canada has been slow to realize and respond to the chaos that these new patterns are creating in its institutions—for example, in the design of pension plans and the health care system.

In the words of Dr. Russell Robinson, assistant deputy minister, Consumer and Corporate Affairs: "Our social institutions, especially government, are slow to catch on. . . . Our basic security programs—pensions, social insurance—can't be a leading edge for these changes, because even if we knew how to construct them, they couldn't be the areas of first change; they represent our security blanket. But we must start soon to look at them because the processing time in changing them takes so long. You have to start now in order to look at the question, for example, of what a model for the social security system might be 15 years from now."

Canada, however, has yet to address openly, much less confront, the question of a permanent income support system that can be sustained for as long as it takes to "unbundle" jobs and redefine "work." Our present systems of unemployment insurance, welfare, and job retraining evolved as a *temporary* response to a *temporary* problem. They were designed to meet the basic income needs of a few people at the margins of an economy for only a short period of time. That was an acceptable model for the last economy, but it is ill-suited to a lengthy transition period of high, structural unemployment among the mainstream of the Canadian middle class.

The biggest obstacles we face now are invisible, leftover assumptions, expectations, institutional systems and social rules rather than visible landmarks of physical geography. The mountains to be conquered rise in the minds of national and provincial capitals and Toronto boardrooms, rather than in the Rockies. The elements to be battled have less to do with the laws of nature than with the laws of Canadian society. It is the restrictive institutional systems and social rules—man-made limits—that have to be loosened.

Take the institution of law, for example. Legal experts are discovering that trying to make property law from the industrial age fit the incorporeal information-age products—ideas, software, brilliant but easy to copy systems—is a formidable task. Not unlike economists who are trying to sort

183

out the value of information-age products, lawyers are trying to figure out who owns these invaluable "brain" products. Similar problems occur in bio-technology.

> **DATELINE LOS ANGELES.** A leukemia patient whose blood may have unique disease-fighting properties filed suit Tuesday for a stake in a potentially lucrative patent his doctors took out on a product developed from his cells. John Moore's lawyers say their client has a right to share in the billions of dollars that the substance, called the Mo-cell line, could generate in licensing fees.
>
> Although Moore knew and consented to the use of his blood for research, he was never told it might have commercial applications, says his lawyer.

Our laws evolved in the days when the respective value of land, labor and capital had a fairly stable relationship. Wealth was derived largely from tangibles, with value tied to physical things we could count, measure or hold in our hand. *Natural resources were the common source of wealth; money was the common currency.*

Wealth   Put simply, this notion of wealth means having stuff, having usually the exclusive possession of some "thing" of value. The value of the thing depends on its scarcity, not on its holder. Each thing has a fixed value in relation to other things of the same kind. For example, the value of one gold bar is the same as the value of another, no matter who owns them. If gold bars are hoarded, their value increases; but owning a second one doesn't alter the value of the first.

In the information age, these relationships are changing dramatically. Increasingly, much of our wealth will be in intangibles, in what Roy Cottier calls "brain industries." And much of the value and wealth created will be through sharing, not hoarding. *In the next economy, people are the source of wealth, and information is the currency.*

Wealth in the next economy is aligned in some mysterious way with sharing, not exclusive possession. The value of a data bit is less dependent on availability, but much more dependent on its holder. Each bit has a value that varies in relation to other bits. For example, the value of information on the stock market changes according to how many other bits of information you have.

As we saw in "the "Money Managers" chapter, many companies who appear to be selling stocks and bonds are in fact selling information. As

Brian Fabbri, asked about hoarding information in the competitive Wall Street atmosphere explains: "Educating our clients means more business for us. So, information about how we see markets develop is something that we disseminate rather than hold as proprietary."

Hoarding a bit of information, therefore, adds little to its value. In the next economy, information, with some exceptions, may be more valuable when it is shared. Data bits become information when there is a context to give them meaning. Information becomes knowledge when there is a receptive environment.

Knowledge—information plus context—then, is both a product and a capital good. This quantum jump in the importance of knowledge poses tough questions for the transition. For example, how do you transpose an industrial-age tax system to these patterns of wealth creation?

For the next economy, *relationships are becoming as valuable as possessions.* In a volatile world, there may be more stability, for example, in friendships than in where you work or what you do. Relationships become key elements of wealth creation in the information age. Who you know, what they know, and how to pursue it together are crucial skills.

Education   The people we talked with are worried about Canada's education system. Their concerns stem from an understanding of some elements critical to a successful knowledge-based economy: excellent data banks, open access to information, rich individual diversity of perspectives, and cumulative learning processes.

"How will we be able to change education?" asks Saskatchewan's finance minister, Bob Andrew. "How do we shake it loose? The education institutions, which we were taught were the leading edge of new ideas, are static today, are perhaps the most conservative. The university system is awful. It's an area that used to be the leading edge of change. Now, it is the leading edge of holding things back."

Roy Cottier, senior vice-president of Northern Telecom, says bluntly: "When we recognize that brains are the passport to a post-industrial future, and not just resource activity, then we'll start to solve our problems. How will we bring that about? That is a hell of a good question. Most people are still unaware of the transition that is taking place in the total economy. . . . What we have to get understood is that we have to make drastic changes in the education structure. Another problem with education is that it is a provincial responsibility. That was fine in 1867, but this is 1984."

"If our comparative advantage is intellectual capital," warns Westinghouse CEO Frank Tyaack, "then the thing that we should be investing in like fury is education. And my perception of the education system is that it is shrinking in terms of its support and its facilities. If I had to pick *the* priority area for government policy to enter, I'd pick that one first. I'll forego the tax incentives, the grants, the export aid and so on; if they would shovel all the billions into education, I'd be happier."

Frank Tyaack's advice for becoming an educated, adaptable, high "intellectual-capital" person: "Learn to be generalists." Trevor Eyton, Brascan's CEO, worries about the narrow perspectives that executives bring to strategic planning: "A lot of our senior management comes out of the same kind of environment; they've gone to Upper Canada College and they've learned to think in pretty straight paths. Well, the world has changed a lot and we can adapt to it, and we can perform, but we've got to have different ways of teaching and learning. I don't think I'm all that much smarter, but I found it an advantage not to go to Upper Canada—where I went it was down and dirty and you really learned to think in a lot of different directions."

Banker Scott McCreath takes his children to factories and farms "so they will know something about how we make things, grow things; I want them to be curious about how it all works." Money manager Milton Wong feels that a "spirit of curiosity is the most important attitude" for the next economy, and stresses that it should be coupled with a determination "to go find out."

The cost of restructuring education will be high. Northern Tel's Roy Cottier points out: " We can still afford it, if we decide we want it. But if we decide we don't, we sure as heck will not be able to afford it later because we won't be in business. . . . One of the things that has to be done is we, as a society, have to take a look at our gross national cash flow and say, 'OK, are we going to continue to spend X amount on social services, X amount on defence, X amount on education?' And we're going to find that we're going to have to make changes, because the needs of the last decade are not the needs of the next decade."

Bob Andrew summed up well the delicate issue of capital use in this sensitive transition period: "Every country has a finite amount of capital, some more than others, but each with a finite amount. The success of a country to a large degree depends upon how that country employs its capital: human capital, investment capital, renewable and non-renewable resource capital . . . and how they are able to adapt the application of that capital to the changing world in which they live and function.

"Our country tends to be slower to adapt to change because of our poor use of capital. Too much of our capital is employed in protected, uncompetitive industries that clearly will not survive internationally. They are propped up to survive almost one day at a time. We resist either facing up to the fact that we should wind them down, and redirect both the investment and human capital into something that can grow, whether it is an entirely new industry or a refit of the present one.

"We must approach that problem both from the economic side and from the human side. And it will not be without some pain, but nevertheless we must address the problem.

"Our tax system hardly encourages adaptation; rather it tends to preserve the status quo, to lock in the old industrial-age values, or what is even worse, tries to redirect it to fashionable ideas of the politicians . . . perhaps we should go back to using revenue gathering for that purpose alone, rather than trying to 'manage' the economy with it. Our tax system is important because we have become a country where taxes (or avoiding taxes) too often is the main rationale for making decisions on how capital will be employed. Even governments seem to be getting into the game . . . if that isn't taking it to absurd lengths."

The security of an established "known" is always tempting to cling to—until it no longer comforts with a firm, steady hand, or it chafes too much like a tiresome parent, or it simply blows away. But, too many of our institutions that serve as homes (and provide livelihoods) are resisting the process of change, and hamstringing the transition to the next economy. "Muddling through," as Tom Axworthy warned, is in the long run likely to be more painful than trying to form a picture, together, of what comes next, and how our institutions should help. We run the risk, however, of violating the first law of wing walking. . . .

Chapter 15

THE FIRST LAW OF WING WALKING

Dressed in a brown leather bomber jacket, a long white scarf billowing out behind him in the full force of the wind rushing past, he grins at us, waiting far below on the ground. We all wave. He moves one arm in a curving gesture. Bravado.

One foot begins to slide forward, just as the pilot starts a wide lazy circle. His knee moves up and out a bit, jarred by the blast of air currents, then down and forward, edging over towards the next strut. Both hands stiffen while the lower body shifts weight, leaning into the wind, arching to the right.

He stands on the wing of the bi-plane, arms in a pair of fixed right angles locked onto the struts. Blinded by the wind, one arm extended, groping ahead, pressing in the direction of where the second strut should be. He thrusts his arm forward once more against the powerful current and catches it. Arms wide, buffeted, he slides more of his body weight over; tension grows in his left arm. Arms outstretched, he is pulled by his own weight off centre again and again, until he lets go and draws himself—smiling once more, remembering to look towards us—to the second strut. On the ground there is an audible wave, a sigh rippling through us as the plane completes another lazy circle.

"Never let go of what you've got, until you've got hold of something else" cautions the first law of wing walking. Preparing for the future is like wing walking. No one can be blamed for refusing to yield the relative security of a good firm grip on what they knew.

We cling to the old-but-familiar structural elements even when we feel them dissolving in our hands, or holding us back. Among the people

189

we interviewed, there was a remarkable degree of consensus that the institutions that served us well in the past, now don't; that the experts who served us well, now don't; and that the politics of the industrial age may not fit the needs of the next Canadian economy.

New ones have to be invented at the same time that we find a way to let the old ones go, lest they impede us. Attitudes and values appropriate to the last economy affect the strategies and tactics required for managing our personal, corporate and national security. They have to be revised to fit the demands of the next economy. Those courageous and probing people we met stressed a number of recommendations about some key things that are holding us back, moving us forward.

The first view they share: *We are not likely to get anywhere if we don't ask the right questions.* That means having the courage to put the necessary questions—no matter how uncomfortable—on the table. It means having the courage to face a "gloomy" economic forecast, or a tough set of anxious feelings about technology choices. These forecasts or trends in the culture are nothing more than starting points; a place to begin to confront what effect they might have on our personal and mutual choices.

Unfortunately, one of the hold-over groups from the last economy, the "mood managers," are accustomed to framing issues in such a way that it makes it virtually impossible to ask the right questions. Those who do, risk being called critical, impolite, or gloomy about the future—at the furthest extreme, a "danger to the unfolding economy," if you want to believe, as we are repeatedly told, that "our worst economic enemy is pessimism."

Let's take the brutal and painful question of who gets a job and who gets a welfare cheque during the transition to the next Canadian economy. The tacit assumption in our culture is that the guys who have jobs are "good citizens," and those who do not are "lazy bums." This social and economic roulette carves deep scars on those who land on the wrong number. Yet, part of the pain is tied to our being too polite (or too frightened) to ask the more fundamental question about how we are going to distribute income in this country.

There are many of these kinds of questions—that have to be asked openly and discussed openly, rather than closeted or tucked away on the hidden agendas of closed-to-the-public meetings of finance ministers or secret sessions in the Privy Council Office.

Other questions of high national priority that are also very politically sensitive, but need to be openly addressed, include, for example, the problem of developing excellent research on the new technologies. Achieving

190

this at a level that will enable Canada to keep pace in the game of world-class competition implies a concentration of resources at a particular university, or within a few companies. This need to focus resources conflicts sharply with our habit of trying to distribute all the new factories, government labs, or grants as evenly as possible. If we try to use the same formula, and spread knowledge capital too thinly, we may fail to concentrate and develop our key to wealth in the next economy, our human resources.

Many more questions are directed at the security issues; trying to agree on a list of the things we want to cling to from the last economy is one of the biggest challenges facing the present government. What was "waste" or a "frill" in the last economy may well be an essential in the next. For example, educational funds that have been quietly cut back in the last several years by provincial governments will not only have to be restored, but augmented. Knowledge capital is certainly one ticket to our security in the next economy.

The next shared conclusion, although there is no agreement on how to go about it, is that *our institutions need to become more flexible.*

In addition to questioning attitudes that hinder a wide-ranging search for the future, we must now focus on the economic, political and cultural institutions which have become so rigid that they limit our range of choices in managing a transition to the next Canadian economy.

Some of these institutions are easy to spot—schools that do not teach computer literacy, for example. Others are virtually invisible; they are simply established practice—automatically depositing money in a bank, for instance. We rarely ask: "What happens to this money?" Is it invested in new, job-creating small businesses, or does it go offshore, to finance a Brazilian loan?

These multi-level trade-off questions about our institutions are barely being acknowledged, much less spelled out. In the last chapter some of the symptoms of this soft revolution are described. The transition to the next economy is pressuring individuals to constantly re-examine their choices. So much of what we used to take for granted is now up in the air: not just when, but whether to have children, or, which second-career training to pursue, just in case the first set of job plans breaks down.

The challenge implicit in the second conclusion is that we have to identify the rigid and inappropriate institutions that are blocking us, and then transform or abandon them. For example, a tax system that is tied to the last economy will hamper a transition. The carrots and sticks tucked into our process of collecting revenue, designed to shape behavior towards certain industrial-age objectives, are not going to work as well in the next economy. We'll have a different set of needs and goals. Recognition of this set

191

of blocks is one of the things that is fostering the grass roots resistance to the "overly complex" (or put less delicately, "manipulative") nature of the present tax structure.

A third perspective that emerged clearly from our coast-to-coast discussions is that *while we are negotiating the rapids of the transition, we should not constantly change the rules of the game.* Points out Don Johnston: "If entrepreneurs are the catalysts of economic growth in our future, nothing stimulates capital investment as much as a supportive fiscal regime that features a tax system which is stable, predictable and fairly administered." The basic terms of reference need to be clarified, not constantly or capriciously altered to suit a short-term situation.

Much of the push for deregulation is born in the natural reluctance to hear the latest change in an already cumbersome, rigid and often out-dated set of rules. Both the pressure to simplify the tax system and the urge to reduce the paperwork reflect a collective sense that it is time to simplify the rules of the game. With fewer and simpler rules, there may be, so the argument goes, more room for people to experiment and adapt to the transition to the next economy. It's tough enough living with a tangled set of guidelines when things are stable. When the basic premises of the economy are being shaken, the web of our regulatory structure can strangle us.

These pressures are not just a simple-minded "step to the right" or a "swing to conservatism" in the traditional sense. These cumulative pressures for deregulation and tax simplification also represent a feeling that people are less inclined to merrily follow the piper, or accept being told what they can do or can't do, when they sense that the system as a whole is increasingly out of sync with the emerging economy. "Get off my back" is a loud and legitimate cry during an era when people are trying to gain a little more manoeuvering room for their own personal security.

The heavy emphasis on personal security accounts for the wide concern about the strength of the safety net. A corollary to the third conclusion becomes: *Don't mess around much with the safety net.* Shaking the moorings of the safety net implies changing the rules of the game at a time when people cannot tolerate any more uncertainty. The healthcare system and pensions, for example, become even stronger symbols of long-term stability than in a more predictable era. They become those struts we don't want to let go of. A strong safety net helps a transition, reduces fear, and allows us to experiment and become more adaptable.

The fourth conclusion is that *we need ways to decide, that fit the size, scope and duration of the problems we face; these being strategic decisions, we need to include a wide range of perspectives.* This is a particularly acute need when the

192

traditional balance points within the system—the old left and right perspectives—are so clearly outdated by the emerging realities of the next economy. There is little room for ideology, blame, or nostalgia for the good old days in the transition to the next economy.

Ritual political contests between "socialists," "conservatives" and "liberals" not only lose meaning in this context, but get in the way. This is underscored by the size of the Conservative "win" in the last federal election, which swept candidates of every political orientation into office at the same time and created a participant pool that is so huge it is virtually unwieldy. A clear-cut win which could have been argued as an endorsement of a particular set of conservative principles would have been, for example, a thirty-seat gain. But a victory of 211 seats means the government has to speak for all of the people, not just count on an opposition voice to represent a dissenting, or coherent point of view. One result of the last federal election is that the task of government has grown larger, and at the same time, of necessity more respectful of the diverse participants in the winning coalition.

The Mulroney government's early choice to emphasize process and consultation was a fitting one for the times. "Canadians expect our new government to be open and honest, and to introduce new concepts of consultation and cooperation" the prime minister emphasized repeatedly in the period just before and just following the election. His advisors in cabinet and on the policy side, such as Michael Wilson and Charles MacMillan, carried the day in the early stages of the Mulroney government. They emphasized the need to get broad participation rather than handing things off to the backroom boys. The former PC government of Joe Clark also drew its highest marks for pursuing a course of openness.

A major change in institutional direction that is in harmony with the pull of the next economy implies a need for strategic, not just operational planning. Shorter-term *operational planning*, with well-defined goals, can be carried out by a group of managers with relatively uniform values and even a narrow perspective. But *strategic planning* demands a wider array of values, more voices at the table, more room for dissent, and greater diversity of opinion. As Milton Wong points out, in making strategic decisions about a billion dollars of investment funds, there is a strong need for "open, constructive conflict of perspectives in order to get to a creative strategic recommendation."

The final conclusion, and the one that is hardest to see through the spectacles of our old institutions, and the one that we explore in this chapter is: *Canadians need to develop for themselves effective strategies for facing the transition to the next economy.* We have begun the painful process of backing away from our old reliance on government to "solve" everything for us. There is always anger associated with breaking free of a dependency, and the last federal election result reflected some of those feelings. But the research evidence has been steadily mounting—Canadians are begining to do it themselves.

Effective Strategies In this context, let's look at some winning strategies for the next economy. Those we interviewed certainly presented some good ideas, but let's start by stepping back and looking at how we got our ideas about what would be a winning strategy for the last economy.

Political and personal strategies are built on sets of assumptions about the nature of conflict, as well as the nature of success. These ideas come almost from the primordial ooze, as we base many of our pictures of the future on what we believe to be the truth about our past. Similarly, our values about decision and conflict are often based on our beliefs about the evolution of human nature or who *won* a place on the great chain of being. Our ideas about winning strategies and the nature of conflict are intimately intertwined with our sense of the history of the species and the descent of man.

Was it *always* a fight to win an ecological niche, or does cooperation play a part in our view of evolution? Does the notion of "survival of the fittest" underly our view of how the strongest and best won the right to reproduce? Does the idea of "survival of the fittest" form the basis for our belief as to why capitalism works? Are we sometimes using "competition" as a quick shorthand for saying "After all, Darwin was right—survival strategies are always a question of the fittest, the fastest, and the most fiercely competitive?"

Does a vague belief in social darwinism inform our perspective on why some families always seem to wind up on welfare, while others prosper? Have we learned, either consciously or unconsciously, that competition and struggle are implied in any winning strategy? Do we believe that "toughest," most "aggressive," of necessity mean the "best" or minimally "the winner?" How does that make us feel about our potential for success in, for example, highly-competitive international markets if we are simultaneously so proud as Canadians of our traditions of being "nice," "polite," and "cooperative?"

A brief look at some of the contemporary research and thinking on the subject of conflict resolution and winning suggests these issues are intimately tied together. Yet, the last thirty years has given us a suprising volume of new information on the evolution of the species, and on conflict versus cooperation. Perhaps we can make use of that new information.

In the field of anthropology, for example, views have run the gamut from Ardrey's turf and power-oriented "mighty hunter" theories to Elaine Morgan's perspective that "what saved the species was a group [of women] who cooperated in fighting against the savage drought by running into the ocean . . . for a few thousand years." You can look up the rest of the theory in her provocative and humorous answer to Darwin, called *Descent of Woman*.

Both of these authors have presented their arguments in popular forms. Both have wide followings who look to the story of evolution to prove their views about the nature of man (or woman), and more importantly, to reinforce their belief that their values are the "right" ones.

Both are using shards of evidence based on a mixture of fossil findings, judgments about how those fossils correlate with other things going on at the same time, and, of course, their respective personal value systems. But one of the advantages of pursuing research questions at this point in the twentieth century is that we are now allowed to probe past the statement that the authors used an "objective scientific method." The part played by an investigator's value system in his conclusions is now a matter for more open examination.

Another advantage in living at this time of the twentieth century is that we have developed some additional research techniques to supplement the intellectual digs of the anthropologists. We aren't just dependent on watching them battle it out in print. And we aren't just forced to resign ourselves to saying, "Well, one informed opinion against another—who is to know?" No, in addition to supplementing what they tell us with our own personal experience and observation, we now have some additional options. One of the most effective learning and research tools is the use of *simulations*.

Simulations create situations in miniature for testing or exploring the whole bunch of "what if" questions with as much fun and as little risk as possible. Simulations are also extremely effective in teaching environments, when it is important for the participants to understand and integrate a number of complex factors all at once. A short word for "simulations" is "games."

A game takes some basic rules, agreed upon goals, and then, if it is a good game, provides an opportunity for the full force of personality to work itself out, within a rational framework. The games and simulations played in the last thirty years which have the most to offer in an examination of conflict and decision making fall into three clusters: *management games, war games, and peace games.*

Management games and simulations have been principally developed and financed by business as the quickest and most efficient way to get complex ideas integrated into the system. Because executive time is expensive, businessmen must learn quickly. Business schools, too, consider simulations to be one of their most effective teaching tools. They use a lot of these teaching games, ranging from case studies to computer-simulated portfolio management programs.

War games have largely been financed through the various defence establishments around the world and were, at first, usually played in secret at think tanks, or on military bases. Vast sums of money have been dedicated to this branch of game theory. Much of the early work on war games was classified and secret, but quite a bit has found its way into the open literature of political science.

The two we are going to concentrate on are *war games* and *peace games*.

Let's start with *peace games* because they are the least familiar. The idea and the name "Peace Game" originated with the Quakers when they were trying to resolve a post-war problem with their neighbors. In particular, they needed to reconcile their beliefs of conscience with the strong social disapproval they received when they refused to go to war. This "act of conscience" and their religious beliefs, especially their value of "non-violence" were in conflict with the values of many of their neighbors. So the Quakers started holding Peace Games to simulate some of the situations that had been faced in earlier wars and in the aftermath of those wars, as neighbors tried to reconcile their wartime views, actions, and values with one another, so they could be friends again.

The Peace Game is an event designed for a fairly large community, involving from fifty to a few hundred people. The community is divided up into "attackers" and "defenders" who are assigned logical roles. The Peace Game script is written setting the stage, and then all the participants who are assigned roles have to stay in character until the game is over, even while eating or performing other ordinary chores. If they break character, they are asked to leave the game. Usually those assigned to be the attackers or invaders "believe" in force and violence, and in competition as the only way to resolve conflict. The defenders, by contrast, "believe" in non-violence.

Quite a lot of "what if" questions can be explored when a community of that size acts out the issues over an extended period of time. Some peace games have been played for up to two weeks. People become deeply involved in their roles, exploring not only their intellectual beliefs about winning strategies, but they also test their feelings in a very intense environment. The object of the Peace Game is to develop a wider array of ways to "win" in a life-like situation.

196

Perhaps the most fundamental question in its simplest terms that these real life simulations try to address is: "What is the best strategy, cooperation or conflict?"

By contrast, the study of War Games began with a narrower question than Peace Games. The War Games question was: "How do you win?" Interestingly enough, War Games have evolved to ask the broader strategic questions of "How do you avoid conflict?" or, at the diplomatic level, "How do you win the maximum number of negotiations in the theatre of world opinion?"

The recent popular movie "War Games," ended with the war-room computer being instructed to play an almost endless progression of tic-tac-toe games in a process designed to teach it about the futility of world conflict.[14] The computer concludes: "Global Thermonuclear war. A curious game: the only winning move is not to play."

Early war games were much simpler, starting off with maps and models of planes and tanks, assessing the arithmetic of two opposing forces. The choice of ground, timing, and the volume of the forces arrayed against one another were the central elements. The classic battle scenes were transformed by the high-speed computer simulations into more abstract mathematical modelling exercises. What would be our gains, what would be our potential losses, under the following conditions—were the standard questions.

In the earliest stages, they were viewed as straight power conflicts, mostly a matter of sheer weight of armaments determining the outcome. But as hundreds of millions of dollars were poured into these military "what if" exercises, they became far more sophisticated and complex. A much wider range of factors were explored than just the physical weight of weapons. Theories of personality were applied, perspectives on leadership, the political will of the combatants was assessed, and questions of the strategic worth of different cultural values were incorporated into the game.

Sophisticated war games, not unlike their cousins, econometric models, became much more difficult to quantify. The softer-sided issues of personality, politics and cultural values, and especially political will, became more critical concerns as the models matured. New fields of inquiry were developed to fuel the models, such as content-analysis techniques which can assess the evolving political will in a country, even if those being studied don't wish to cooperate.

Information about the War Games procedures and research findings began to be available outside the military think tanks as academics from many different disciplines were called upon to consult on the games. A wider variety of players took a look at the technologies and theories of the games and began to apply them to civilian life and to decision-making in the political arena. The games came out from behind closed doors and some of the software has even turned up at the local video arcade. Open, widely-publicized tournaments are now held.

New Games   Recently, a political scientist and games theorist, Robert Axelrod, held two rounds of an international tournament posing this question: "In the absence of a higher authority, when should a person (business, province, country) cooperate, and when should a person try to gain maximum personal advantage?"

Axelrod used a fairly simple game to try to identify a *strategy that would win over the long haul.* The game that he employed makes a number of important assumptions. First, it assumes that, like "real life," the players are likely to see each other again, and no one knows when one might move to another city, change jobs, or die. So, when one round is over, it doesn't mean the game is over. The next assumption is that you will always know what the other person did last, but not what he is likely to do next. Again, quite like real life. We know a lot about history, but very little about the future. Even if someone tells you what they are going to do, you don't really believe it until you see it.

Axelrod picked a well-tested game called "The Prisoner's Dilemma" to try to discover the best, most "robust" strategy, the one that would be most likely to win consistently. The game itself is quite straightforward. Two "prisoners" have been arrested and are being questioned separately. Their guards try to get each one to "defect," to agree to testify against the other one in hopes of a lighter sentence for himself. Each "prisoner" has to choose to either continue to hope that his accomplice "cooperates," and also keeps quiet, or he must decide if there is going to be a "defection." If so, it is to his advantage to defect first.

In the computer model, points are assigned for each choice, and the points are known in advance by both players. You get a good solid score if you both cooperate. You get a lousy score if you cooperate and the other guy chooses to defect (this is called the "sucker's payoff"). You get a higher score (at least for the one move) if you choose to defect while the other guy chooses to cooperate. But the worst score is if both choose to defect at the same time.

The reason it is called the prisoner's "dilemma" is that if both defect, both do far worse over the course of the game than if they had both cooperated. Just reading a description of the game and the points system doesn't seem all that hopeful for a strategy of cooperation. Axelrod invited competitors from all over the world, both experts and kids who are hackers (computer wizards). Some of the entries were very complex; some were sneaky; some used subterfuge and psychology. (You can read about the interesting ones in Axelrod's book.)[15]

Yet, despite the tough competition and more than three decades of game theory, and the arrival of bigger, better and cheaper computers and more complex software for simulations, a relatively simple strategy called *tit for tat* won the international tournament.

Tit for tat has only four rules:

1. Start off *nice*. Never be the first to "defect."

2. *Retaliate*. If the other player starts by defecting, return his move, "tit for tat."

3. Always be *forgiving*. If the other player cooperates, makes a nice move, then forget the past; return to making nice moves.

4. Be very *clear* and *open* about your strategy. Let the other players around you know that these are your rules; communicate clearly. Above all, keep it simple.

After the tournament, Axelrod published the results and explained why *tit for tat* was such a robust strategy. Then he held a second, larger, round. Most people tried to improve on *tit for tat*, making it trickier, slightly less forgiving, for example. Most of those people ignored the fourth rule, "Keep it clear and simple."

But the person who had submitted *tit for tat* in the first round, Anatol Rappaport, a professor at the University of Toronto, remembered the rule and simply resubmitted the same entry. He won again. Decisively.

It seems ironic that even the cold mathematical rules of computer-simulation game theory drawn from the chest of war games, rather than peace games, suggest some kind of cooperative strategy works best over the long haul. The findings show that a "nice" and "cooperative" strategy, but one that is ready to retaliate if the other guy is playing by different rules, works best when the future is uncertain.

Those who think and write about theories of conflict resolution have argued a long time whether a positive, cooperative value system would have the stamina to endure, without a higher authority provided by a creed, a belief in God, a formal value system or just a solid authority figure. Even those who teach the tactics of non-violence, drawing on the teachings of Gandhi and the experience of Martin Luther King, sometimes wind up expressing doubts about human "nature." They wonder whether the precepts of non-violence and cooperative resolution of conflict will hold up without the presence of a great spiritual leader.

What is particularly interesting and useful about some of the game theory results (such as the Prisoner's Dilemma tournament) that are tested to see how they work without higher authority, is that cooperative strategies often work whether or not people even know or like each other. What does seem to matter is that they have to notice that they inhabit the same small planet, and may see each other again, for another "round," on another day.

This is where we stand in our dilemma; no matter whether one politician wins or loses, or whether one side wins or loses a round, a sufficient framework must remain so that we can continue to play another round.

For, to take an issue of growing proportions, it doesn't matter whether Ottawa wins or loses against the provinces on a question such as who should pay the bill for the *UIC-welfare shuttlebus*. We do all live in the same country and are likely to see that unemployed person again. No matter whose budget he is lodged in right now, unless there is some fundamental adjustment in his situation, we will all be paying the cost of structural unemployment for a long time. Games theory tells us there is no free lunch; and it is becoming harder and harder to declare some factor, or some person to be unimportant in the equation. Evolving research in this area, whether it is for war games, peace games, or predicting the shape of the next economy, tells us we have to be more inclusive in our respect for the things that count.

These sophisticated simulations also tell us that each decision counts, and that each of us can affect the outcome. Simple-minded win-lose strategies based on mutal distrust appear to win only if it is game-over in one move. As soon as there is any likelihood that we are going to keep playing together, then the cooperative strategies begin to look like the long-term winners.

The challenges that we face in the transition to the next economy are not likely to be resolved in a few years, or by a limited number of players. Ironically, the more you add complexity to the trade-offs, the more likely it is that cooperative strategies are the most effective approach.

That is the situation we face in the transition to the next Canadian economy.

One hint on how to face it comes from the Dutch cultural historian, Johan Huizinga, who argued that the most civilizing pastime man has is play; that games and explorations over the long history of the race have given rise to new ideas and vision . . . and progress.[16] Why call us "homo-sapiens," man-the-knower, he asked, when our character of "homo-ludens," man-the-player, has been so very important to the evolution of the race? Why not indeed?

It is in this spirit that we invite you not only to explore the existing options for the transition to the next economy, but to "play" with developing a much wider array of new political and personal choices. Your suggested solutions to our present quandary may well go beyond *war*, *reflation*, or *mate-like-rabbits*. Let us know what you come up with.

NOTES

1. Spider Robinson, *Melancholy Elephants*, Penguin Books Canada Ltd., Markham, Ontario, 1984.

2. With the permission of the publisher and the encouragement of the *Canadian Trend Report* research network members, *Canadian Trend Report* research findings have been made available to the authors. Unless otherwise noted, research referred to in this book is from the *Canadian Trend Report. CTR* was established in Montreal in 1977 by a cooperative group of business and government sponsors. *CTR* provides social, political and economic forecasting for its members on a proprietary basis. Members include provincial governments, federal departments, Canada's leading financial institutions, Crown corporations, and privately-held corporations. The principal research methodology is content analysis, which is conducted through Canada's major print media sources. In contrast to survey research or polling (which collects attitude and opinion data), content analysis provides an accurate assessment of public *behaviour. CTR* documents trends on the basis of what people are *doing*, not what they are *saying*.

3. Some time ago, Ned Riley called our attention to a series of articles in the *Co-evolution Quarterly* that are now published as *The Next Economy*, by Paul Hawken, Holt, Rinehart & Winston, New York, NY, 1983. In addition to his seminal ideas, Paul Hawken has contributed to the debate by giving us an elegant and clear expression for the transition that we face. He calls it simply, the "next" economy, rather than getting tangled in expressions such as "post-industrial economy," "the information age," or "the horizontal age." Author/businessman Hawken also provides a model for the new-age entrepreneur.

4. Robert L. Heilbroner, *An Inquiry Into The Human Prospect*, Norton, Guilford, CT, 1980.

5. Former banker turned author and small-business expert, Michael Phillips, has written two very useful books on how to get started in small business. The books are the *Seven Laws of Money* and *Honest Business;* both are in print and available through Random House. Michael Phillips developed the Briarpatch network of small business organizations that combines an emphasis on commercially, economically sustainable activity and on performing a service or selling a product that is "worth while." Members of the Briarpatch provide generous support for

one another, particularly during critical business start-ups. Briarpatch organizations have been cloned in Sweden and Japan.

6. Edgar Z. Friedenberg, *Deference to Authority: The Case of Canada*, M.E. Sharpe, White Plains, NY, 1980. This book is distributed in the U.S. by Random House.

7. One of the best of the breed is *The C Zone, Peak Performance Under Pressure: A New Approach and a Practical Program*, by Robert and Marilyn Kriegel, Anchor Press, New York, 1984.

8. Jacques Vallée, *The Network Revolution*, And/Or Press, Berkeley, CA, 1982. Those who have a serious interest in exploring the excitement and risks inherent in computer networking will find the witty and insightful first-hand reports of Vallée an excellent place to start.

9. Ibid.

10. Since the idea for the Canadian Software Bank began to circulate, it captured the fancy of those who enjoy creating nicknames and acronyms. Some of the best include: CATCAN (Canadians Access Technology, or in French, TACCAN (Techno-access Canadien); DATACAN; CANABYTE; MEGABYTE CANADA; BYTE CANADA; CANANERDS (National Electronic Retrieval and Distribution System); and last but not least, TWIT (The World In Touch).

11. Matthew Lesko, *The Computer Data and Database Source Book*, Avon Books, New York, NY, 1984.

12. *Canadian Trend Report* research findings point to a steady erosion of industrial-age "left" and "right" models. *CTR* election forecasts for 1984, for example, correctly anticipated a "new" conservative victory that combines traditional "left" support for the safety net with traditional "right" expression of the need to control government expenditures. (See *CTR* documents on the evolution of the new conservatism, 1978-1984.)

13. Decima quarterly report of provincial assessment trends, Summer 1984, Vol. 5, No. 2, *Assessment of Governments:* "There has been a marginal decline in the number of British Columbia residents expressing satisfaction with their provincial government's performance since March (45 to 41 percent). Although barely significant, this decline signals an end to a six-month trend towards improving assessments of the government's performance.
"In addition, the B.C. government is currently receiving the second lowest overall performance rating in the country (after Québec). In contrast, the governments of Alberta and Manitoba have enjoyed substantial improvements in their performance rating since March."

Goldfarb Report August 84—Summer Update
Provincial Governments' Performance Ratings

British Columbia
Is the kind of job the government is doing rated:

	Excellent	Good	Fair	Poor
1983	3	14	55	27
Jan 84	3	23	36	39
Jul 84	1	17	38	44

"There is upward momentum since 1983 on 'poor.' "

14. "In November, 1979, in an 'incident' that passed generally unnoticed in American newspapers, the entire North American continent was in a state of nuclear war for seven minutes because of what seems to have been an operator error. Whether the computer detected the wrong set of patterns, or was fed an emergency training tape, the result was the same: It appeared that a massive enemy attack was being directed at the United States. Going through regular procedures, officers at NORAD—the North American Radar system located under Cheyenne Mountain in Colorado—gave takeoff orders to fighter-bombers from Montana to Canada to meet the unexpected onslaught, while the entire military system of the United States and Canada was placed on alert status. The Strategic Air Command did not take off because a Presidential order is required for that, and after seven minutes nobody had been able to reach the President, the Vice-President, or the Secretary of Defense. Finally, an officer who thought it was strange that the Russians would attack during 'a period of relative detente,' ordered his staff to run a check of the computer, and the mistake was found."

— Jacques Vallée, op. cit.

15. Robert Axelrod, *The Evolution of Cooperation*, Basic Books, New York, NY, 1984.

16. Johan Huizinga, *Homo Ludens*, Routledge & Kegan, Boston, MA, 1980.

Printed in Canada

g